# US MULTI-ROLE
# FIGHTER JETS

# US MULTI-ROLE
# FIGHTER JETS

STEVE DAVIES

First published in Great Britain in 2011 by Osprey Publishing,
Midland House, West Way, Botley, Oxford, OX2 0PH, UK
44-02 23rd Street, Suite 219, Long Island City, NY 11101, USA

E-mail: info@ospreypublishing.com

© 2011 Steve Davies

All rights reserved. Apart from any fair dealing for the purpose of private study, research, criticism or review, as permitted under the Copyright, Designs and Patents Act, 1988, no part of this publication may be reproduced, stored in a retrieval system, or transmitted in any form or by any means, electronic, electrical, chemical, mechanical, optical, photocopying, recording or otherwise, without the prior written permission of the copyright owner. Enquiries should be addressed to the Publishers.

Every attempt has been made by the Publisher to secure the appropriate permissions for material reproduced in this book. If there has been any oversight we will be happy to rectify the situation and written submission should be made to the Publishers.

A CIP catalogue record for this book is available from the British Library.

ISBN: 978 1 84908 220 4

Page layout by: Myriam Bell Design, France
Index by Alan Thatcher
Typeset in Cambria
Originated by United Graphics Pte, Singapore
Printed in China through Worldprint Ltd.

11 12 13 14 15   10 9 8 7 6 5 4 3 2 1

Osprey Publishing is supporting the Woodland Trust, the UK's leading woodland conservation charity, by funding the dedication of trees.

www.ospreypublishing.com

**Author's Note:**
Throughout the book I have used, wherever possible, official figures. These are the most up-to-date official figures to be released at the time of going to press (September 2010).

# CONTENTS

| | |
|---|---|
| FOREWORD | 6 |
| DEDICATION | 7 |
| ACKNOWLEDGMENTS | 10 |
| INTRODUCTION | 12 |
| STRIKE EAGLE | 24 |
| LOCKHEED MARTIN F-16 | 62 |
| HORNET & SUPER HORNET | 112 |
| RAPTOR | 160 |
| F-35 LIGHTNING II | 200 |
| CONCLUSION | 214 |
| ABBREVIATIONS | 222 |
| SELECTED READING | 228 |
| PICTURE CREDITS | 230 |
| INDEX | 231 |

# FOREWORD

It is an honor to provide the foreword for this latest version of Steve Davies' impressive work. He has once again produced a book full of well-researched information and personal stories. In addition to the detail, many of the experiences and stories brought back near and dear memories to include the missions I was fortunate to fly with Navy and Marine Corps F-14s and F-18s during Operation *Iraqi Freedom*.

I have been a blessed man to have flown the F-4, F-15E, F-16, and F-22. Steve's portrayal of the most recent United States Air Force fighters is insightful and indicative of a special man that has studied these birds for a long time. He entices me to want to fly the newest fighter, the F-35, someday!

For any aviation enthusiast of current US fighters, this is a book that will bring great enjoyment.

I am compelled to mention that these great fighters do not fly without significant effort. Support and maintenance personnel deserve great and unending credit for keeping these steel birds of prey flying, as well as figuring out how to continually make them better.

Finally, while fighter aircraft have advanced over the years, it remains the skill and courage of the men and women who fly them that in the end will ultimately win the day in combat.

Brig Gen Darryl Roberson
United States Air Force
November 2010

# DEDICATION

In Memory of Maj Brian "Wolfman" Wolf

Maj Brian "Wolfman" Wolf saved the lives of more than 30 British Special Boat Service (SBS) troops in the desert of Western Iraq in March 2003. Flying in the dead of night, he was forced to fly below a solid undercast that deprived him of any ambient lighting for his night vision goggles. In the pitch black, Wolf spotted the group against all odds as, surrounded by an overwhelming force and within minutes of being overrun, their panicked radio calls requested that bombs be dropped within 300m of their position. Wolf "padlocked" them, flew through 180 degrees, dropped a single bomb, and then ejected flares to scare off the Iraqi troops. It worked. The SBS team was later rescued without loss. "Wolfman" died, aged 37, in a road traffic accident in November 2006.

# ACKNOWLEDGMENTS

This book represents the combined efforts of a great many people. It has taken several years of coordination with the US Air Force and US Navy to conduct air-to-air photo sorties to capture many of the images in this book, and for the hard work of all those concerned – from the public affairs officers and crew chiefs, to the squadron and wing commanders who adjusted their flying schedules for me – I offer my sincerest gratitude.

This book was always intended to combine great photography with enlightening historical, anecdotal, and technical information. Yet it cannot, by virtue of its modest size, be an all-encompassing history of the multi-role fighters on which it concentrates. I hope, though, that it gives enough of an insight that it is both interesting to read and a rewarding purchase for the reader. Three of the aircraft described in this book have been exported to international customers, but this publication is concerned only with America's use of these jets, thus only fleeting reference to international operators is made.

On a similar note, the vast majority of the combat actions described herein occurred with America's allies fighting shoulder-to-shoulder with the aviators and units mentioned in the text. Again, I have not referenced this cooperation in all cases because constraints on word count, and an aversion to diluting the focus of the text, have made it desirable to avoid doing so. However, the author fully recognizes that while America may have led such operations as *Northern* and *Southern Watch*, *Desert Storm*, *Allied Force* and *Iraqi Freedom*, the Coalition effort was one of the key ingredients that made them successful. It is equally important to point out that the tactical aviators interviewed in this book would be among the first to give their Coalition brethren credit where it is due.

In writing this brief acknowledgment, I know immediately that my list of those to whom I owe thanks is incomplete. If you are not mentioned here despite helping me make this book a reality, please accept my apologies.

Thank you:

V Adm Thomas Kilcline and R Adm Frank Thorp; ACC/CC, USAFE/CC, and PACAF/CC; 31FW/CC, 53W/CC, 3W/CC, and 18AGRS/CC; Adm (ret.) Jim Robb; cols Michael Shower, Roberto Comelli (AM), and T. J. Kopf; lt cols "Popeye" Hansen and Randall Haskin; Lt Cdr Suzanna Brugler; Sq Lr (RAF) Justin Heliwell; majs Joseph Siberski, Chris Bacon, Duke Wisher, and Mike Cabral; Flt Lt (RAAF) Matthew Harper; capts Jennifer Ferrau, Sean Canfield, Nate Freeman, and Ryan Ough; lts Lesley Lykins and Frank Hartnett; and T Sgts John Gott and Jill Victor.

Particular thanks go to: Ruth Shepherd, formerly of Osprey, for commissioning this book all those years ago; Kate Moore, the current editor at Osprey, who allowed me extra time to finish and has been extremely supportive; Soph Moeng of Aerospace Publishing, for allowing me to make use of elements of his excellent *World Aircraft Information Files* partwork; Mike Maus, the US Navy PAO at NAS Oceana who worked magic to get my Super Hornet flight approved and coordinated; Cdr Matthew Leahy, skipper of VFA-211, who stepped into the breach and flew me at the last minute; T Sgt Mikal Canfield, for his tremendous support at Elmendorf; Capt Carrie Kessler, for arranging for me to fly with the "Green Bats," and Lt Col James Vogel who put together the first ever formation of all five Air Force fighters for me to photograph over the Nellis ranges; Ty Rogoway and Jamie Hunter, the incredible aviation photographers who allowed me to use their images to fill gaps in my own collection for this book; and last but not least, Luisa Merlo, who made me feel very welcome at Aviano and was always a joy to be around.

Finally, to Caroline go my thanks and love for being the incredible woman that you are.

# Acknowlegments

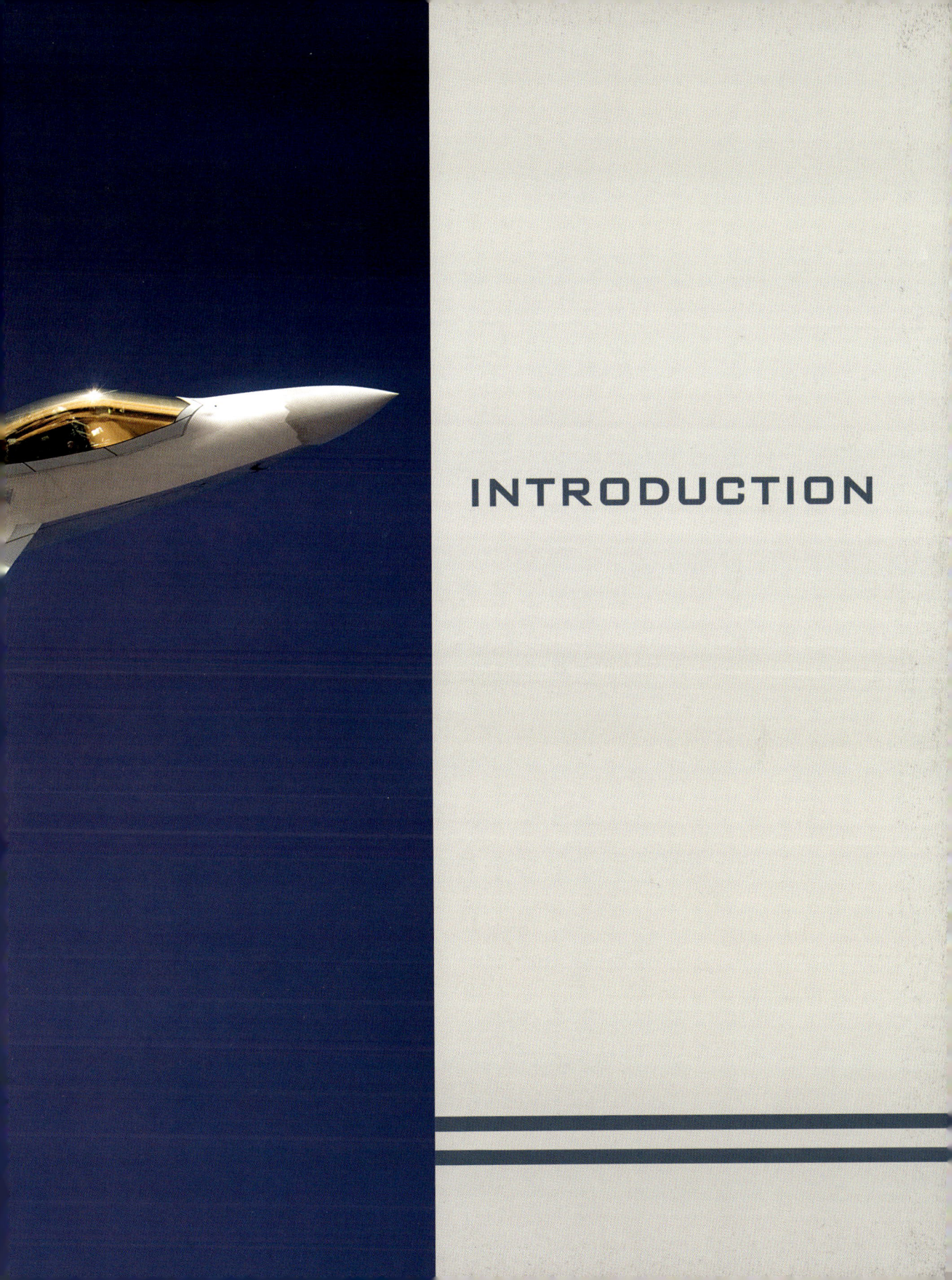

# INTRODUCTION

## US Multi-Role Fighter Jets

In 2010, the United States remains the world's only superpower, able to politically influence world events like no other, but equally able to project military action against adversary and threat nations anywhere on the globe when diplomacy fails or does not meet its national interests. The ability to conduct military operations at short notice and irrespective of where the threat is located is what underpins US foreign policy, and has been termed "global reach, global power" by the US Air Force.

Since the end of the Cold War, global reach has been focused almost exclusively on so-called contingency operations – where once the main threat existed in the form of a homogenized foe of the likes of the Soviet Union, it is now more difficult to define. Over the last 20 years, America has turned its attention to smaller pockets of belligerent adversaries. Between 1991 and 2010, the US military has been involved in contingency operations as far afield as the Balkans, Africa, and the Middle East. Some of these operations have involved fully developed combat, others have been about simply presenting a show of force that intimidates or enforces the will of the United States and its international allies.

As a backdrop to this, America's military has maintained a constant vigilance in those regions of the

**Previous page:** A "Diceman" F-22A Raptor breaks into the photo chase, showing off its gold-tinted, radar-reflecting canopy. The Raptor is an air dominance fighter, able to hunt and kill in non-permissive environments where non-stealthy aircraft would be dispatched with ease.

The EA-18G Growler is an outgrowth of the F/A-18F Super Hornet, perhaps the most technologically advanced multi-role fighter in existence today. Despite the Growler's use as a jamming platform, it retains a modest air-to-air capability and can be converted back to F-model configuration in a matter of hours.

Few military operations evoked as much patriotism as Operation *Enduring Freedom*. This F-15E Strike Eagle of the 492nd Fighter Squadron, 48th Fighter Wing, RAF Lakenheath, is pictured over Afghanistan in summer 2007. It carries an AAQ-33 Sniper target pod and GBU-38 JDAMs with which to strike Taliban or Al Qaeda targets.

world where old adversaries still threaten conflict. The threat from the perennially petulant North Korea, for example, requires that America station an extensive array of military hardware in both the Korean Peninsular and Japan. For 13 years the US military maintained a 24-hour watch over Iraq's No-Fly Zones, from bases in Turkey, Saudi Arabia, Kuwait, Qatar, and Cyprus, which then extended to a constant presence in Iraq, following Operation *Iraqi Freedom*, that will last until at least 2011.

All of this takes place amidst the considerable shrinkage of force levels that followed the drawing back of the Iron Curtain, and the consequent wholesale slashes in defense spending. By way of illustration, the USAF consolidated its command structure, moving from 13 to eight major commands, while simultaneously shedding more than 220,000 of its staff between the late 1980s and 1996 alone.

Today, "Global Contingency Operations" – originally termed the "Global War On Terror" (GWOT) – mean that the United States finds itself engaged in protracted operations that not only force the military to adapt to an irregular threat, but are also shaping the defense spending plans of the future. While the US-led operations in the Balkans in the 1990s were largely "symmetric" in nature – army against army, and air force against air force – the fight in Afghanistan and Iraq has been asymmetric to the extent that a $60m fighter jet is now pitted against a farmer with a $380 AK-47 assault rifle who blends in with the rest of the population on account of the fact that he is one them. Urban warfare, and a fastidious adherence to rules of engagement designed to limit

Continued on page 20.

**Overleaf:** Block 40 Vipers of Aviano's 31st FW look down onto a sunspot shining on the clouds that obscure northern Italy. These jets belong to the 510th FS "Buzzards."

## US Multi-Role Fighter Jets

**Previous page:** Since Operation *Desert Storm* in 1991, the United States has worked hard to modernize its arsenal of weapons, to the extent that today one aircraft can strike multiple target types in a single sortie. This 40th Flight Test Squadron (FTS) F-16C carries a Laser JDAM during a test sortie in 2005.

civilian casualties, have prompted pilots and weapons systems officers (WSOs) to think laterally and to devise unusual tactics and techniques to ensure that the enemy is still neutralized. At one point during the Gulf War of 2003, for example, training bombs – filled with concrete, not explosives – were being considered as one way of killing an insurgent in a house, without destroying neighboring residential properties or killing innocent civilians in the immediate vicinity.

Contributing to all of these actions has been an array of ground forces and naval forces. It is as true today as it ever was, that conventional wars in the traditional sense (that is, non-nuclear) can only be won by boots on the ground, and Afghanistan and Iraq illustrate this amply. Yet it is air power that must create the correct conditions for that to be possible. Air superiority must be attained and held: the enemy's "centers of gravity," such as political, leadership, command and control, and industrial base, must all be struck from the air; the enemy's army must be interdicted far behind the forward line of troops; and close air support must be provided when friendly forces mount offensive operations or find themselves, unwittingly or otherwise, in a defensive posture.

To enable this, a variety of what the military calls Mission Design Series (MDS) platforms are used. For example, three long-range bomber MDSs, the Boeing B-52 Stratofortress, Rockwell B-1B Lancer, and Northrop Grumman B-2 Spirit, each bring a unique capability to the war planner's table, and are in equal measure indispensable. But the brunt of the war fighting is conducted by the multi-role MDSs – F-15E, F-16, and F/A-18 – which offer greater flexibility to "swing" from one role to another, and are not only

The words of Tod Beamer, a passenger aboard the hijacked United Airlines Flight 93 on September 11, 2001, have become the mantra for the warriors who have responded to the threat that Al Qaeda poses to the free world. Since that fateful day, the "Let's Roll" emblem has adorned US multi-role fighters, such as this F-15E Strike Eagle.

An F/A-18F Super Hornet of VFA-211 "Fighting Checkmates" crosses the Norfolk coastline on a training sortie out of NAS Oceana in June 2010. The Super Hornet, while initially a subject of controversy, has proven to be an excellent purchase for the US Navy.

better equipped to deal with pop-up or time-sensitive targets, but also able to operate more autonomously in non-permissive environments where enemy fighters and air defense systems lurk.

*US Multi-Role Fighter Jets* attempts, within the constraints of a limited page count, to chart the development of these aircraft, their weapons systems, and US tactics and techniques, since the end of the Cold War. It focuses on the three US-operated stalwarts of the GWOT and previous contingency operations around the globe over more than two decades, and brings the reader up-to-date with the latest improvements and enhancements that are being made to keep the ageing Strike Eagle, Viper, and Hornet as potent today as they were when they entered service.

It is not possible to detail every single action, deployment, operation, or development of these MDSs over that time period, and so some operations are treated to only a very brief mention, while the reader can learn about others in separate reading. Those operations that have been singled out for greater detail have been selected on the basis of their importance to world and regional stability, or because of their exemplification of the work, achievements, or lessons learned by the aircrew involved in them. Similarly, where an operation provided an impetus that prompted the development of new weapons, tactics, and techniques, it has also been mentioned.

This book also looks briefly at the F-22 Raptor, the world's first operational fifth-generation fighter which has, more by necessity than by design, taken on a multi-role mission that means it is now an air dominance fighter. Finally, a cursory look at the F-35 Lightning II, the latest fifth-generation fighter, provides a glimpse into the future of what many believe will be the last ever manned multi-role fighter.

**Overleaf:** The Super Hornet is well suited to the fast forward air controller role. Its crews pride themselves in their ability to perform this, and many other roles, with alacrity.

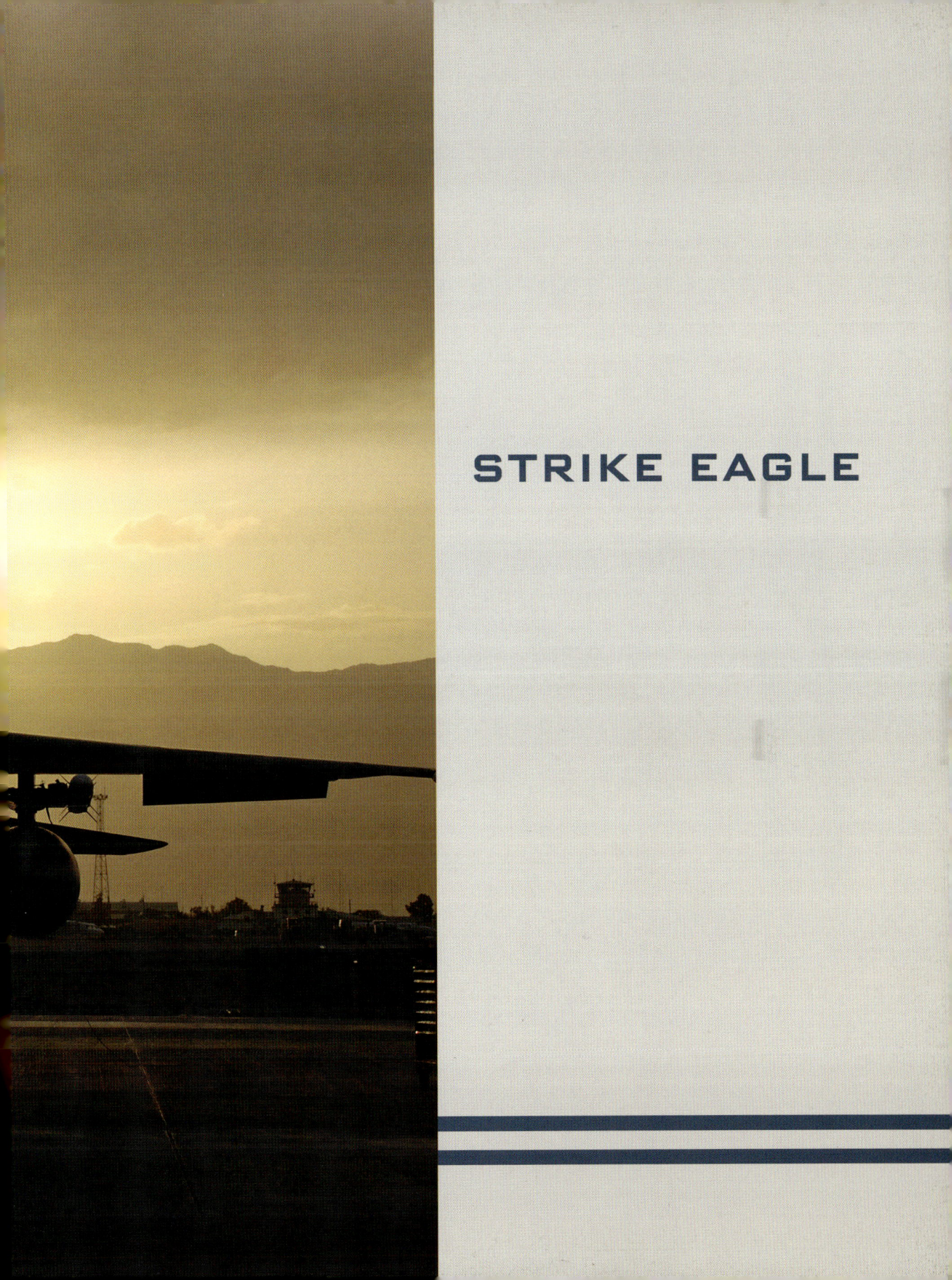

# STRIKE EAGLE

The F-15E is a dedicated multi-role adaptation of the F-15 air superiority fighter, and has proven itself as the most capable, well-rounded strike fighter of all time. Only with the introduction of the F/A-18E/F Super Hornet has its position as the world's most capable "mud-mover" been challenged.

"Strike Eagle" came about as a result of a combination of clever corporate strategy by McDonnell Douglas, the foresight and vision of Tactical Air Command (TAC) commander General Wilbur Creech, and the predictable ageing status of the General Dynamics F-111 Aardvark. McDonnell Douglas and Hughes, the latter of whom was charged with developing the Strike Eagle's radar, had recognized that a two-seat, dedicated strike version of the F-15 would be of great interest to the United States Air Force (USAF), and set about developing the concept of an air-to-ground orientated F-15 under the internal project name "Strike Eagle."

In the early 1980s, the consortium received positive encouragement from General Creech, who harbored concerns that as the swing-wing Aardvark continued to age TAC would lose its edge in the deep strike and battlefield air interdiction roles, both crucial missions in Cold War Western Europe that were being fulfilled by a complement of over 70 F-111Fs and F-111Es divided into two wings (at RAF Lakenheath and RAF Upper Heyford, England).

In its greatest iteration, the F-111F, the long-nosed Aardvark, was a potent strike platform that offered long-range, automatic terrain following flight and precision strike capabilities. The AVQ-26 Pave Tack pod mounted in the small weapons bay of the F-111F used infra-red imaging to allow the pilot and WSO to visually acquire their targets at night. It could also fire a laser onto the target to allow laser-guided bombs (LGBs) to fly down the cone of reflected laser energy and strike the target with pinpoint accuracy. A dedicated terrain following radar (TFR) installed in the jet's snout allowed the crew to fly down to 200ft above the ground in all weathers, thereby avoiding enemy radar and visual detection. The F-111F was not going to be easy to replace.

## ELECTRONIC WIZARDRY

The Aardvark had aged gracefully on the outside, but on the inside the electronics that gave it its war fighting ability would soon be outdated. Having already provided the F-15 Eagle air superiority fighter with a massively powerful and capable air intercept radar, Hughes went back to the drawing board with a view to completely overhauling and improving the Eagle's APG-63 for the Strike Eagle. The result of that process was the APG-70, incorporating the key air-to-air elements of the Eagle's radar, but adding dedicated air-to-ground modes, key among which was the synthetic aperture radar (SAR) mapping mode. Thus, the Strike Eagle retained most of the F-15's air-to-air capabilities, but incorporated an entirely new set of air-to-ground capabilities into the mix.

SAR measures the Doppler shift created when radar waves hit the ground and bounce back towards the radar antenna. Using complex computer algorithms to establish the movement of the aircraft (as judged by the air data computer and the inertial navigation system) relative to the ground, the APG-70 interprets these shifts and translates them into a top-down picture for the pilot and WSO to scrutinize. The resulting image gives a very clear view of the ground, and looks very similar to a bird's-eye view of the target area. This process became known as "patch

---

**Previous page:** The rugged silhouette of a Strike Eagle on the ramp at Bagram AB, Afghanistan. The jet squats in the cooling air armed with a GBU-31 JDAM on the centerline, four GBU-12s on the left CFT and three GBU-38 JDAMs on the right.

mapping," and the APG-70 can map down to a resolution of .67 of a nautical mile.

While Hughes developed the radar, McDonnell Douglas – or McAir, as it was often called – was developing a new airframe for the Strike Eagle. Advanced manufacturing processes allowed the company to build a stronger, internally redesigned airframe. Thus, the Strike Eagle would look similar to an F-15D, but on the inside it was quite different. McAir also worked to develop and integrate two other key components into the Strike Eagle: the conformal fuel tank (CFT) and LANTIRN (low altitude navigation targeting infra-red for night). CFTs are slipper tanks that sit flush along the aircraft's fuselage, below the wing root. They carry extra fuel and also feature hardpoints allowing additional stores to be carried. The USAF had signed a contract with Martin Marietta to produce LANTIRN as a combination of forward-looking infra-red (FLIR) optics and TFR, which would eventually be mounted beneath the engine nacelles in two underslung pods. LANTIRN reached operational status in 1987.

The LANTIRN pods, designated as the AAQ-13 navigation pod and AAQ-14 target pod (TP), are each attached via two mounting lugs and simple electrical terminals. The "nav pod" houses a FLIR sensor and TFR and is primarily used by the pilot to allow hands-off low altitude flying in all weathers, night or day. The FLIR sensor looks ahead of the aircraft and can display the resulting image onto the pilot's Kaiser wide field-of-view (WFOV) head-up display (HUD). The TFR looks ahead and slightly to either side of the jet to detect obstacles and terrain. Mounted on the left

pylon, the target pod is used by the WSO to identify and designate targets when weather conditions permit, and can be tied to the radar or manipulated independently. It has three selectable fields of view and houses a laser designator with which to guide LGBs onto the target. The WSO finds his target with the TP, puts the crosshairs over it and presses a button to commit the pod to automatically track it. Several tracking options are available, all of which permit the WSO to keep one eye on other systems during the course of the attack run, something that F-111F WSOs were never able to do.

The Strike Eagle's forward avionics bays were redesigned, along with changes to the electrical system which supplied them, to allow additional

A rack of BDU-33 training bombs adorns the centerline station of this Strike Eagle. The small bombs carry a smoke charge that helps mark their point of impact on the target range and, despite their diminutive size, are specifically designed to mimic the aerodynamic behavior of the much larger Mk 82 500lb LDGP bomb.

## US Multi-Role Fighter Jets

electrical power and cooling to be supplied to the black boxes that would run the power-hungry APG-70 and a new, sophisticated, very-high speed integrated central computer that digitally fused the radar's components together with the jet's other electronic gadgetry. On the downside, the ammunition carriage space for the M61A1 20mm Vulcan "Gatling" gun was reduced in size to make way for additional avionics. The engine bays were redesigned to allow commonality in plumbing and installation for either Pratt & Whitney or General Electric engines and the tail hook was modified to accommodate a heavier than anticipated landing weight. These modifications forced the installation of a new landing gear and wheels in order to allow the jet to operate safely at higher gross weight. In all, the Strike Eagle weighs in at just under 16,000lb heavier than the F-15C, and has a maximum take-off weight of 81,000lb.

The two-man cockpit was considerably updated, with an emphasis being placed on interoperability, the ability of each crewmember to perform almost any function necessary to get the mission done. The front cockpit features two monochrome multi-purpose displays (MPDs) and one multi-purpose color display (MPCD); the rear cockpit boasts two MPDs and two MPCDs. A UFC (up-front controller – basically a rugged key pad) is installed in each cockpit to allow the crew to enter data into the powerful and sophisticated avionics suite.

Thrust for the new variant was initially provided by Pratt & Whitney F100-PW-220 turbofans, as used by the F-15C, with a digital engine control system.

Mountain Home AFB is located near Boise, Idaho, but is remote enough that the airspace that surrounds it gives the crews of the 366th Wing freedom to train as they would fight. Bitterly cold winters test the indispensable maintenance crews to the maximum.

However, the powerplant was soon replaced under the Improved Performance Engine (IPE) program, whereby General Electric F110-GE-129 and Pratt & Whitney F100-PW-229 engines were both flown in F-15Es under competitive evaluation. The Pratt & Whitney engine was eventually selected. From August 1991 the new engine (from aircraft 90-0233) was fitted on the production line, with other aircraft being retrofitted. To adapt the F-15E to the rigors of the low-level role, the aircraft was structurally redesigned for a 16,000-hour life and loads of up to 9*g*. More use was made of superplastic forming and diffusion bonding in the rear fuselage, engine bay and on some panels. The internal fuel tanks were filled with reticulated foam, reducing capacity to 2,019 US gals.

The USAF ordered the Strike Eagle – designated F-15E – in 1984, following a six-month competition against the General Dynamics F-16XL. July 1985 saw 86-0183, the first F-15E, make its maiden flight, and two other F-15Es ('184 and '185) flew soon after. The 33rd Tactical Fighter Wing (TFW) – formerly an F-15C/D unit at Eglin Air Force Base (AFB), Florida – received three F-15Es in August 1986 to begin USAF trials. In 1988 the 405th Tactical Training Wing at Luke AFB, Arizona, became Tactical Air Command's replacement training unit (RTU) for the F-15E, tasked with training all new aircrew converting to the Strike Eagle. The 4th TFW at Seymour Johnson AFB, North Carolina, converted from its McDonnell Douglas F-4E Phantom IIs in December 1988 to become the first operational F-15E wing, and in the early 1990s Seymour Johnson took over from Luke as the Strike Eagle RTU.

## WAR GAMES AND THEN WAR

As the first operational wing to fly the Strike Eagle, the 4th TFW and its constituent units, the 335th Tactical Fighter Squadron (TFS) "Chiefs" and 336th TFS "Rocketeers," began planning their first Operational Readiness Exercise (ORE) in August 1990. The ORE would take the few mission ready (MR) crews of the 335th TFS and mix them and their jets with those of the 336th TFS. It would also include the F-4s of the 4th TFW's third squadron, the 334th TFS "Eagles," which had yet to convert to the F-15E. The ORE objective was to demonstrate the wing's capability to use the electronic attack, navigation, and target designation systems on the F-15E to execute precision strikes on a range of targets over a small period of time. The portentous timing of the ORE quickly became apparent less than a week later as the new Strike Eagle crews and the rest of the world watched aghast as on August 7, 1990, Iraqi dictator Saddam Hussein ordered his troops to invade Kuwait, thus staking his claim to its oil fields.

The "Rocketeers" were given the order to prepare to deploy, but crews at the 335th TFS, of whom only one third were MR, were not expected to go. On August 9, 1990, six-ship flights of F-15Es and 48 crewmen began deploying to Seeb Air Base, Oman – a journey requiring a 15-hour non-stop flight, which started at Seymour Johnson in atrocious weather. While en route, their destination was changed, and although they were not told the name of the new location over the radio, it eventually turned out to be Thumrait, Oman.

Operation *Desert Shield*, the precursor to Operation *Desert Storm*, began with the deployment of F-15Cs and F-15Es to the Persian Gulf region. The 1st TFW at Langley AFB sent 24 F-15C and three F-15D aircraft to Dhahran AB, Saudi Arabia, on August 7. The next day, 25 F-15C/Ds arrived from the 27th TFS. On August 9 the 336th TFS F-15Es arrived at Thumrait AB, Oman, via Dhahran, Saudi Arabia. Thumrait had stockpiles of weapons that had been stored by the US for just such an eventuality. Initially confusion reigned as the squadron, operating as the 4th TFW (Provisional)

A 335th FS F-15E flies over Kitty Hawk, the place of the historic first powered flight by the Wright brothers on December 17, 1903. The 4th FW's logo, stencilled on the inboard surfaces of the Strike Eagle's two vertical stabilizers, depicts the Wright Flyer.

(TFW (P)) and led by Col Russell "Rusty" Bolt, was without clear orders or directives. The reality of its situation was stark; nine of Hussein's elite Republican Guard units stood ready at the Kuwaiti border to steamroller south into Saudi Arabia, whose oil fields might also be in the sights of the Iraqi dictator. It quickly became evident that the "Rocketeers" were the only force that could delay and harass such an advance, although the price they might pay in the process did not bear thinking about.

By August 11, the squadron had 12 jets on alert, although this had not been achieved without considerable effort. Being so new, the Strike Eagle was only cleared to release Mk 84 and Mk 82 low drag general purpose (LDGP) bombs at that time, although several other weapons had been tested by the Seek Eagle weapons testing program at Eglin AFB, Florida. There was therefore some consternation about dropping the Mk 20 Rockeye cluster bomb as it had not been fully tested from all stations. These concerns were more than valid, since some crews had seen a video from the Strike Eagle prototype weapons release tests which had shown a 500lb bomb coming off a CFT pylon only to whip back up behind the wing and slam into the horizontal stabilizer. The Mk 20 Rockeye was an "area munition" that released hundreds of cricket ball sized bomblets over an area as large as a football field, and was therefore far more effective in killing lightly armored targets than a LDGP bomb. The Air Force waived normal procedures and permitted Bolt and his men to load "unauthorized" stores onto the jet to allow the Mk 20 to be used. Two jets also stood ready to defend the base, or a strike package, from enemy attack, each loaded with four AIM-9 Sidewinder and four AIM-7MF Sparrow missiles.

In Riyadh, Saudi Arabia, US and Coalition representatives formed the Tactical Air Control

# OPERATORS

As of October 2009, the USAF had 223 F-15Es in service. Most of these are assigned to the four Active Duty (AD) squadrons at the "Strike Eagle Super Base," Seymour Johnson AFB in North Carolina. In the northwest, two squadrons operate out of Mountain Home AFB, Idaho. Two additional squadrons are located at RAF Lakenheath, England, under the command of USAFE (United States Air Forces Europe), while ACC (Air Combat Command) and AFMC (Air Force Materiel Command) each operate a number of squadrons in the test capacity – operational test for the former, and technical test for the latter.

On March 30, 2010, the first ever F-15E Air Force Reserve Command (AFRC) unit stood-up at Seymour Johnson, tasked with helping the Formal Training Unit at the sprawling base (the 333rd and 334th FSs) in meeting the demands of graduating newly qualified (or re-qualified) pilots and WSOs.

---

The F-15E cockpit is well designed ergonomically and benefits from both MPDs and MCDPs to present a myriad of information to the pilot and WSO. The front cockpit (left and top right) features two MPDs and single MPCD, as well as a wide field-of-view HUD onto which can be projected the FLIR image from the AAQ-13 nav pod. The WSO's cockpit (bottom right) features two MPCDs and two MPDs, any of which can be used as a "HUD repeater" to allow the WSO to see what the pilot is seeing. Additionally, the WSO has two hand controllers on the side consoles, through which he can manipulate the jet's weapons and sensor systems.

### Air Combat Command

4th Fighter Wing – Seymour Johnson AFB, NC
   333rd Fighter Squadron
   334th Fighter Squadron
   335th Fighter Squadron
   336th Fighter Squadron
53rd Wing – Eglin AFB, FL
   85th Test and Evaluation Squadron
53rd Wing – Nellis AFB, NV
   422nd Test and Evaluation Squadron
57th Wing – Nellis AFB, NV
   17th Weapons Squadron
366th Fighter Wing – Mountain Home AFB, ID
   389th Fighter Squadron
   391st Fighter Squadron
   428th Fighter Squadron (mixed USAF/RSAF unit for training Royal Singaporean Air Force crews on the F-15SG)

### United States Air Forces Europe

48th Fighter Wing – RAF Lakenheath, England
   492nd Fighter Squadron
   494th Fighter Squadron

### Air Force Materiel Command

46th Test Wing – Eglin AFB, FL
   40th Flight Test Squadron
412th Test Wing – Edwards AFB, CA
   415th Flight Test Squadron
   419th Flight Test Squadron

### Deployed Expeditionary Forces

379th Air Expeditionary Wing – Bagram AB, Afghanistan
455th Air Expeditionary Wing

### United States Air Force Reserve

414th Fighter Group – Seymour Johnson AFB, NC
   307th Fighter Squadron

---

Center (TACC). The TACC planned the air war, as defined by a 600-page document called the Air Tasking Order (ATO). The ATO was the route map for the air campaign against Iraq and detailed every sortie that was to be flown. The F-15Es were to fly sorties in unison with F-4G Wild Weasel anti-radar aircraft and EF-111 jammers, against SAM sites and key airfield complexes, but were also assigned to, politically speaking, the most problematic target – "Scud" missiles. Iraq operated four "Scud" types, all based on the original Soviet SS-1 missile, which was a surface-launched missile with a range of over 200 miles, albeit not particularly accurate. Iraq, it was believed, had adapted the "Scud's" warhead to carry chemical or biological loads and would show no hesitation in using them against neighboring countries. Doing so could upset the entire balance of neutrality of other Arab nations in the region (Jordan and Syria), and would likely draw Israel into the conflict; it was therefore to be prevented at all costs. Iraq boasted a combination of fixed sites that could be attacked with ease, but the mobile units posed the greatest concern and ultimately proved very nearly impossible to pinpoint. (Between January 18 and February 26, 1991, 40 "Scuds" would be launched against Israel and 46 against Saudi Arabia.) In December the "Rocketeers" and "Chiefs" moved to Al Kharj AB, Saudi Arabia, following the realization that the Iraqis were not going to advance any further south.

---

**Overleaf:** RAF Lakenheath is home to two squadrons of Strike Eagles. The blue fin stripe marks this jet out as a "Bolar," belonging to the 492nd FS. In the background, two rows of "Bolar" and red striped "Panther," 494th FS, F-15Es stand ready for a packed flying schedule.

## OPERATION *DESERT STORM*

President Bush gave the order for the first strikes on January 17, 1991 – Operation *Desert Storm* had begun. With great media attention focused on Baghdad, waves of RAF Tornado GR.Mk 1s; USAF F-111Fs, F-15Cs, F-15Es, EF-111s, F-16s, F-4Gs, and B-52s; and US Navy F/A-18s, F-14s, A-6s, and A-7s, flew to attack the "eyes" and "ears" of the Iraqi military machine. The country's integrated air defense system (IADS) was the primary target for many of the first sorties, with airfields, hardened aircraft shelters (HAS), and aircraft also being attacked so that air superiority could be attained. The ATO called for later strikes against Iraqi armor, C3 (Command, Control and Communications), and logistics supplies, thus paving the way for a less protracted (and, hopefully, less bloody) ground war to rid Kuwait of its uninvited guests.

That first night, fixed "Scud" sites in western Iraq were attacked by the Strike Eagles. A total of five sites were hit by 21 jets, which divided into three-ship or four-ship packages, each carrying two fuel tanks, 12 Mk 20 Rockeye CBUs (cluster bomb units), and two AIM-9M missiles. The exception was CHEVY flight, which was to attack "Scud" sites at H-2, an Iraqi air base. Each of CHEVY flight's aircraft carried 12 Mk 82s. All of the jets would ordinarily have been loaded with four AIM-9s, but that would have taken them above the 81,000lb maximum weight limit. This maximum weight carried penalties, not least of which was a restriction to $3g$ – a severe impediment on their maneuverability.

The fixed sites were simple to strike. The crews of DODGE flight chose to ingress the target area at low level at 540 knots. Climbing briefly to altitude as they neared the target, they patch mapped the area before descending once again to 300ft. AWACS (the orbiting E-3 Airborne Warning and Control System aircraft) called several unidentified aircraft in their locality, but none came closer than 30 miles. A final update was taken, with the radar, some three minutes from the target to update the navigation computer known as the Mission Navigator (MN). The MN then provided azimuth steering cues on the HUD so each pilot could precisely position his aircraft for bomb release. Nearing the target, they executed "Pop" and less aggressive "Level" deliveries and the first jet released its CBUs at 0305 local time.

Attacking the "Scud" sites was risky since they were well defended, and several pilots exceeded their jets' $g$ limits as they hauled the aircraft into jinks and evasive turns to avoid seemingly impenetrable streams of unguided AAA (anti-aircraft artillery). In the haste to avoid the AAA at least one jet came within 90ft of flying into the ground, saved only as a result of a $7g$ "pull" prompted by the panicked scream of the WSO, who had noted his pilot's error.

CHEVY flight was the only E-model flight to attack its target – a "Scud" missile launching facility at H-2 airfield – at medium level that night. Col Steve Kwast (then a lieutenant), flying as CHEVY ONE-TWO on that sortie, vividly recalled the sight of more than 100 AAA pieces firing together following the impact of CHEVY ONE-ONE's bombs.

> We took-off out of Al Kharj and flew to our tanker track – Banana tanker track, I think it was called – and once we tanked we dropped down to low-altitude and crossed the border. As we crossed, we could see the fires burning at the observation posts and radar facilities that our special forces had taken out. As we flew at 500ft we could see in our FLIR the special forces' helicopters flying below us at 200ft and other than that it's totally pitch-black outside. Cruising in low we're thinking about our two plans. One sees us perform a low-altitude attack, the other a high-altitude attack. It depended on how much AAA there was out there; lots of it would make us go high, but if there

was not too much then we'd stay low and try and use the element of surprise. AWACS calls out a MiG beaming us on the far side of the target, but it doesn't look like he's aware that we're here. We look out into the distance and, man, you could see the AAA rising like a curtain from the ground. The squadron commander, who's leading this six-ship package says, "climb," so we all climb up to medium altitude and each drop our 12 Mk 82 dumb bombs. Once we were off target we descended and egressed at low altitude until we neared our tanker track, at which time we climbed back up and tanked.

The GBU-28 "Bunker Buster" is the heaviest single weapon in the Strike Eagle's inventory. Weighing in at 5,000lb and made from an artillery barrel, it is also often referred to as "Deep Throat." The weapon is able to penetrate hardened bunkers, command centers, and missile launch sites deep underground.

Kwast was the first ever Strike Eagle "baby" – the first pilot to go straight from undergraduate pilot training to the F-15E – and the only lieutenant pilot to deploy with the "Rocketeers" in 1990. "Once the initial cadre of F-15E pilots had been established, they started the pipeline for guys straight out of pilot training. I was the very first lieutenant in the very first class to go to the F-15E. My class consisted of captains; older officers with time as instructors in other jets like T-38s." Kwast added, "the experienced guys flew all the sorties on the first couple days of war. 'Experienced' was a relative term in those days. With a few exceptions, the experienced guys had maybe 200 hours of F-15E time. By today's standards they wouldn't even qualify to be flight leads, but back then the whole F-15E community was brand new. However, nearly everyone had several hundred hours

## US Multi-Role Fighter Jets

of time in the F-4, or some other aircraft, so they did have a clue."

Al Gale recollects his first night, flying in the same package, but against a different target set, as Kwast.

On the first night of the war there were 21 F-15Es that went into Iraq. The original plan was for 18, but three more were added near the start time. During the mission briefing, our particular three-ship was looking at our target photos. Our targets were fixed "Scud" sites in western Iraq. As we looked at the target photos there was some concern as to whether the launcher array would be oriented as in the photo, so we decided to use an air-to-air type of targeting arrangement: Lead would bomb the target on the right, No. 2 (us) would do the one in the middle, and No. 3 would take the one on the left.

After take-off we climbed out and avoided doing some of the usual weapons checks as we were a big 21-ship gaggle, and in the process my pilot forgot to dial up the tone volume on his AIM-9. This would be an issue later. When we all got up to the tankers they all had their lights turned off except for one small bulb; it was a moonless night so air refueling was very difficult. One of the wingmen went "lost wingman" as he lost sight of the formation, but he regained his position later.

Continued on page 45.

**Left:** The 391st FS "Bold Tigers" were quick to respond to the terrorist actions of September 2001, deploying to Ali al Salem AB in Kuwait and engaging in an unrelenting attack on a largely mobile Taliban target set. This jet carries mission markings denoting GBU-28, GBU-24, GBU-12, GBU-10, and LDGP deliveries.

**Overleaf:** A Native American Indian forms the basis of the squadron badge for the 335th FS, "Chiefs," based at Seymour Johnson AFB, North Carolina. The "Chiefs" have a prestigious history as Strike Eagle operators, having drawn first blood in Operation *Desert Storm* in 1991, and then supported highly classified special operations forces in both Operation *Iraqi Freedom* and *Enduring Freedom*.

# TECHNOLOGY

Central to the Strike Eagle's ability to strike any target in any weather, day or night, is a suite of avionics and weapons systems. Some of these, such as the radar, fighter datalink (FDL), and Tactical Electronic Warfare Suite (TEWS), are installed internally, but others, such as LANTIRN, and the AAQ-28 Litening II and newer AAQ-33 Sniper XR target pods, are carried externally.

## Radar

The F-15E's radar is certainly the most remarkable component of the jet's suite of "Gucci gear." The Raytheon APG-70 is an outgrowth of both the APG-63 and APG-65 radars installed in the F-15 and F/A-18, respectively. In addition to its SAR mode for high-resolution ground mapping, the APG-70 offers a wide range of general mapping and air-to-air modes, operating across a number of frequencies in the I/J-bands. Further flexibility is gained from varying pulse widths and processing modes. Among the most useful features are the several automatic acquisition modes for short-range air-to-air work, triggered by a switch on the control stick, which automatically lock the radar on to a target without the pilot having to designate it. The radar is fully compatible with the AIM-120 AMRAAM (advanced medium-range air-to-air missiles) to give a semi-passive kill capability that means the enemy receives little (or at least, very late) indication that he is being targeted.

The APG-70 consists of a three-axis gimballed antenna array driven mechanically at up to 140° per second. Compared to the original APG-63 it has increased bandwidth, improved ECCM (electronic counter-countermeasures) capability and greater sensitivity, and gives longer-range detection of look-up and look-down targets.

## RMP

While some Strike Eagles were equipped with the improved APG-63(V)1 in the mid-1990s, it is the Radar Modernization Program's (RMP's) introduction of the APG-82 AESA (Advanced Electronically Scanned Array) radar that has brought the F-15E firmly into the 21st century. The Raytheon APG-82(V)1 uses active electronically scanned array technology to massively increase the Strike Eagle's ability to detect targets (an improvement of more than 100 percent against a fighter-size target), map the terrain ahead (one eighth of the current SAR mapping resolution, in other words around .08nm), and jam threat emitters, all at the same time. The first RMP Strike Eagle flew in 2010, and 224 Strike Eagles are expected to receive the upgrade over the coming years.

## LANTIRN

While the APG-82 will dramatically increase the Strike Eagle's ability to precisely engage multiple air and ground targets simultaneously, traditionally one of the biggest facilitators of the Strike Eagle's mission has been the low-altitude navigation and targeting infra-red for night system. LANTIRN consists of two pods, of which the AAQ-14 target pod has since been superseded by the Litening II and Sniper XR, but the second pod in the duo, the AAQ-13 navigation pod, remains in frontline service despite the fact that the first full specification nav pod first flew as long ago as 1987. The pod consists of a TFR, above which is an articulated navigation FLIR sensor installed in the mounting bracket (which attaches the pod to the airframe). Its primary purpose is to allow low-altitude penetration of enemy airspace in either manual or automatic modes, even in the dark of night and bad weather.

At the time of its entry into service, the AAQ-13 was a quantum leap ahead of other comparable FLIR systems, not least because of its innovative functionality. The NAV FLIR, which projects a monochrome image onto the pilot's HUD, has "Snap Look" and "Look Into Turn" (LIT) modes. Snap Look provides the pilot with the ability to drive the NAV FLIR 9 degrees up or down, and 25 degrees left or right, generating a ground-stabilized video image on the HUD that allows the pilot to "see" a wider cone of airspace and terrain ahead of the aircraft. LIT features two modes of operation: one manual, the other automatic. In manual mode, the pilot can press the "coolie hat" on his control stick once he is banked at an angle of 5 degrees or more, in order to generate a 6 degrees LIT horizon-stabilized image on his HUD. Automatic mode changes the view as soon as the aircraft is rolled through 33 degrees of bank. In both cases, normal FLIR video resumes once the aircraft has returned to pre-defined bank angles. Thus, with LIT engaged, the pilot can further enhance his ability to "see" another 19 degrees into his turn by manually engaging Snap Look.

The TFR radar is housed behind a bulbous dome below the NAV FLIR window, and is a penetration aid that allows low-altitude ingress beneath even the densest of SAM and AAA bubbles. Designed with average European weather statistics in mind (visibility of no more than 3,000ft and rain a likely occurrence), the TFR has two weather modes and one ECCM mode, and allows automatic or manual terrain following in increments from 1,000ft to 200ft above the terrain during normal operation. ECCM mode provides protection against enemy radio frequency jamming, picking out bogus radio signals intended to confuse it; while a low probability of intercept mode limits the likelihood of enemy detection. Finally, a special Very Low Clearance mode allows hands-off, fully automatic operation when the threat is so high that the benefits of this mode outweigh the risks of flying so low to the ground.

## Litening II

The second of the LANTIRN pods, often itself simply referred to as LANTIRN, thanks to its pairing with the AAQ-13 navigation pod, is the ageing AAQ-14 target pod. It was hurriedly replaced by small quantities of the Litening II pod on Strike Eagles participating in Operation *Iraqi Freedom* in March 2003.

The Northrop Grumman AAQ-28, which is better known as the Litening II Advanced Target Pod, features a laser spot tracker and optical sensor in addition to an improved derivative of the FLIR sensor from its predecessor. These additional systems allow better daytime operation and extended range target acquisition capabilities, and also facilitate coordination with other ground and airborne laser designators. However, the Litening II pod's IR sensor is actually inferior to the AAQ-14 in some respects, thus

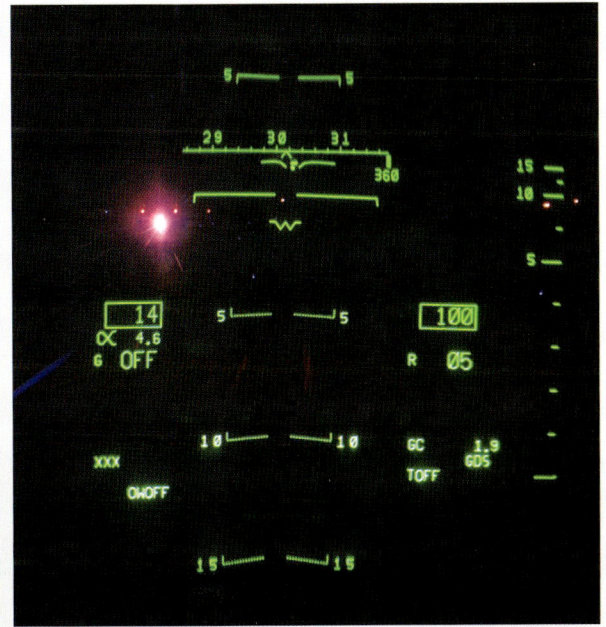

These two images both show the wide field-of-view HUD in the Strike Eagle, although in the image on the right the FLIR picture from the nav pod has been overlaid. The ability to "see" in the dark is a major advantage for the F-15E pilot, especially at low level. However, the green monochrome image lacks the texture and depth offered by daylight stereoscopic vision, and must therefore be used with its limitations always in mind.

representing a compromise. Litening II requires reduced maintenance support on account of the fact that it has no slip ring – the ring that allowed the electronics and optical assemblies in the nose of the AAQ-14 pod to slew freely in any direction. The laser spot tracker allows the F-15E crew to observe the laser markers used by the target pods on other aircraft.

During the March 2003 Operation *Iraqi Freedom*, the AAQ-28 provided excellent daytime identification capabilities, according to Maj Joe "Ramsty" Siberski:

> The pod made life a lot easier for me for almost one reason alone; positive target identification. The only way to ID something like a vehicle with the LANTIRN pod [AAQ-14] was to fly your precious ass into the heart of every single threat the bad guy has. Not a good way to do business. With the Litening pod we could stay at medium altitude and ID from there. Now, that sounds like a huge upgrade in capability for the Strike Eagle because our pilot/WSO coordination and software integration makes for a lethal combination from medium altitude, but there's more. It is a huge capability boost for all war fighters. With a Litening pod we can ID and hand-off targets to any platform over the radio, and we can also hand them off digitally to other datalink-capable systems (which is best).

But Siberski added that the pod also demonstrated some inferior characteristics to the AAQ-14:

> I couldn't stand the Litening in IR mode once stuff started burning. You see the Litening uses a different part of the IR spectrum than LANTIRN. I'm told the different spectrum allows the pod to be more sensitive, hence provide a much better picture. My observation is that this spectrum is more sensitive to washing out the picture when secondary explosions are going off in the area of interest. Furthermore, the Litening was originally engineered for F-16s (single-seat mentality) and there was little "manual tuning" ability like there is for LANTIRN. Instead, there was a range of tuning settings, called histograms, which we could step through. The guys at the 422 [Test and Evaluation Squadron] spent a lot of time trying to tweak the different histograms to deal with blooming, but I still had issues. I did most of my flying with it during the day, so I usually had the EO [electro-optical] camera selected. The EO camera is "the money" with good visibility, and the only blooming you have to worry about is the dirt, fire, and target parts covering your next target.

Capt Christian Burbach had some very positive experiences with the AAQ-28's spot tracker.

> We worked with some of the FAC(A) [Forward Air Controller (Airborne)] F-14D guys who were at the Deid [Al Udeid]. On one occasion the F-14D WSO said to me, "OK, here's my laser code, I'm lasing now." He lased a DMPI (desired mean point of impact – target) and said, "Here's the first one," then he dragged my laser spot tracker over to the next target and said, "here's the second one," then he dragged it over to the third one. I made a mark point on the first one, gave my wingman the second DMPI and we dropped on both in the same run-in and hit both targets simultaneously. Then, we turned around and dropped on the third target with the F-14D lasing my bomb in for me.

This kind of utility is worth a thousand words, and the expertise and professionalism of the F-14D FAC(A)s allowed the Strike Eagle aircrew that worked with them to be even more lethal in their execution of the mission. While not typical of the experiences that most F-15E crews had out in the desert, it did show what was possible when conditions allowed.

More recently, the Sniper pod has equipped F-15E squadrons deploying to combat. It gives the crews a significant increase in capability and detection range on account of its third-generation FLIR sensor. Subtle changes in tactics have followed, and one tale from "the sandbox" relates to an F-15E that used its laser to pinpoint an insurgent leaving a safe house many miles away. While the insurgent was unaware that he was being observed, a Special Forces team used its own laser spot tracker to observe the F-15E's laser, and to close in on the man as he mingled in a crowd. They simply had to look for the man with a laser beam sticking invisibly out of his head.

Once the refueling was completed we headed north and descended to low level. We all had our lights off. Our three-ship was Nos 16–18 in the long chain of Eagles heading towards their targets. We all were on the terrain following radar at 200ft in radio silence – the pilots were hand flying the TFR steering while concentrating on the FLIR picture in the HUD and maintaining their formation position, the WSOs in the back seats were monitoring the TFR e-scope, the radar, and keeping the Nav systems updated. The only talking on radio was by the AWACS who was doing a very good job providing bull's-eye locations for four groups of enemy fighters, but we didn't encounter any of these groups on the way in. When I mapped one of the update points, which was the corner of a building, it turned out that the building was rubble. As we ingressed further we flew by it and it was on fire, and it turned out that our update point was one of the targets the Army Apache attack helicopters took out to pave the way for us. As we flew along at 0300 or so (our TOT [time on target] was 0308) we would pass over cars traveling on the highway sometimes. It looked just like any highway at night. It felt strange to know that those drivers who must have heard us going by at over 500 knots were just driving along watching jets with a total of over 200 bombs to drop on their military. As we approached the target we took our radar map, and when it displayed the target array looked just like it had in the pictures during the briefing, so I designated the one in the middle.

We climbed to 500ft for the delivery and pushed it up to 550 knots. Given our speed we weren't able to turn to go direct to the target and stay inside the TFR bank-angle limits (the low bank angle limits made us just arc the target rather than head towards it) so my pilot (Rich Crandall) pulled the nose up to ensure ground clearance and made a hard right turn to head direct to the target. We rolled out and descended back to 500ft for the delivery. I was watching out for threats now and saw AAA start up off to our left and mentioned it to Rich. He was concentrating on the target. The AAA looked like small stuff not too far away, but it was actually big stuff 12 miles away at H-2 airfield as the lead elements of our 21-ship group were over their targets. Rich wasn't able to confirm the target in the FLIR so he undesignated it and bombed another one, which was visible a little farther along. In the debrief the big TV picture showed a better picture than in the jet and it turned out that the designation was fine on the original target, so I didn't feel bad. It was standard procedure for the pilot to visually confirm that the designation was on the target before releasing. Anyway, our No. 3 said both Nos 1 and 2 got secondary explosions from their bombs so we were sure we had taken out a "Scud" like we were tasked to do.

## DAYLIGHT STRIKES

In the daylight deliveries that followed, "Dive Toss" was used to put bombs on target from the relative sanctuary of medium level. Rolling the jet inverted from 30,000ft and diving towards the target for final visual verification, the pilot would pull out no lower than 15,000ft; the approximate ceiling for the majority of Iraqi AAA. When the target was not accurately designated, the pilot slewed the target designator in his HUD over the correct target before hitting the "pickle" button.

Jerry "One-Y" Oney and Bill "Shadow" Schaal, both captains at the time, flew their first two missions during daytime, which was a little disconcerting, as Oney explains:

I sorta liked the advantage the night gave us. About the funniest thing that happened during the first mission was Bill saw a guy heading west, pulling a boat down one of the major highways in Iraq. We both got a good chuckle out of that one before we slung our CEM [CBU-87 Combined Effects Munition] at some "Scuds" intel [intelligence] had previously located for us. Didn't see much of anything in the way of either air–air or air–

ground threats during our ingress of egress, but I can tell you we had the radar working overtime and "checking-six" wasn't just a casual pastime.

We were sent after some more mobile "Scuds" on our second mission and this was probably our most eventful one – maybe! Our two-ship had been scheduled on a pre-planned target, but just before "step-time" [time to "step out" to the jet for the mission] we got re-tasked to go after some mobile "Scuds." Apparently a two-ship of "Hogs" [A-10 attack aircraft] had been looking for these things, had bingo'd out [reached a critical fuel state] and gone home, so we were sent to have a look. The "Scuds" were supposed to be located somewhere along a certain road in southeastern Iraq so we pressed up there as quickly as we could. We crossed the border, went to a trail formation, and started to look for the bad guys. In the process of looking for the "Scuds" we'd found a smallish Iraqi AAA site/encampment and had patch-mapped it for future use. Personally, I wanted to sling at least one Mk 82 on the camp, but we had other priorities at the time. Well, there we were, a couple of the USAF's finest and flying the mighty Strike Eagle at around 2000ft AGL [above ground level], below a mostly scattered cloud deck, in a two-mile trail, doing 500 knots, and doing road-recce looking for some "Scuds." Even then I was thinking, "This ain't the greatest idea in the history of earth." I was soon proved correct as we flew past this Iraqi airfield and saw the smoke trail of an SA-7 or maybe an SA-9 heading past us and right towards lead. As luck would have it, lead had just looked over his right shoulder starting an easy right turn, and saw the missile smoke trail heading his way. The next bit of action that happened seemed compressed into about two seconds or less: lead broke hard into the missile in an attempt to defeat it, I watched the thing overshoot and detonate about 500ft above lead (I could've sworn I actually heard the thing explode), Bill maneuvered hard to avoid lead as we now had a BIG face-full of F-15E heading more or less right towards us. Damn but an Eagle can turn!

I felt all of our ordnance and fuel tanks come off the airplane as Bill calmly punched the jettison button as part of our attempt to avoid hitting lead, and to get our weight down in anticipation of another shot coming our way. We continued our evasive action more or less to the north, and lead continued his hard maneuvering heading south. We eventually joined up a few minutes later; the APG-70 radar is a wonderful thing, thank you Hughes! Our day wasn't done yet, though. We regrouped, got our noses in the same direction, got back into a trail formation, got down low, got real fast, and headed home. Murphy's law is alive and well no matter the country or continent. We managed to fly right past that same AAA site I'd wanted to bomb not ten minutes earlier! As we came upon it, I could actually see this guy run to his quad-barreled 23mm gun, swing the thing around, and begin shooting at us; at least this is how my mind's eye recalled it once we'd crossed back into Saudi territory. Well in that particular space of time the longest distance in the world was between my brain and my mouth. I wanted to tell Bill all about the guy running to his gun, it turning towards us, and about all the tracers heading our way. The net result of all those efforts was me taking the throttles and slamming them into full A/B [afterburner] to help the situation out. Unbeknownst to me, Bill had seen the entire thing too, and having the throttles flung from his hands with a resounding "bang" against the stops, thought we'd been hit!

After we figured out we both had the same situation awareness, Bill's comment was classic and shows what an always-thinking fighter pilot he was – and is: "that's a good way to soak up a heater!" [Attract a heat-seeking missile.] Roger that. As an Air Force brat I'd grown up around a lot of World War 2, Korea, and Vietnam combat aviators. One told me the story of how, unlike everyone else he'd heard on the radio after they got hit with a SAM and/or AAA, [he thought] that he'd be calm and collected should he ever take rounds in his airplane. When that finally happened, he confessed his voice did indeed go up a few octaves. Well, during this AAA event, I'm actually

The 333rd FS "Lancers" are one of two formal training units responsible for taking brand new aircrew and training them to a standard where they can join an operational squadron. This "Lancer" jet basks in the sun during a rare "down day" at Seymour Johnson, amid a backdrop of more than 80 other F-15Es of the 4th FW.

replaying his story in my head before telling lead we're taking AAA (probably a wasted radio call anyway) so I reckon I'll sound cool and calm over the radio! To say I didn't sound like a play-by-play sports announcer hardly does it justice and lead let me know just that. Once we got back across the border and climbed up to altitude we both had a good belly-laugh at the whole thing. And so went mission number two!

## MOBILE "SCUDS"

With the fixed "Scud" sites now taken out of action, the hunt moved on to finding and attacking mobile "Scud" launchers. Unbeknownst to the TACC at the time, the Iraqis were hiding their mobile "Scuds" in specially adapted buses and underneath road bridges; they were inventive and highly skilled in the art of deception and camouflage. The E-8 J-STARS (Joint-Surveillance Target Attack Radar System) aircraft had prematurely finished its own Operational Test and Evaluation program and been rushed to the region. It carried a massive SAR and ground moving target (GMT) radar in a canoe-shaped fairing under the lower fuselage. This was able to see many, many miles into Iraq and Kuwait.

TACC in Riyadh assigned F-15Es and A-10s to work "Scud" boxes (patches of desert where "Scud" launches might be possible) every night with the E-8. If a suspected "Scud" was picked up on radar, the E-8 would pass the coordinates and the "striker" would put the bombs on the target. F-15Es would patrol their "Scud" box for four to six hours, after which they would be relieved by another flight, and would then move on to drop their ordnance on secondary targets – anything from armor, or artillery pieces, to known fixed "Scud" sites.

Throughout the war, the F-15E was continually frustrated by the elusive search for "Scuds." Diverted from its deep-strike role, it failed to have much of an impact on continued "Scud" launches. Despite random bomb releases in the hope of dissuading the Iraqis from setting up for a launch, many of the kills claimed during the war were discredited following a more thorough, post-war analysis. This did not betray any dishonesty by the F-15E crews, but was instead indicative of the fact that they could not adequately identify what they were hitting from medium altitudes at night, even when they had the benefit of a TP. (Several "kills" were subsequently identified as commercial fuel tankers or busses. On other occasions, the IR signature from herds of camels and flocks of sheep closely resembled mobile "Scuds" and the unfortunate beasts were subsequently attacked.)

## LOSSES

On the second day the 4th TFW (P) lost its first jet to hostile fire. Maj Donnie "Chief Dimpled Balls" Holland (WSO) and Maj Thomas F. "Teek" Koritz were part of T-BIRD flight, a six-ship strike against a petrol oil and lubricant (POL) station near Basra, defended by SA-3, SA-6, SA-8, and Roland SAMs (surface-to-air missiles), in addition to a full range of radar-directed AAA. It is likely that they were downed by the latter, early reports suggesting that they may have flown into the ground as a result of pilot error having been discounted. Two other F-15E packages joined T-BIRD flight en route that night, making for a total package of 16 jets. T-BIRD flight separated to ingress the target at 300ft, intending to loft its Mk 82 bombs into the target – a technique suitable for a large, highly explosive target such as this. Intense fire greeted them and several jets were forced to turn tail and attempt another run at the target. Koritz and Holland were T-BIRD ONE-SIX (in F-15E AF88-1689); the sixth jet to attack the POL station. Al Gale picks up the story:

The crews that returned from this mission described it as one of the most difficult and dangerous missions of the war. Early on in the war the Iraqis had all their ammo and AAA sites ready.

The mission ingressed at low altitude (at night), using terrain following radar and FLIR in the LANTIRN pods. In those days this system was flown entirely manually by the pilots. The TFR provided pitch steering to maintain you at the altitude you specified, but there was no coupling with the autopilot as there is today. The pilot had to hand fly to keep the velocity vector inside the pitch steering box. This required total concentration. I don't know what ordnance they delivered, but they used loft deliveries. Ask any pilot or crew that has done a night, manual-TFR loft recovery, and they will tell you that it is dangerous even on a peacetime training mission. You start at low altitude and pull the nose up to your loft angle for bomb release. After release you over-bank and pull away from the target while starting your descent back to low altitude. Realize that at night this is entirely an instrument procedure as you have no ground references to look at. The FLIR provides a black and white picture in the HUD, but there is little depth perception from it. You have to watch your altitude, bank angle, and dive angle carefully: if you get outside the parameters for the TFR, you can hit the ground before it can time back in and provide pitch steering.

**Right:** In position and stabilized, an F-15E pilot concentrates on holding position behind a KC-135 tanker during a sortie over Iraq. The WSO watches the refueling boom (out of shot, but visible in the reflection on the canopy) as it plugs into the Strike Eagle's receptacle with a clunk. The seeker heads of two GBU-12 LGBs on the right CFT stations weathervane awkwardly in the F-15E's slow boundary-layer air.

## US Multi-Role Fighter Jets

# STRIKE EAGLE

Two nights later came the second, and final, F-15E loss. Flying AF88-1692, Col David Eberly and Maj Thomas E. Griffiths Jr were downed by an SA-2 on January 20 while attacking a fixed "Scud" site. They ejected and managed to evade capture for several days, and Eberly made contact with two Coalition aircraft as he attempted to arrange a rescue. Eberly and Griffiths were subsequently captured, and paraded on television as war trophies. They spent the rest of the war as PoWs.

## "SPLASH ONE HELICOPTER!"

On February 14, 1991 the Strike Eagle scored its first air-to-air kill – a Mi-24 "Hind" attack helicopter. In response to a request for help from US Special Forces (SF), AWACS called capts Richard T. Bennett and Dan B. Bakke to ask for assistance. Arming and selecting a single GBU-10 LGB, Bennett took the F-15E at full power through bad weather and into the area as directed. At 50 miles out, Bakke picked up contacts on the radar and later cued the TP as they broke through the weather at 3,000ft. They closed the last 20 miles as Iraqi AAA crews fired their weapons towards where they thought the F-15E was, a technique Strike Eagle aircrew came to call derisively "Sound Activated AAA."

With two of the three helicopters now clearly visible in the pod, Bakke pickled the GBU-10 six miles from the target – it would have a 30-second time of flight to reach the "Hind." As the 30 seconds came and went, the crew assumed that the bomb had missed or failed to detonate. Bennett pulled the jet into a left

Designed to operate by dead of night, the F-15E Strike Eagle is a fearsome fighter whose two-man crew allows it to undertake particularly complex missions in high-threat environments. This example, replete with waiting pilot and WSO, belongs to the 48th FW, RAF Lakenheath, England.

Afghanistan offers little by way of conventional threats, although as this 492nd FS Strike Eagle shows, the jet is still armed with flares to counter IR missiles. In reality, the biggest threat comes from flying at night over mountainous terrain; a danger that became all too clear on July 18, 2009, when an F-15E pilot and WSO flew into the ground during night strafing practise.

turn, his intention being to come back and target the helicopters with an AIM-9 or two. But as they reefed the jet around again, the "Hind" blew up and literally vaporized. SF troops on the ground had estimated the helicopter to be at about 800ft when the bomb impacted just in front of the main rotor. The call "COUGAR [AWACS], PACKARD FOUR-ONE [F-15E], splash one helicopter [one helicopter shot down]," was duly made.

The F-15E had played a pivotal role in the opening stages of the war, and had flown 7,700 combat hours in around 2,400 sorties. In addition to flying deep interdiction to hit "Scuds," it had also flown close air support (CAS) and been tasked against air defense sites on the third night of the war – when they were still highly active. It enjoyed great success in destroying Iraqi armor, artillery, troops, and aircraft on the ground, and had expanded its repertoire by working with SF controllers on the ground, and E-8 J-STARS in the air.

Over the next 19 years, the Strike Eagle would go on to play a pivotal role in every major conflict the United States was involved in. It patrolled the skies of Iraq for more than a decade under the auspices of operations *Provide Comfort*, *Northern Watch* and *Southern Watch*. Interspersed with these taskings, the Gunship Gray jet was also central to the ability of NATO to forcibly resolve the turbulent troubles of the 1990s in the Balkans, under operations *Deny Flight* and *Allied Force*. Many of these combat operations have been widely reported, yet the Strike Eagle's operations in Afghanistan in the immediate aftermath of the September 2011 terrorist attacks have received less coverage than they perhaps deserve.

## OPERATION *ENDURING FREEDOM*: OUSTING THE TALIBAN

The Strike Eagle's ability to find elusive targets by dead of night mean that its importance in ousting the Taliban from power, and pursuing Al Qaeda into the mountains that border with Pakistan, cannot be overstated. At the time of writing (August 2010), Strike Eagles continued to deploy to Bagram AB, Afghanistan, to support Operation *Enduring Freedom*, but it was the months that followed the initial October 2001 invasion of the small landlocked country that are most noteworthy.

Less than 24 hours after being told that they would be supporting Operation *Enduring Freedom*, 12 F-15Es from the 391st FS "Bold Tigers" and 12 F-16CJs of the 389th FS left Idaho on October 12, 2001, and began a lengthy trip to Ahmed Al Jaber Air Base (AB), Kuwait, where they began operations under the command of the 332nd Air Expeditionary Group (AEG). The Strike Eagles belonged to the 366th Air Expeditionary Wing (AEW), Mountain Home AFB, Idaho, a "composite wing" whose *raison d'être* was to be ready at a moment's notice to deploy anywhere in the world. Highly flexible therefore, the 336th operated not only within the USAF's pre-planned Aerospace Expeditionary Forces (AEF) assignments, but also as a "crisis reaction wing" to cover un-planned Air Expeditionary Forces requirements. AEF was primarily a means of evenly tasking USAF aircraft and manpower for three-month deployments to operations *Northern* or *Southern Watch*. Up until the day before it was assigned to Operation *Enduring Freedom*, the 391st was scheduled to go to Operation *Southern Watch*.

In some respects, the 36 "Bold Tigers" (18 pilots, 18 WSOs) were better prepared for this war than might have been imagined. The US's "relationship" with the Taliban had certainly not improved since limited cruise missile strikes targeted Al Qaeda leader Osama Bin Laden in October 1998. Astute planners and weapons school graduates within the "Bold Tigers" had taken it upon themselves to build up a picture of what kind of foe Afghanistan would make. Beavering away in their squadron's secure compartmented information facility, they had pieced together a basic picture that suggested a non-existent air threat and an unsophisticated air defense system consisting of man-portable air defense systems (MANPADS) and AAA equipment.

Arriving in Kuwait to a somewhat uncertain tasking, they therefore had at least some idea as to what they would be up against. It had been obvious during the squadron's studies that Afghanistan's dilapidated infrastructure would offer few fixed targets of real value. Indeed, the squadron had specifically trained for the eventuality that much of its work would see it making full use of forward air controllers (FACs), as Lt Col Andrew "AJ" Britschgi, 391st FS CO in 2001, reflected: "We knew that we'd end up working mostly with FACs if we were ever tasked to strike targets in Afghanistan. We therefore practiced that mission regularly over the course of our peacetime schedule. We also knew that our role within any deployment would be [as] the primary player, and there is no doubt that our training translated well into the way in which we operated over there [Afghanistan]." The 391st FS crews believed that FACs would guide them to mobile or time-critical targets over jam-resistant radios, and time would soon tell just how accurate their prediction had been.

**Previous page:** Strike Eagle pilot Maj Randy "Hacker" Haskin sends "Two" to line abreast as a photo opportunity presents itself following the conclusion of another Operation *Enduring Freedom* sortie. The F-15E saved many friendly lives in both Iraq and Afghanistan, and continues to be the focus of regular updates and improvements.

---

The Combined Air Operations Center (CAOC) at McDill AFB, Florida, was the authority delegated to plan all sorties for the duration of the war – the Air Tasking Order (ATO). In late October 2001, some two weeks after the air war had started, "AJ" led the first wave of 391st FS F-15E attacks, meeting little resistance once over the target. As they returned mid-afternoon, the second Strike Eagle wave took flight, and so began an almost continuous cycle of F-15E strikes that would run for three months. "For the first fortnight or so, military buildings, Taliban supply depots, caves, and Al Qaeda training camps were the key focus of our attack," commented "Fang," a highly experienced WSO who had already seen combat in the Balkans and operations *Northern* and *Southern Watch*.

> Crews would receive the "frag" [ATO] the night before a mission was flown. The guys not scheduled to fly would break out the ATO and plan the next day's sorties throughout the remainder of the night; when our own resources were inadequate we used commercial sources, such as 5-metre resolution satellite imagery from Georgia State University, to fill the blanks. CAOC would provide suggestions for weapon types and delivery modes, but on the whole the Squadron would run things as we saw best, and only rarely did the CAOC ever "tell" us how to get the job done. Once the sorties had been planned, the guys flying could come in the next morning one hour before their briefing, familiarize themselves with the route, brief the mission and then step to the jets for engine start.

Both the AGM-130 and EGBU-15, 2,000lb, optically guided weapons (featuring mid-course GPS guidance and datalinked terminal guidance) were used throughout the first weeks of the war to hit caves leading to underground facilities. They were also used to precisely strike targets which were difficult to identify under normal conditions or when desired weapons effects were required. It was the first time that the EGBU (Enhanced Guided Bomb Unit) had been used in anger, and this was one of just a number of "firsts" achieved by the "Bold Tigers" in Afghanistan. The GBU-24, fitted with the BLU-109 penetrator warhead, and the 4,400lb GBU-28 "Bunker Buster" bomb were also both used for the destruction of reinforced targets and underground Taliban facilities. The GBU-28 in particular was targeted at Taliban command and control centers, and cave entrances; a total of five were dropped. "We prepared ourselves for the arrival of the BLU-118/B thermobaric bomb, but it arrived too late in theatre for us to use," said Britschgi. That honor fell to the 335th FS "Chiefs," who replaced the 391st in January 2002.

Often, the Strike Eagles would operate as two-ship flights alongside two-ship flights of F-16s. "The F-16s had VHF radios and this made it much easier to talk to civilian ATC agencies, since most didn't closely monitor their UHF. All players, like AWACS and the FACs, had UHF capability, so VHF made things a little easier for going to and from the target area," said "Spear," an F-15E pilot. "For the most part, we'd fly as two ships and would link up with the F-16s over Afghanistan. They would often fly separate orbits from us, but we'd share the same tanker. Only rarely did we ever fly as four F-15Es," he added.

Within a matter of weeks, CAOC planners were discovering that they had almost exhausted their list of meaningful fixed targets. From very early on in the operation they had recognized that a growing number of targets were falling into the time-sensitive tasking

(TST) category. TST targets were those that could move or hide if they were not attacked within a certain window of opportunity – people, vehicles, etc. It was time to change the way in which air assets were tasked.

The Taliban had access to Soviet-made SA-7 and US-made Stinger "basic" MANPADS. Their air force was believed to be non-existent, and although they had AAA guns of a variety of calibers, very little of this was radar directed. "A lot of their AAA was sound activated," said "Spear," "they'd hear us and fire at where we had been, but they never really came close to us." "AJ" concurred, "in the time I was there I did not get locked up by a single hostile radar." Fixed SAM sites around such cities as Mazar-I-Sharif and Bagram were struck very early on with precision weapons, although they may not have actually been serviceable to begin with. In all, the AOR was classed as "low-threat," and this classification was reinforced by the fact that there was not a single instance of an F-15E jettisoning its external fuel tanks, a standard tactic when evasive maneuvers need to be flown.

Taliban troops who fired their shoulder mounted missiles rarely posed a threat, since most aircraft were well above the 7,000ft engagement zone of these early-generation IR guided missiles. "Spear" commented that, "the Taliban conserved their missiles early on in the campaign, but, as the war progressed, their frustration mounted and they began to fire more and more." Britschgi reflected that this was the way in which the air war was waged – the Taliban and Al Qaeda soldiers were powerless to defend themselves; futile attempts to do so only brought them more misery as their location was identified and bombed.

As had been predicted, and some three weeks into the operation, the "Bold Tigers" tasking changed from specific targets to providing on-call support for pre-set "vulnerability times." "Fang" compared the system in Afghanistan with those that he had previously experienced, "the US Army had established a grid system worked out according to Army placement of FACs. It was far better than the east/west system used in Kosovo; we had very specific areas of responsibility here. Our new tasking was geared explicitly to making sure that TST targets could be hit as expeditiously as possible. Our ordnance for these sorties would typically be nine GBU-12s or a mix of GBU-12s and Mk 82s, but we also used ten other symmetric and asymmetric loads according to mission requirements." A third "first" for the Strike Eagle occurred when a GBU-28, two GBU-24s and six GBU-12s were released in a single sortie.

Much of the "Bold Tigers" action happened at night when the Taliban felt safest to move. "Calls for support were often as a result of Northern Alliance troops flushing the Taliban out of hiding and forcing them to take to the open. Our radio chatter would be intense at times, and we were far from refining the art of night CAS," "Fang" said. "Spear" continued, "the lead pilot or WSO would sometimes be talking to a FAC who was not fully trained in the art of directing air strikes, so we had a very busy environment up there. Night vision goggles [NVG] helped us, but most of our work was done with the target pod."

Occasionally, humidity and smoke obscured the TP's view and the FAC would "walk" the F-15E's bombs onto the target with verbal corrections ("next bomb 50 metres north of your last," for example). "Spear" recalled, "when the target could be clearly identified, the two-ship element would discuss the placement of their bombs before actually running in on the target; we did not want the debris and smoke from one another's bombs to obscure the target." People, vehicles, and convoys were the most frequent targets called in, and the former were dispatched with proximity fused Mk 82s (CAOC permitted the use of cluster bombs early on in the campaign, but the

# F-15E STRIKE EAGLE SPECIFICATION

**Dimensions**
Length: 63ft 9in
Height: 18ft 5½in
Wing span: 42ft 9¾in
Wing aspect ratio: 3.01
Tailplane span: 28ft 3in
Wheel track: 9ft ¼in
Wheelbase: 17ft 9½in

**Powerplant**
Original F-15E had powerplant of F-15C/D, but with option of General Electric F110-GE-129. Aircraft from the 135th onwards (90-0233), built from August 1991, have two Pratt and Whitney F100-PW-229s each rated at 29,000lb st with afterburning.

**Weights**
Empty operating: 31,700lb
Normal take-off: 44,823lb
Maximum take-off: 81,000lb

**Fuel and load**
Internal fuel: 13,123lb
External fuel: 21,645lb
Maximum weapon load: 24,500lb

**Performance**
Maximum level speed: Mach 2.5
Maximum combat radius: 685nm
Maximum combat range: 2,400nm

**Armament**
One 20-mm M61A1 six-barrel gun, with 512 rounds, in starboard wingroot. Wing pylons for AIM-9 Sidewinder, AIM-120 AMRAAM, and AIM-7 Sparrow, AGM-65 Maverick and AGM-130. A wide range of compatible guided and unguided weapons includes GBU-31, -38 and -54 JDAM; GBU-39 SDB; GBU-10, -12, -15, -24 and -28 LGBs; EGBU-15 and -24; Mk 82 and Mk 84 LDGPs; CBU-87, -89 and -97 cluster munitions; and B57 and B61 nuclear weapons. For AGM-130 and E/GBU-15 missions an AXQ-14 datalink pod is also carried.

---

"Bold Tigers" refrained from using them due to the indiscriminate way in which these munitions operated).

For moving trucks, tanks, and convoys, GBU-12s were the weapon of choice: "We became quite adept at hitting vehicles traveling at 60mph with the GBU-12. We'd simply place our crosshairs in front of the lead vehicle, release the weapon and then walk the laser spot back onto the target," said "AJ." The GBU-12 was the precision munition most often employed, not only because of its relative cheapness, but also because it did not exhibit a propensity for falling short of the target as some of the larger GBU series did. This was an important consideration when dropping weapons within close proximity of civilians or civic buildings.

When troops were in contact and CAS became necessary, the "Bold Tigers" would venture down low to ensure maximum weapons and target identification accuracy. Several times they struck Taliban troops who were so close to friendly troops that the FACs would whisper their radio calls. One example of enterprising tactics employed by the "Bold Tigers" involved a US Special Forces request for a strike on Taliban trucks, traveling in convoy and about to "requisition" a key bridge. The FAC, speaking in hushed tones, requested that the Taliban be hit without the destruction of the bridge, over which the

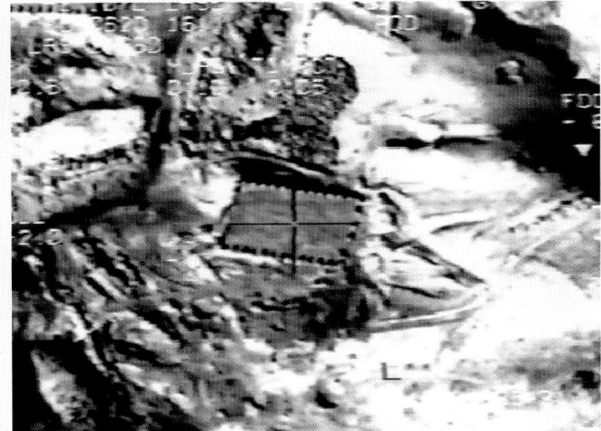
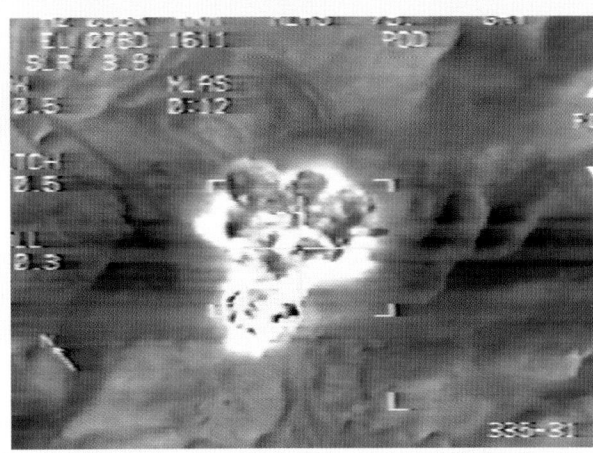

March 2003, and a "Scud" missile propellant factory falls under the crosshairs of the AAQ-13 LANTIRN target pod carried by a 336th FS "Rocketeers" Strike Eagle. In the first image, the factory is clearly identified and the pilot "pickles" the GBU-10C LGB. As the second image shows, the bomb impacts neatly in the middle of the crosshairs, having ridden the reflected cone of laser energy all the way to the target. Less than a second later the third image captures the resulting secondary explosion, one so ferocious that it blankets the area and causes the LANTIRN's IR sensor to "bloom," meaning that the resultant heat washes out the once-detailed cockpit display.

enemy was now swarming. The obliging Strike Eagle pilot rolled his aircraft towards the bridge and decimated the Taliban convoy with several hundred rounds of 20mm M56 high explosive incendiary rounds from the M61A1 Vulcan cannon mounted in the right wing root. The bridge remained standing and was used later that day by the Northern Alliance to move reinforcements. "The F-15E has employed the gun in combat before and it is a viable offensive weapon. F-15E aircrew need to train to use it much more than every six months," "Fang" commented.

Sometimes FACs used their own lasers: "The FAC would call a run-in heading, we'd synchronize laser codes so that our bomb 'recognized' his laser beam, and we'd roll in and pickle off a GBU-12 which the FAC would then guide to target. It worked well," said "Spear." In these scenarios the GBU-12 was favored not only for its ballistic properties, but also for its smaller explosive footprint. In addition to FACs, the F-15E also worked with Predator UAVs (unmanned aerial vehicles), although the Strike Eagle's unique AXQ-14 datalink pod (which can receive real time video for targeting purposes) was not used as the ground support equipment necessary to support it was unavailable.

Some sorties resulted in frustration. All aircraft in the theater were operating under strict rules of engagement (ROE), especially those providing close air support. The "Bold Tigers" took HQ-assigned ROE as minimum criteria for weapons release and added their own discriminators to the equation. "Fang" explained, "in all situations, targets had to be visually identified by the FAC as hostile. This had to be concurred by lead, and then concurred by his wingman before we would strike a target. If either of the three decision makers had reservations or could not see the target, then weapons would not be released."

Crews were genuinely concerned about the potential for innocent civilians being killed, and worked hard to ensure that this was avoided at all costs. "Fang" cited a terrorist training camp by way of example: "It measured 200ft by 200ft and was tasked for complete destruction, the LIMFAC [limiting factor] was that it lay directly next to a Mosque. We used GBU-12s to systematically demolish the camp, but left the Mosque standing and untouched. As an added layer of protection, we only ever employed large weapons like the GBU-24 and GBU-10 2,000lb bombs when there was very little chance of collateral damage."

The "Bold Tigers" also flew reconnaissance missions, often at the behest of a FAC, and would scout roads and valleys for Taliban activity using the AAQ-14 target pod. The E-8C J-STARS was also in theater, although only a limited amount of work was accomplished with this particular platform.

During the course of their three-month tenure, four "Bold Tigers" entered the history books when they flew what at that time was the longest fighter combat sortie ever – 15.5 hours, of which nine hours were spent over the target. CROCKETT 51/52 was a two-ship F-15E flight tasked with patrolling a set of grid coordinates for the usual "vul" (vulnerability) time of three hours. In the lead jet were "Slokes" and "Snitch" (pilot and WSO, respectively), while No. 2 was crewed by "Spear" and "Buzzer." Each Strike Eagle carried nine GBU-12s, two AIM-9 Sidewinders, two AIM-120 AMRAAMs, and two wing fuel tanks.

Once on-station, CROCKETT flight received a TST from AWACS to contact a Predator drone control unit. The unit had been monitoring suspicious activity around a set of buildings believed to be Taliban command and control facilities. "Spear" recalled:

> Each jet set up two different laser codes (No. 1 had 1511 on the left CFT and 1533 on the right CFT. No. 2 had 1522 on the left and 1544 on the right). No. 1 released four bombs [GBU-12s] from his jet, giving us two with 1511 laser codes and two with 1533. We programmed in 1533 on our laser so that we could guide two of the bombs, they had 1511 in on theirs so that they could guide the other two bombs. This way we took out two buildings, side-by-side, with simultaneous impacts. We actually flew two passes, the first to ensure that we had the correct targets, the second to actually drop the weapons.

Both targets were effectively neutralized. During the course of this action a AAA piece had been firing at the flight, and this too would have been attacked but for the fact that it stopped firing at them and they were unable to locate it. One more building was struck and demolished following a second TST Predator tasking.

CROCKETT flight pressed on to fly a road recce following a FAC call to request their help in identifying some road traffic he had spotted. Unsure of the identity of the traffic, the flight soon came across a Taliban road block in the mountains and quickly dispatched it. Having already air refueled several times, the flight was taking fuel for its journey home, when AWACS called and asked them to contact Predator once again. A third building was assigned to them, and each jet once more rippled two GBU-12s. The building, suspected of sheltering Taliban fighters, was directly hit and destroyed.

CROCKETT 51/52's historic flight had refueled 12 times (each refueling giving them 1 to 1.5 hours of loiter time) and had been hugely successful in terms of weapons delivery accuracy and weapons effects accomplished. Although the duration of the sortie was exceptional, "Spear" seemed more impressed that his backside could still hurt a week later!

On January 7, 2002, the 366th AEW welcomed back the 391st FS from what had been a highly successful deployment. The "Bold Tigers" were replaced by F-15Es of the 335th FS, 4th Wing, Seymour Johnson AFB. They had achieved a sortie generation rate better than 85 percent, flying two to eight sorties every day, each of which lasted six to nine hours and involved anywhere up to 12 air refuelings. The tactics they had used were heavily modified, and F-15E Fighter Weapons School instructors have privately heaped praise on them for their innovation and success rate, "some of our most recent graduates did a fine job of 'making things happen' in Afghanistan. Thinking through and executing 'non-standard' tactics to achieve the desired results is more important than mastering a single mission type; our boys made us proud," said "Bud," a weapons school instructor WSO.

Operation *Enduring Freedom* was followed in March 2003 with the second invasion of Iraq, Operation *Iraqi Freedom*, and the two Seymour Johnson squadrons, the 335th FS "Chiefs" and 336th FS "Rocketeers," deployed 48 jets to Al Udeid AB, Qatar, accordingly. The actual "shooting war" lasted only a matter of a few weeks, and while one Strike Eagle was lost to unknown causes, the conflict was otherwise a successful one for the F-15E pilots and WSOs. The 336th FS recorded a total time of 5,937.9 hours flown; 4,788.7 of those were combat hours flown during the course of 1,768 individual combat sorties. The F-15E itself finished the war with a mission capable rate of 84.1 percent, higher than any other USAF fighter bar the far less active F-117 Nighthawk.

The Strike Eagle's presence in the opening stages of Operation *Enduring Freedom* gave Allied Commanders significant flexibility when assigning target types and complexes. In response, the F-15E community performed with great skill.

# LOCKHEED MARTIN F-16

## LIGHTWEIGHT FIGHTER

Conceived and marketed as the ultimate dogfighter, the Lockheed Martin (formerly General Dynamics) F-16 Fighting Falcon is one of the most ubiquitous combat aircraft in service today. With 2,231 individual airframes procured by Air Combat Command (formerly Tactical Air Command (TAC)) between December 1976 and January 2009, it remains the most prolific fighter in US service today.

The F-16 was originally designed as a lightweight, short-range point defense fighter to complement the McDonnell Douglas F-15 Eagle. In the Pentagon in 1969, a cadre of vocal fighter pilots had lobbied for a design that would be simple, agile as a knife in the close-in fight, and dedicated to dominating the enemy in the within visual range fight.

The 1972 request for proposals asked companies to submit designs for a 20,000lb fighter with good turning capabilities and acceleration, and while the first YF-16A prototype was very light when it first flew on December 13, 1973, by the time it had won the Lightweight Fighter (LWF) competition – beating the Northrop YF-17, which eventually became the F/A-18 Hornet – in January 1975, the jet was only ever going to get heavier. There were many reasons for this, but perhaps the most pressing was that the Air Force would be foolhardy to purchase a bantam fighter when the United States fully expected to be fighting its wars halfway around the world. Crucially, though, the Air Force took the view that the F-15 Eagle, which featured only very basic air-to-ground capabilities, was too expensive and important to be assigned to the CAS, battlefield interdiction, and other ground-attack roles.

As a result, it was the F-16 that was given the air-to-ground mission, and with that decision came an increase in weight and complexity. Even so, the "Fighter Mafia" had prevailed in their enthusiasm for combining high-cost fighters (F-15) with low-cost fighters (F-16) as a complementary force mix that could be purchased in sufficient quantities, without compromising on technical advantage, to defeat an opponent who was likely to have an overwhelming numerical advantage.

The F-16 won the LWF competition because it offered better maneuverability near the Mach and could out turn and out accelerate the YF-17. Moreover, it was cheaper to operate, had a more attractive combat range, and shared the same engine as the F-15A/B Eagle, the Pratt & Whitney F100.

General Dynamics built eight full-scale development (FSD) F-16A/B airframes. The first FSD F-16A flew at Fort Worth, Texas, on December 8, 1976, while the first two-seat FSD F-16B flew on August 8, 1977. Each was equipped with a Westinghouse AN/APG-66 radar, an increased fuselage length of 49ft 6in, and a fin height of 16ft 8in. The enlarged canopy and elongated forward fuselage of the B-model added no additional aerodynamic drag, but did cost 1,500lb of fuel tank capacity.

On August 17, 1978, TAC accepted the first production F-16A and the first operational unit to fly the type became the 388th TFW, Hill AFB, Utah, in January 1979. Hill's 4th TFS became the first to achieve initial operational capability (IOC), on November 12, 1980. F-16A/Bs were subsequently manufactured until 1985, following production of the first Block 25 F-16C/Ds in 1984.

---

**Previous page:** The Lockheed Martin F-16 is the most widely exported US fighter of modern times and remains the most prolific fighter in the US inventory. This pair of 18th Aggressor Squadron F-16Cs returns home to Eielson AFB, Alaska, sandwiched between an ominous overcast and a prominent ground haze.

## F-16C/D

The succession of improved build standards of the "Viper" (the most universal of the F-16's nicknames) in the intervening years, are identified as "Blocks" (Block 1, Block 10, Block 25, etc). These Blocks further refine the major overall airframe improvements that manifest themselves as marques (F-16A/B and F-16C/D for the USAF). Insofar as US multi-role fighters are concerned, the most capable and numerous of the C-model Viper family are the F-16C/D Block 30/32, Block 40/42, and Block 50/52.

The F-16A covered Blocks 1-20 and was superseded by the F-16C, which began at Block 25 and features the much more capable AN/APG-68(V) radar; a "glass cockpit" consisting of two multi-function displays (MFDs), a wide-angle HUD, up-front controls, support for infra-red video; increased capacity environmental control and electrical power systems; a MIL STD-1760 data bus/weapons interface allowing the use of AGM-65D Maverick and AIM-120 AMRAAM; improved fire control and stores management computers; and a Have Quick II anti-jam UHF radio.

The F-16CJ is a Block 50/52 Viper whose primary concern is the prosecution of enemy threat emitters — a role known as Wild Weasel. Key to the success of this mission is the HTS pod, seen here on the right side of this 22nd FS jet's intake. HTS "sniffs out," categorizes, and locates the position of enemy radar and network sites.

## IMPROVED VIPERS AND NIGHT STRIKERS

The Block 30/32 F-16 was the first Viper variant to feature a common engine bay able to accept either the Pratt & Whitney F100-PW-220 (Block 32) or General Electric F110-GE-129 (Block 30). The F110 produces 5,000lb more thrust than the F100, and requires a larger amount of air, prompting the redesign of the F-16's inlet to satisfy the larger volume of air required. Early F-16C/D Block 30s have "small inlets," but F110-powered Fighting Falcons from F-16C 86-0262 onwards feature the aptly coined "big mouth" inlet. The official name for this installation is Modular Common Air Intake Duct. The

# US Multi-Role Fighter Jets

Dave Goldfein, a colonel at the time of this 2005 photograph, but a major general since July 2010, prepares to fly a sortie at Spangdahlem AB, Germany. Between 2004 and 2006, Goldfein was the commander of the 52nd FW, parent to two F-16CJ squadrons. As a member of the 555th FS, based at Aviano AB, Italy, a Serbian SAM had downed him in May 1999 during Operation *Allied Force*.

smaller inlet of Pratt & Whitney-powered F-16s is the normal shock inlet.

Full multi-target capability for the AIM-120 AMRAAM was added in the spring of 1987, prompting the designation Block 30B. Expanded memory was provided for the Programmable Display Generator and the Data Entry Electronics Unit, and the Block 30/32 also introduced the Seek Talk secure voice communication system, and was equipped with seal-bond fuel tanks. In August 1987, provision to fire the AGM-45 Shrike and AGM-88 HARM (High-speed Anti- Radiation Missile) was made, together with installation of a voice message unit and crash-survivable flight data recorder. Block 30D introduced twice as many chaff/flare dispensers and moved the forward radar warning receiver (RWR) antennas to the leading edge flap. Dubbed "beer can" antennas for obvious reasons, these have since been retrofitted onto all previous F-16C/Ds.

In 1990 production moved to the F-16C/D Block 40/42 version (in Air Force service these aircraft are unofficially designated CG for the single-seaters and CD for the two-seaters); this now equips the bulk of the F-16 FWs in the Active Duty Air Force (ACC, Pacific Air

Continued on page 69.

# OPERATORS – BLOCK 30 AND ABOVE

The 1,280 F-16C/Ds in the US Air Force inventory in 2010 are divided among the active duty squadrons, Air National Guard (ANG) units and Air Force Reserve.

Block 40 and Block 50/52 F-16s were used by the USAF in Operation *Iraqi Freedom* in March 2003, and Block 30s were employed by the ANG. The Air Force received its final new-build F-16 in March 2005, the Block 50 machine going to the 79th FS, 20th FW, at Shaw AFB, South Carolina.

## Air Combat Command
20th Fighter Wing, Shaw AFB, SC (Block 50)
53rd Fighter Wing, Eglin AFB, FL (Block 40/42 and 50/52)
57th Fighter Wing, Nellis AFB, NV (Block 32, 42, and 52)
388th Fighter Wing, Hill AFB, UT (Block 40)

## Air Education and Training Command
56th Fighter Wing, Luke AFB, AZ (Block 20 (Taiwanese); Block 25, 32, and 42; Block 52 (Singaporean))

## Air Force Materiel Command
46th Test Wing, Eglin AFB, FL (Block 15, 25, 40/42, and 50)
412th Test Wing, Edwards AFB, CA (all Blocks between 15 and 52)

## United States Air Forces Europe
31st Fighter Wing, Aviano AB, Italy (Block 40)
52nd Fighter Wing, Spangdahlem AB, Germany (Block 50)

## Pacific Air Forces
8th Fighter Wing, Kunsan AB, South Korea (Block 40)
35th Fighter Wing, Misawa AB, Japan (Block 50)
51st Fighter Wing, Osan AB, South Korea (Block 40)
354th Fighter Wing, Eielson AFB, AK (Block 30)

## Air Force Reserve
301st Fighter Wing, NAS Fort Worth, TX (Block 30 "small")
419th Fighter Wing, Hill AFB, UT (Block 30 "big")
482nd Fighter Wing, Homestead ARS, FL (Block 30 "big")

## Air National Guard
113th Fighter Wing, Andrews AFB, VA (Block 30 "small")
114th Fighter Wing, Sioux Falls IAP, SD (Block 30 "small")
115th Fighter Wing, Truax Field, WI (Block 30 "big")
122nd Fighter Wing, Fort Wayne AP, IN (Block 30 "small")
132nd Fighter Wing, Des Moines IAP, IA, (Block 30 "big")
138th Fighter Wing, Tulsa IAP, OK (Block 42)
140th Fighter Wing, Buckley ANGB, CO (Block 30 "big")
144th Fighter Wing, Fresno IAP, CA (Block 32)
150th Fighter Wing, Kirtland AFB, NM (Block 30 "big" and "small")
158th Fighter Wing, Burlington IAP, VT (Block 30 "big")
162nd Fighter Wing, Tucson IAP, AZ (Block 25, 32, and 42; Block 60 (UAE))
169th Fighter Wing, McEntire ANGB, SC (Block 52)
174th Fighter Wing, Syracuse IAP, NY (Block 30 "small")
177th Fighter Wing, Atlanta City IAP, NJ (Block 30)
178th Fighter Wing, Springfield IAP, OH (Block 30 "big")
180th Fighter Wing, Toledo AP, OH (Block 42)
187th Fighter Wing, Montgomery AP, AL (Block 30 "big")

## US Multi-Role Fighter Jets

# LOCKHEED MARTIN F-16

Forces (PACAF), USAFE, and Air Education and Training Command).

The Block 40 F-16C is equipped for enhanced all-weather and night capability. It carries LANTIRN navigation and targeting pods; features a holographic HUD; automatic terrain following capability; a pressure breathing system to improve $g$-tolerance; an enhanced-envelope gun sight; and a ground moving target bombing capability, in addition to many of the improvements seen in the Block 50/52. To top it off, the airframe was strengthened to expand the $9g$ flight envelope from 26,900lb gross weight to 28,500lb. Maximum take-off weight was to 42,300lb, which, combined with the need to provide adequate ground clearance for the two LANTIRN pods, prompted new undercarriage struts that were not only of heavier construction, but also physically longer. Bulged landing gear doors accommodate the larger wheels and tyres that are associated with the heavier ground-handling loads of the Block 40.

## FROM VIPER TO WILD WEASEL

In 1992 production of F-16C/D Block 50/52 commenced, and the type assumed the suppression of enemy air defenses (SEAD) role with the unofficial designation F-16CJ/DJ.

It was during the Vietnam War that the USAF introduced the first SEAD fighters, initially in the shape of the F-100F Super Sabre and most notably the F-105G Thunderchief. A rapid proliferation of Soviet-supplied SAM sites across North Vietnam had rendered the Iron Hand mission, which had typically

The 52nd FW at Spangdahlem AB, Germany, provides USAFE with its sole dedicated Wild Weasel capability. These three F-16CJs – one 22nd FS "Stingers," one 23rd FS "Fighting Hawks," and one jet belonging to the 52nd FW Operations Group – each tote two inert AGM-88 HARM practise rounds in addition to the standard fit of peacetime captive-carry AIM-120 AMRAAMs.

concentrated on killing AAA emplacements, largely impotent. With specialist mission equipment for hunting and killing SAMs a prerequisite, the Wild Weasel was born. Various iterations of the F-105G were seen, and many lessons were learned, before the archetypal SEAD platform – the F-4G – was finally created. Viewed by many as the most potent SAM killer ever, the F-4G Phantom performed with alacrity during the 1991 Gulf War, following which it was promptly retired from service, much to the chagrin of many a seasoned Wild Weasel. Its successor was the F-16CJ.

The Viper chosen for the SEAD role was the F-16CJ Block 50D/52D, one of the latest versions of the airframe, and the only one powered by the Pratt & Whitney F-100-PW-229 (Block 52) and General Electric F-110-GE-129 (Block 50) Improved Performance Engines. The standard Block 50 airframe features GPS navigation; a ring laser gyro inertial navigation system (RLG INS); AN/ALE-47 threat-adaptive countermeasures system; ALR-56M advanced RWR; horizontal situation display (HSD) – a digital moving map over which flight, weapons, target, and navigation data can be laid; night-vision goggle-compatible cockpit lighting; and the AN/APG-68V(5/7/8) radar, which offers improved reliability and detection ranges over previous versions. Combined, these modifications give the aircraft a significant boost in performance in both the air and ground arenas.

Taking the standard Block 50D/52D F-16C and upgrading it to perform the SEAD role involved the addition of two main pieces of mission-specific equipment. The most obvious of these is the AN/ASQ-213 HTS, the HARM Targeting System. HTS is carried in a small pod on the right side of the intake cheek. It is used to find, classify, range, and display threat emitter systems to the pilot. Supplementing HTS are the AN/ALR-56M advanced RWR, AN/ALQ-131(V)14 electronic countermeasures (ECM) pod and additional underwing-mounted chaff dispensers to complement those already mounted on the lower rear fuselage adjacent to the horizontal stabilizers.

The second key component to the F-16CJ is the Avionics Launcher Interface Computer (ALICS), which resides in the AGM-88 HARM launcher pylon and acts as the conduit between the HTS, the jet's central computer and the missile itself. Pronounced "a-licks," ALICS is essential for successful hand-off of radar threats from the jet to the HARM.

HTS uses reprogrammable software loads to permit it to maintain a library of up-to-date threat emitter signatures and to employ new techniques as they become available; the version in use at time of writing is Revision 6 (R6). Revision changes occur as both hardware and software updates are made available, and are a cost-effective way of ensuring that the HTS remains as capable as possible. As well as improvements to the speed and accuracy of emitter identification, location, and ranging, recent revisions have also seen the introduction of additional bandwidth coverage, to include the elusive millimeter wave datalink signals sent between SAM sites operating as part of an IADS.

Using HTS is straightforward in most instances. It has its own display page that can be called up onto one of the two MFDs in the cockpit, and which displays threat systems as symbols in a top-down format. By controlling the field of view of the pod, the pilot can make it scan certain frequencies and sectors of terrain faster or more slowly, depending upon whether the locations of target emitters are already known. Slower scans will be provided when a large field-of-view must be monitored; fast scans will naturally occur when the field of view is very narrow. With a given threat emitter detected, the pod can be commanded to generate the threat's geographic coordinates via the GPS and RLG INS. The "tightness," or accuracy, of these coordinates depends upon the specific frequency on which the emitter is working.

HTS also ties in with the RWR display, providing front hemisphere detection across a range of bandwidths. The system is passive, meaning that it operates in a receive-only mode. HTS allows the pilot to select a threat emitter and hand-off the relevant data directly to the AGM-88, meaning that reaction time to pop-up threats is greatly reduced.

Other software updates include those to the aircraft itself. These software loads are known as Operational Flight Programs (OFPs). They occur on a cyclical basis and have a direct bearing on the capabilities of the aircraft. Recent OFP updates include OFP M2+, which allowed the jet to carry the MIL STD 1760 BRU-57 smart weapons bomb rack; M3.1+, which provided the aircraft with the software necessary to communicate with an IR target pod and to use air-to-air interrogator hardware; M3+, which brought AIM-9X compatibility; and M4+, the much-anticipated upgrade that allowed the CJ to employ both the HTS pod and the AAQ-28 Litening II/Sniper XR target pods.

In 2003, the USAF embarked on the Common Configuration Implementation Program (CCIP) in an effort to further enhance the capabilities of all Block 50/52 Vipers. F-16CJs were the first airframes to benefit from CCIP, which brings a number of significant enhancements to the jet. Included among these is an air-to-air interrogator (AAI) that takes the form of strake antennas ahead of the canopy on the upper side of the nose, and which allows the pilot to proactively interrogate the transponder codes of other aircraft. Further modifications include the installation of color MFDs; provision for the future installation of a Link 16 datalink; compatibility with the GBU-31 Joint Direct Attack Munition (JDAM) and CBU-103 Wind Corrected Munitions Dispenser (WCMD); and the keenly anticipated introduction of the Joint Helmet Mounted Cueing System (JHMCS).

## WILD WEASEL ROLES

The F-16CJ is currently employed by the USAF in three main roles, according to the budget-driven philosophy that each major weapon system (MWS) in the USAF should be able to perform in a truly multi-role capacity. Thus the airframe has seen combat in not only the force protection/force projection roles that are synonymous with the Wild Weasel mission – SEAD and the destruction of enemy air defenses (DEAD) – but also in the precision strike role. In doing so, the F-16CJ and its pilots have proved their worth as tools that maximize war-fighting flexibility and allow commanders to task them to support changing scenarios with little or no notice. The knock-on benefits of this sort of switchable role are far-reaching, not least within the often-stretched logistics train that supports any war.

In the force protection role, F-16CJs fly SEAD and DEAD in close coordination with strikers on their way to the target, sniffing out nodes and specific threats within the enemy's IADS and hindering their ability to target the strikers by using the AGM-88 from stand-off ranges, or direct attacks on the offending sites (DEAD) with conventional and smart weapons. The main priority is to get threat emitters off-air as soon as possible; whether simply firing a HARM to force them to cease transmitting, or actually scoring a hard kill against the emitter with a HARM, it matters little. In instances where the threat to the strike force permits, offending sites may be suppressed with HARMs while other F-16CJs fly DEAD and close in to permanently neutralize the threat with a hard kill using freefall munitions. Force projection, on the other hand, concerns itself with proactively striking known nodes of an IADS, or taking out key emitters.

The AGM-88 facilitates both roles with a series of modes of employment. Its most effective mode, the one that HTS is geared to provide data for and which

*Continued on page 75.*

## US Multi-Role Fighter Jets

# Lockheed Martin F-16

makes the F-16CJ unique among US HARM shooters, is the "range known" mode, where the missile has accurate azimuth and ranging information. This is the mode that offers the best probability of kill, and known emitter locations can be programmed to the missile prior to flight, or passed dynamically via the ALICS during flight as HTS "sniffs the air for electrons." A pre-emptive mode allows the AGM-88 to be fired towards suspected or known sites in a parabolic trajectory that gives it maximum time of flight. In this mode the missile seeker activates as it heads back down towards earth and then waits to see if its assigned target(s) comes on air.

## FREEING KUWAIT

The F-16's combat debut came in Operation *Desert Storm* in 1991. The most numerous aircraft in the USAF inventory, F-16s were deployed en masse to the region (with 249 examples eventually in theater, it became the most numerous single type), whereupon the Viper was employed exclusively in the air-to-ground role, but clearly retained a limited offensive air-to-air capability through the carriage of wingtip mounted AIM-9 Sidewinder missiles.

The Alabama ANG boasted the most capable F-16s in the USAF inventory as America went to war with Iraq once more in March 2003. Such is the nature of modern multi-role fighters and such is the flexibility of the ANG, that the 187th FW's Block 30 Vipers had the latest software "tapes" and upgrade hardware installed, giving them new capabilities that other Vipers did not have. One of these was the ability to use the SADL datalink.

Previous pages 72-73: Pulling into the vertical, the personal mount of the Operations Group Commander, 52nd Fighter Wing, darts into blue skies above the German countryside. This F-16CJ is loaded with captive-carry (inert) AIM-120 AMRAAM, AIM-9M Sidewinder and AGM-88 HARM training rounds. On the centreline hangs an ALQ-131 jamming pod, while the inboard wing pylons carry 370 US gallon drop tanks.

Rapid deployment to the Arabian peninsular from the eastern United States required 16 hours of non-stop flying by the aircraft, and F-16s ranging from the GPU-5 cannon-armed F-16As of the New York ANG to the most modern Block 40/42s flew 43 percent of all USAF strike missions, amounting to 13,480 sorties, of which in the region of 4,000 were flown at night. The average sortie duration for F-16s was 3.24 hours and almost every mission involved air refueling.

The experience produced many valuable lessons for the Viper pilots, not least of which was that the traditional dive-toss, level, and dive deliveries that they employed were really not sufficiently accurate when compared to the exploits of the Pave Tack-equipped F-111Fs and the LANTIRN-equipped F-15Es. It was hardly the F-16 pilots' fault. LANTIRN had originally been developed for the F-16, yet when the war started on January 17, 1991 there were only 72 Block 40/42 F-16s in theater that were actually wired to carry the system and even that was academic, since there were so few LANTIRN target pods available that there were not enough for the Strike Eagles, let alone the F-16s. In the end, the sophisticated Block 40s were relegated as simple bomb trucks whose deliveries of 2,000lb Mk 84 LDGP "dumb" bombs were either visual or against a set of coordinates in the INS.

The Viper could employ these big weapons quite accurately from a low-level dive attack, but Saddam Hussein had built around him a "Super MEZ" (MEZ: missile engagement zone), supplemented by a dense thicket of low-level AAA, forcing the Vipers to drop their bombs from slant ranges of 17,000–20,000ft, after which the differing winds at various altitudes played havoc with an existing circular error probability (CEP) of 30ft (a 30ft CEP means that the average distance from the target that the bomb will fall is 30ft). In the event, the CEP actually ballooned to 200ft.

To make matters worse, two Vipers were downed in one sortie on January 19 when a massive "Gorilla Package," a mixed formation of aircraft reminiscent of those employed in the Vietnam War, was sent on the first daylight raid over southern Iraq. Some 64 F-16s, accompanied by F-4Gs, EF-111 jammers, and F-15 escorts, were soon forced to jink wildly to avoid the heavy radar-guided flak that started only 50nm into Iraq. The jinking stretched the formation like an elastic band, causing the first Vipers to arrive over the target minutes before those at the rear of the package. Despite the efforts of the jamming EF-111s and the HARM-firing F-4Gs, while the first F-16s egressed the target unscathed (and still laden with bombs because the target had been obscured by an undercast), the final elements arrived overhead to find the skies clearing and the Iraqi gunners now very capable of seeing and targeting them. In the bedlam that ensued two Vipers were downed, one by an SA-3 and one by an SA-6, and their pilots became captives of the Iraqi regime. Later in the war, a third F-16 would fall foul of an SA-16 MANPADS.

While this all had a sobering effect and gave pause for thought, the Viper had more success in the close air support role, most notably in the air campaign to free Kuwait. Arriving attack aircraft would take instruction from fast-FAC F-16s, working a designated map grid area known as a "kill box," measuring 15nm square. Directing other F-16s armed with CBU-87 cluster munitions and AGM-65 Maverick fire-and-forget missiles, in addition to 500lb and 2,000lb LDGPs, the killer-scout teams accounted for more than 360 armored vehicle kills. Meanwhile, the Block 40s used their GPS to help locate "Scud" missile launchers by night, a mission fraught with difficulties, as experienced by the LANTIRN-equipped Strike Eagles in the same role, and yielding limited concrete results.

As Operation *Desert Storm* made way for the No-Fly Zone (NFZ) missions of operations *Northern* and

# Lockheed Martin F-16

*Southern Watch*, the F-16 was better able to flex its multi-role muscles. It did so resoundingly on December 27, 1992 when the USAF scored its first Viper kill (and the first AIM-120 AMRAAM kill, to boot) as an F-16D of the 23rd Fighter Squadron (FS), deployed to Incirlik AB in Turkey, shot down an Iraqi MiG-23 at beyond visual range over northern Iraq.

## BALKANS CAMPAIGNS – *DENY FLIGHT* AND *ALLIED FORCE*

Like the F-15E, the F-16 continued to play a vital role in the Middle East, patrolling NFZs in operations *Northern* and *Southern Watch*, and would soon be engaged on two battle fronts as it also contributed to NATO's efforts in the Balkans.

Operation *Deny Flight* commenced in April 1993 as a NATO operation that followed UN Security Council Resolution 781, enforcing a NFZ over Bosnia-Herzegovina and providing close air support for UN troops on the ground in Bosnia. The troops, whose mission was to halt the Bosnian-Serb persecution of ethnic minorities, worked under threat of air attack, necessitating the creation of the NFZ. Eleven NATO nations committed their armed forces to the operation, and the Block 40 F-16CGs of Aviano's 510th and 555th FSs, 31st FW, comprised a significant element of the Coalition.

Once more America's Vipers stood ready to engage the enemy on the ground or in the air. Timing was key, therefore, on February 28, 1994, when six Serb G-2 Galeb jets attacked a Bosnian factory. As they egressed the target a pair of Aviano Vipers engaged them over Banja Luca. In a matter of minutes four had been downed, three with AIM-9 Sidewinders and one with an AIM-120, from well within visual range. The engagement, which could have resulted in all six jets being downed were it not for the second F-16 losing sight of his flight lead during the engagement, was the first air-to-air encounter of the operation.

The air campaign was expanded in August and September 1995, when NATO military commanders began to emphasize the importance of targeting Serb air defense systems. The switch, which was code-named *Dead Eye* on account of the plan to destroy Serbian SAMs and their radars, involved F-16CJ Wild Weasels from Spangdahlem and was named Operation *Deliberate Force*. Aviano's Vipers

An abstract image of the F-16's "turkey feathers" serves as a lesson in Block identification. These "feathers" – the metal louvres that open and close to maintain a constant pressure in the engine exhaust tunnel – are subtly rounded, identifying this as a General Electric-engined Viper and allowing its identification as a Block 30 (vice Block 32) model. By contrast, the Pratt & Whitney exhaust petals of the Block 32/42/52 series Viper are straight.

## US Multi-Role Fighter Jets

participated in pre-emptive strikes during *Deliberate Force*, but it was the Wild Weasels that saw most of the action. However, with the Serbs releasing UN hostages, the F-16s were soon returned to NFZ patrol operations. It was on one such sortie, on June 2, 1995, that Capt Scott O'Grady, of the 555th FS, was downed by an SA-6 – one of the systems *Dead Eye* should have neutralized.

In a shoot-down still surrounded in controversy, O'Grady's F-16 had been engaged by two missiles, but the commander of the "Gainful" SAM unit had been wise enough to fire them in an unguided mode; turning on his radar at the very last minute to give the missiles guidance while denying the Vipers ample notice that they were being targeted. O'Grady's flight lead called "missiles in the air," but his wingman was hit nonetheless. He ejected and was successfully rescued after evading enemy forces for six days.

Operation *Noble Anvil* was the name given by US commanders to their role in Operation *Allied Force*, between March 24 and June 11, 1999. Once again a NATO operation, *Allied Force* came in response to ethnic cleansing by the Federal Republic of Yugoslavia (FRY) under the leadership of Slobodan Milosevic. In a long-brewing conflict, Milosevic's forces were being challenged by the Kosovo Liberation Army, which also sought independence for Kosovo. To settle the issue, the Rambouillet peace accords were signed by Albania, the United States and Great Britain, calling for NATO to commit 30,000 peacekeepers to Kosovo and to enforce free right of passage through Yugoslav territory. Unsurprisingly, Milosevic refused to sign, and NATO prepared for conflict.

Behind the slender lines of the F-16 lie an assortment of line-replaceable units, electronic components, and the other innards of a complex machine. This Alabama ANG Block 32 resides in the maintenance shop, awaiting repair. The antenna for the APG-68 radar is tilted up and right to allow access to its mounting bracket.

# TECHNOLOGY

### Fly-by-Wire

Central to the F-16's performance and agility is the use of a quadruplex fly-by-wire (FBW) control system, whereby pilot inputs are processed by a digital computer before being translated into the actuation of flight control surfaces, all signals being handled electronically. As well as allowing the use of a sidestick controller for control inputs, this has significant aerodynamic benefits. The aircraft does not have the positive stability of most conventionally controlled aircraft, owing to its tailplane size and moment arm (ie. the distance between tailplane and center of gravity). With this so-called relaxed stability, the tail can be much closer to the wing, giving greater maneuverability. Furthermore, trim drag is reduced by allowing the center of gravity to travel much further aft than would otherwise be possible, so unloading the tail and wing of balancing lift.

### MDSP

The Manned Destructive Suppression Program (MSDP) funds the development of the USAF's SEAD and DEAD efforts, and is currently adding capabilities and working issues on the HTS R7 upgrade that was introduced to service in May 2007. R7 entered development in 2000 to address evolving threats, allow multi-ship cooperative ranging, and provide a precision geolocation capability with which to employ precision-guided munitions (PGMs) in the DEAD role. Thus, an R7-equipped F-16CJ can target JDAM and other GPS-guided weapons against threat systems based solely on coordinates generated by the HTS pod. It can also share these "GPS-quality" coordinates with any other aircraft equipped with the Link 16 datalink. These "tight" coordinates mean smaller target location errors and minimize the impact of enemy countermeasures. Similarly, R7 also improves the speed and accuracy of the HTS pod's emitter targeting solutions, allowing improved performance when tasked with the destruction of not only fixed sites, but crucially against mobile threats, too. Less obvious benefits include the ability to form a more accurate electronic order of battle picture.

As the R7 program progressed, testing also focused on the dual carriage of the HTS and the AN/AAQ-28 Litening II, or Sniper ER infra-red targeting pods. The USAF initially opted to delay the dual-carriage program in a bid to prevent CCIP from slipping, but both pods have now been integrated effectively. The addition of the target pod provides the CJ with a crucial tool with which to supplement the HTS and its other avionics systems. Not only does it facilitate in the primary SEAD/DEAD role – by allowing visual confirmation and laser-guided munition targeting against a threat handed down by the HTS – but it also makes the CJ a more effective platform in the tertiary roles of precision strike and force projection. With Operation *Iraqi Freedom* proving that, in some wars at least, a much talked about Super MEZ may never actually come on line, the ability to prosecute it using tools other than the HTS seems crucial. In the words of one Viper pilot interviewed after *Iraqi Freedom*, "R7 would have made no difference whatsoever to our performance in Operation *Iraqi Freedom*, but the pod? Now, that would have made a world of difference."

### Cockpit and HOTAS

Allied to the Viper's HUD, controls on the throttle to the left and sidestick controller to the right allow the pilot to perform the critical portions of a mission without looking down into the cockpit, a system known as hands on throttle and stick (HOTAS).

The F-16CJ's ability to react very swiftly to pop-up threats is almost entirely down to clever software programming and the hugely successful integration of HOTAS switchology in the cockpit. Capt Gene "Owner" Sherer gave an example:

The jet's smart enough that if we see something in the HTS pod, all we do is put our cursors over the threat and get a pretty accurate idea of its position that will be good enough to launch a missile at it. At that point we designate the target and let the HARM go. How do we physically do that? We move the cursor switch on the throttle with our left thumb and use our right thumb on the designator management switch and target management switch – the DMS and TMS, which are on the stick. So, we DMS forward to make the hat [HTS cursor] the sensor of interest, TMS forward to designate that target, which will hand it off to the HARM, and then hammer down on the pickle button to unleash the HARM.

The F-16's cockpit has, like most of the jet's internals, improved steadily since the YF-16 was rolled-out in 1973. Today, the Viper boasts two color MFDs, while early-Block examples had only a single liquid crystal display (see right hand image on page 106).

The F-16 figured prominently in the operations that ensued. The United States assigned 64 Vipers from Aviano AB, Italy, and Spangdahlem AB, Germany, the latter's F-16CJs joining their F-16CG brethren to become the 31st AEW. Collectively, the multi-national F-16 force was tasked with the destruction of Serbian infrastructure, as well as the armed forces that continued to perpetrate criminal acts against civilians.

First, though, the Wild Weasels would seek out and destroy the SAMs and anti-aircraft artillery. Among the first to enter Serbian airspace on March 24 were four F-16AMs of No. 322 Sqn, Royal Netherlands Air Force, based at Amendola AB, Italy. While the four Dutch Vipers downed a single MiG-29 "Fulcrum" with an AIM-120 AMRAAM, and two F-15Cs of the 393rd FS, 48th FW, RAF Lakenheath downed two more 'Fulcrums' within a matter of minutes, the 22nd and 23rd FSs from Spangdahlem employed their AGM-88 HARMs against radar sites, and the 510th and 555th FSs from Aviano assisted using freefall weapons. So intense was this effort in fact, that the majority of the Silver Star gallantry medals awarded during Operation *Allied Force* went to F-16 pilots who had taken part in the hunting and killing of Serb SA-2, SA-3, and SA-6 SAM sites.

While the mobile SA-6s proved notoriously difficult to find and neutralize, the fixed sites and AAA were also menacing. The 555th FS lost a jet to an SA-3 over Serbia on May 2, and his wingman was later awarded the Silver Star for marshaling rescue forces to him in the face of enemy fire. On May 4, the 52nd FW's Vipers finally got in on the air-to-air action, when a 22nd FS Viper downed a lone FRY MiG-29 near Belgrade. The Balkan conflicts had truly given the F-16 the opportunity to establish its multi-role pedigree.

## US Multi-Role Fighter Jets

# Lockheed Martin F-16

## DESERT FOX

Heavily involved in the NFZ policing operations *Northern* and *Southern Watch*, by the time a set of concentrated, coordinated strikes on Saddam Hussein's weapons making and storage facilities was launched in 1998, the F-16 had maintained a constant presence in the region. This series of strikes was named Operation *Desert Fox*.

*Desert Fox* commenced with cruise missile attacks against military targets in Iraq, just as Operation *Desert Storm* had in January 1991. This operation, which interrupted the ongoing *Northern* and *Southern Watch*, was in response to Iraq's continued failure to comply with United Nations Security Council resolutions on nuclear, chemical, and biological weapons inspections. It was designed to damage Hussein's capability to make or deliver weapons of mass destruction (WMD). F-16s of the 4404th (Provisional) Wing, based at Prince Sultan AB, Saudi Arabia, and Ahmed Al Jaber AB, Kuwait, took part. These comprised 16 F-16CJ Wild Weasels of the 20th FW, Shaw AFB, South Carolina, and 20 plus F-16C/Ds from the 388th FW, Hill AFB, Utah. On December 16 the F-16s took part in mass actions that struck 50 separate targets, and on December 19 President Clinton announced a cessation to the campaign. The Coalition of Britain and America had successfully achieved its goals; the F-16s had contributed greatly and without loss.

In October 2001, as the F-16s resumed their long vigil over Iraq, the United States led a Coalition force into Afghanistan for Operation *Enduring Freedom*.

The development of new weapons systems, new avionics systems, or new capabilities can take anything from weeks to months. For the F-16 community, the 46th Flight Test Wing at Eglin AFB, Florida, undertakes much of the technical evaluation of such new systems. This 40th FTS F-16C is just one of several Vipers at Eglin tasked with such work.

Meanwhile, in the continental United States, Operation *Noble Eagle* was launched. This involved armed F-16s patrolling major cities and infrastructure sites to ensure that any further hijacked airliners were shot down before they could reach their targets. *Noble Eagle* continues in 2010, as a crucial element of homeland defense.

## SHOCK AND AWE

On the evening of March 19, 2003, the United States commenced Operation *Iraqi Freedom*. The first priority of this operation would be to take control of the battlespace, necessitating an extensive SEAD effort to remove key individual components of Iraq's integrated air defense system. This would require all 71 F-16CJs deployed to the theater of operations, as well as the might of US Navy EA-6B Prowlers and F/A-18 Hornets.

The USAF commitment to this objective was spearheaded by the F-16CJs of the 77th FS "Gamblers," 20th FW, Shaw AFB, South Carolina. The "Gamblers" deployed to Prince Sultan AB, Saudi Arabia, where they would be the dominant squadron in the 363rd AEG. The 363rd AEG would also be parent to eight Block 50 F-16CJs from the 14th FS, 35th FW, Misawa AB, Japan; six Block 40 F-16Cs from the 4th FS, 388th FW, Hill AFB; and six Block 30 F-16Cs from the 457th FS, 301st FW, Air Force Reserve. Combined, these F-16s were tasked with defense of the battlespace and other aircraft.

The 524th FS, 27th FW, Cannon AFB, was tasked to provide 18 of its Block 40 F-16CGs to Al Jaber AB, Kuwait, as part of the 332nd AEG. Like the 14th FS in Saudi Arabia, the 524th FS "Hounds" had deployed into the theater in December 2002 as part of AEF 7. Twelve jets initially deployed, but another six arrived later when the squadron "plussed-up" for seemingly inevitable hostilities. Lt Col Anthony "Roby" Roberson, an F-16CJ pilot who was a key combat planner for *Iraqi Freedom*, explained, "they were put there to provide us with alert and interdiction capabilities, they were part of the air defense plan there in Kuwait," scouring the border between Iraq and Kuwait, and providing non-traditional information, surveillance, and reconnaissance (NTISR) intelligence on border activities or incursions. The 524th FS was also slated to serve as a key platform to drop M129 leaflet dispensers as part of an expansive psychological warfare effort.

Perhaps the most important mission – politically, at least – was assigned to the men and women of the 410th AEW, which comprised the Alabama Air National Guard (ALANG) as the lead wing, plus Vipers from the Colorado and Washington DC ANGs, and a contingent of Air Force Reserves (AFRES) F-16s from the 466th FS, 419th FW, Hill AFB. The 190th FS, 187th FW, ALANG, had some of the most capable F-16s in the Air Force, on account of recent OFP upgrades and the introduction of the Situational Awareness Data Link (SADL). Colorado's 120th FS, 140th FW, and Washington's 121st FS, 113th FW, Block 30 Viper crews would use their finely-honed reconnaissance skills to help the Alabama F-16Cs hunt for "Scud" missiles in what were called "anti-TBM" (Theater Ballistic Missile) missions.

Amidst great secrecy, the US state department negotiated a bed-down base for the group in Azraq, Jordan. From this Royal Jordanian Air Force fighter base, the four squadrons would hunt the western deserts of Iraq while tacitly providing simultaneous support to SF troops conducting the same mission on the ground.

The fourth and final F-16 deployment had been planned to bed down at Incirlik AB, Turkey, in order to force Iraq to deal with a multi-front conflict. However, last-minute negotiations between Turkish officials and the US state department failed to yield an agreement, so these forces were relocated to the southern front. F-16CJs of the 22nd FS and 23rd FS, 52nd FW, Spangdahlem AB were duly re-assigned to Al Udeid AB, Qatar. The 379th AEW, to which the "Spang" CJs were assigned, was also home to F-16CJs of the 157th FS, 169th FW, South Carolina ANG (SCANG). The three "CJ" squadrons were assigned SEAD, DEAD, time-sensitive tasking and close air support as their primary missions. The 22nd FS at Spangdahlem deployed 12 jets – a mixture of its own and some from its sister squadron, the 23rd FS – on January 17, 12 years to the day since the 1991 Gulf War had commenced. It was joined later in February by the 23rd FS, toting 12 more CJs, again comprised of a mix of the remaining 23rd FS and 22nd FS stock.

## "WHO'S RAM 01?"

The phased changeover from *Southern Watch* to the enigmatically named OPLAN 1003V, the combat plan for *Iraqi Freedom*, occurred on March 19, 2003. At 0300Z the Airspace Coordination Order (ACO) changed, switching over the routes, altitudes, and names used to enter Iraqi airspace, and altering the location of the tanker refueling tracks. At 1800Z the special instructions changed, significantly altering the rules of engagement and where and how Coalition

In full afterburner, the PW-220E of this F-16C is rated at 23,770lb of thrust. The "flatter" nozzle covers help identify this Eglin-based 40th FTS Viper as a Block 32 example.

aircraft could fly. Shortly thereafter, an F-15E dropped the last-ever Operation *Southern Watch* bomb, guiding a GBU-28 laser-guided bomb into H-3's intercept operations center.

But the move to OPLAN 1003V had been brought forward by two days in order to take advantage of time-sensitive intelligence, thus catching many Coalition aircrew by surprise; they had been flying *Southern Watch* sorties and had no inkling that the war would start while they were airborne. Indeed, one F-16 pilot was caught completely unawares: "On March 19 we were flying on-call SEAD and had HARMs on board the airplane. I was a night guy, flying only at night, and it was early in the morning. I had one more vul to cover before I went home. We were covering six-hour vul times, where we'd come away to get gas when we needed it and then go back in again. I came out of the AOR, contacted the appropriate agency, and they said, 'Copy. You're going to support RAM 01'. That's all I got. Who's RAM 01?"

Capt Paul K. "Zero" Carlton III was a seasoned F-16 pilot with over 1,500-hours of logbook. Only weeks before, he had been plucked from the 55th FS at Shaw to add NVG experience to the 77th Expeditionary Fighter Squadron (EFS), and was leading a two-ship flight of F-16CJs on the last portion of their assigned vulnerability time when he'd received the cryptic message.

> I had no idea what was going on... I asked, "can you tell me who RAM 01 is, what their time over target is and where they're going?" I got nothing back. Silence. The ROE at the time were that we couldn't shoot or drop anything unless we were given permission to do so; that morning we were briefed that we were not to shoot any weapons unless we were told we could. So, I sent Two [Carlton's wingman] off to get permission to fire our weapons if needed, and at the same time I started looking for RAM 01 on the radio. I had no idea what he was or what was going on.

Completely in the dark despite the impending tasking to support this enigmatic mission, Carlton was thinking that RAM 01 was probably a traditional asset, a Block 40 Viper, or some such. Little did he know that RAM 01 was actually an F-117 tasked with a time-critical mission to bomb a bunker in which Saddam Hussein was reportedly hiding.

> RAM 01 came up on the radio and told me roughly where he was and the coordinates of where he was going. He also gave me the coordinates of his IP [initial point] and his target, which I plugged into the airplane to figure out where he was going and what his target was. His target plot fell right into the little map of downtown Baghdad. That clued me in to what he was about to do, and I knew that things were about to get much more exciting.
>
> Having learned the TOT and seen where he was going, I knew all I needed to know. I knew what threats he was up against, and now I was thinking about how best I could support him. I had just four HARMs to work with [two per F-16], which is not a whole lot to cover the entirety of Baghdad.

Having devised a basic strategy, Carlton continued:

> I flew back into the AOR but chose not to go up near his target, even though we were now allowed to cross the NFZ. The F-16 is a radar-significant target, and I don't want to trip anything off, or stimulate it [the IADS] before it needs to be stimulated. I never heard anything else from RAM 01, which thinking about it now makes sense to me with how they clean-up to go to war [the F-117 retracted its communications antennas when entering hostile territory].

Continued on page 94.

**Right:** Looking over the shoulder of an Aggressor Viper pilot, the excellent view becomes apparent. The single-piece canopy of the F-16 means that adversary aircraft are easier to spot visually.

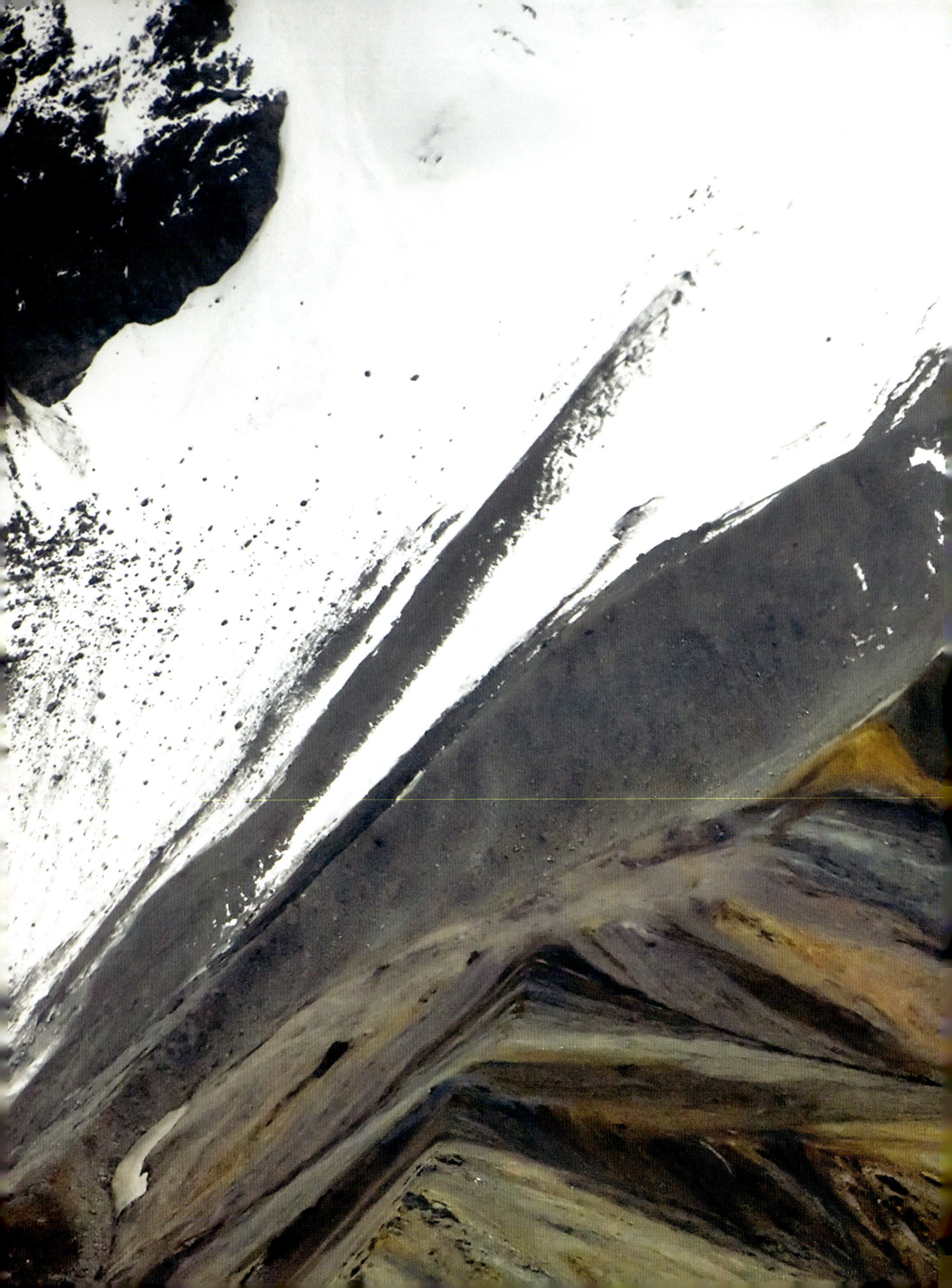

## US Multi-Role Fighter Jets

**Previous pages 88–93:** The F-16 is easily the smallest multi-role fighter in service with the US military, and in Alaska, where the 19th AGRS flies as Red Air for visiting US and friendly nation units during Red Flag Alaska, the mountains dwarf the little jet. The same mountains also provide cover behind which the Aggressor pilot can hide, either sneaking in behind an opponent as he crosses a ridge unawares, or diving into the beam and subsequently disappearing from view altogether.

Carlton continued to play it cool, but was still not aware of who it was he was supporting. He watched the Super MEZ for about an hour,

> Then I hit Bingo fuel. I've not seen anything happen or anything to suggest what's happened to RAM 01, so I told the controlling agency, "I'm Bingo and have to go home." I get handed-off to different agencies and head back to the tanker down south to get gas for the trip home. We're on the tanker when RAM 01 comes over the radio and says, "RAM 01, TANKER 51, behind you and checking in for gas." As I come off the tanker with my wingman, I look behind me and there's this "Stinkbug" [F-117] taxiing up. That was the first clue that I had that we'd basically just helped start the war.

RAM 01 successfully struck the bunker, but Saddam Hussein would later appear on television alive and well. The mission was backed up with scores of Tomahawk Land Attack Missile (TLAM) strikes, prompting Coalition pilots to watch silently as the cruise missiles made their way through the pre-briefed TLAM corridors to their targets, their heat signatures showing up clearly on NVGs.

The impromptu SEAD escort for RAM 01 came about 48 hours prior to the date that had originally been briefed for the beginning of the war, so the Armageddon that the public had been told to expect was never quite realized. The "Shock and Awe" tactics promised by the Bush administration may have been a little less shocking and not quite as awe-inspiring as many had thought they would be, but for Carlton, the intensity of those first raids was far less of a consideration when compared to the fact that he'd just performed a textbook demonstration of what he'd spent nine years in the Air Force training to do. As he explained, "we spend all our time in peacetime training learning rules of thumb and doing the calculations so that when this kind of tasking comes when we're at war, we don't need to do detailed planning there in the jet in order to get the mission done." Operation *Iraqi Freedom* was under way.

Meanwhile, at Prince Sultan AB the squadron readied itself to fly its ATO-assigned missions. Foremost among these was the SEAD escort role, which saw each jet loaded with two HARMs and assigned to protect a Coalition package of strikers. Escort required the F-16CJs fly in close coordination with the strikers on their way to the target, sniffing out radar nodes and specific threats, and employing the AGM-88 from stand-off ranges in a bid to hinder the enemy's ability to shoot at the strikers. A pre-planned mode available to the AGM-88 allowed this – the missile was fired at a suspected site regardless of whether it was emitting. Based on precise and thorough pre-flight planning, the timings were calculated so that the HARM would be in the air as the strikers were over the target or at their most vulnerable point. If the threat radar came on-line

Continued on page 98.

**Right:** The F-16's slender nose dictates that its radar antenna is correspondingly small. In turn, this reduces the F-16's radar detection range, and forces the Viper pilot to rely instead on agility and cunning in order to survive a beyond visual range engagement. One infamous tactic is the "exploding cantaloupe," in which four F-16s will, with exquisite timing, suddenly break in different directions in order to spoil the long-range shots of their opponents. In the ensuing confusion, the Viper pilots expect that one or more of their number will merge unseen and then reap havoc upon their quarry. These two 19th AGRS (Aggressor Squadron) Vipers demonstrate the technique for the camera.

**Previous page:** While the Vipers of Spangdahlem provide USAFE with its Wild Weasel capability, the Block 40 F-16CGs of the 31st FW, Aviano AB, Italy, give it a vital night-attack, multi-role capability. These two 510th FS "Buzzards" F-16CGs pull gs in the skies of northern Italy while below the countryside is socked in with fog.

during the missile's time of flight, the HARM's sensitive seeker would detect the radar energy and issue corresponding guidance commands to steer the missile towards the source. The main priority was to get threat emitters off-air as soon as possible, or to dissuade them from coming on-line at all. Early indications that the IADS would probably not operate cohesively, or with alacrity, would later prove to be more of a hindrance than a help.

For some 77th EFS pilots, *Iraqi Freedom* would be the most demanding experience yet of their short careers. Lt Eric "Paps" Spear had received his Air Force commission in 1999 and had only recently graduated from F-16 training with the 162nd FS, Ohio ANG, when he went to war. With fewer than 200 hours in the Viper when he arrived in the desert, he relied on, "dedicated and knowledgeable instructor pilots," to help him keep on top of the challenge. He performed well, and would end the war with a tally of eight AGM-88 shots, two JDAM and four WCMD drops, in addition to 260 rounds of 20mm ammunition expended. Lt Col Scott "Zing" Manning, the 77th EFS Assistant Director of Operations, explained the rationale behind deploying such inexperienced flyers:

> We did it the best way we could. The Air Force deploys units, and if your unit's combat ready, then why go and steal a bunch of experienced guys from somewhere else? If this squadron gets the nod to deploy then this squadron's going to deploy. Twelve years ago they cherry-picked units, racked and stacked the deck, which I didn't necessarily agree with. Lt Spear was the youngest guy in the squadron, and Col Bob "Surf" Beletic, the OG [Operations Group] commander, wrote a letter to the Wing Commander, Col Angelella, telling him that he wanted him to send Spear out to the desert. So he sent him.

In keeping with their role to defend the battlespace and other aircraft, the 77th EFS "Gamblers" and 14th EFS "Samurais" were concentrated on dealing with the SAM threat around Baghdad. The Super MEZ comprised over 200 SAM systems, many of which were never pinpointed accurately by intelligence, and spilled over into the cities surrounding Baghdad. While the 22nd EFS and 23rd EFS at Al Udeid would target the very heart of the MEZ, the "Gamblers" and "Samurais" would pick off elements of the SAM structure around Baghdad as Coalition strike requirements dictated.

Manning flew his first *Iraqi Freedom* sortie on March 22. His four-ship flight each fired an AGM-88 against SA-2 sites located on Al Taqaddam airfield to the northwest of Baghdad. His diary noted, "I flew … in support of some UK GR.4 [Tornado] aircraft. We took some AAA fire and unguided missile launches, but nothing close." Next, he flew a similar mission to the Al Najaf area, although resistance was once again light and uncoordinated. The fifth day of the war saw him tasked to provide on-call SEAD. "After our second refueling we were tasked to depart the tanker and make a full-speed dash, without over-speeding our weapons, to Baghdad in support of a B-1B bomber. I lit the afterburner and we raced 180-miles to Baghdad in less than 18 minutes. We arrived just in time to fire our HARM at known sites in the Baghdad area. The B-1 was bombing Saddam International Airport and some of its surrounding defenses," he noted.

On the same day, Capt Gene "Owner" Sherer also flew his first combat mission.

I was SEAD mission commander, VOUCH 61, and we were flying in the Super MEZ in the southwest corner of Baghdad. We were a four-ship supporting a B-1B, some EA-6B Prowlers doing some jamming, some F-16CGs, some F/A-18s and an F-14 or two. VOUCH 62 was Capt Matt "Demon" Morrison, VOUCH 63 was Capt Jeremy "Mount" Gordon, and VOUCH 64 was Capt Brad "Fletch" Turner – all good dudes. We had one vul time that was supposed to be 25 minutes, but the CGs flexed late and "Fletch" had a FCC [Fire Control Computer] fail, which is bad because it means he's lost almost all his combat capability. Flying on station the next thing I know Four [VOUCH 64] calls for a break turn. In the break I look and see a missile go straight past him, and I think, "Oh, shit!" We started to get a heartbeat going and we're using the pod trying to do our stuff. Well, I end up seeing another three missiles unguided, and at least two more that guide [optically] on me and my wingman, who's a mile and a half to the east in line-abreast formation. All of it is unguided, but I later saw on my HARM tape that an SA-3 came online. I didn't see it at the time because we had AAA all over the place and my wingman was defensively maneuvering. It was squirrelly, but the most incredible thing I've done. We all shot HARMs that day except poor old "Fletch." We were out in the MEZ for 45 to 50 minutes.

On one of Spear's first missions he too narrowly avoided an optically guided missile: "It passed about 200ft off of my right wing. My flight lead saw the missile first, and gave me a directive to break. There wasn't time to think about what had just happened, I just carried on with the mission and with supporting the other aircraft out there." Sherer received the DFC for his actions that day, and told the author two years later, "I'm still pissed to this day that I didn't get to shoot back at that SA-3."

Carlton recalled that the on-call SEAD missions would often result in them being called on to strike specific SAM systems as they came on air:

We'd get out our maps, work out where the target was and figure out the best way to go and hit it without getting shot at too badly. The HSD – the horizontal situation display in the F-16 – is position based, but it's not so good at expanding different areas. We didn't know where all the SAMs were in the MEZ, so the best thing we had was the map that intel gave us with the best information available to them on it. The best thing we could do was put an "x" on the map for our target coordinates and then look to see what [SAMs] were around it. Then we could see what our best entry and exit strategy would be. We put that "x" on both our paper map and our HSD.

The battlespace across Iraq had been split up into 10nm x 10nm kill boxes to allow strikers assigned to CAS and interdiction to work specific areas and to provide deconfliction with other Coalition air assets, but the F-16CJs were allowed to roam wherever they wished during their on-call SEAD vul times. "We weren't really CAS assets, and were only really TST assets in the sense that we had to go and hit SAM sites, but our primary job was to go and support the army by making it safe for other airplanes to directly support the guys on the ground," Carlton clarified. Mission planning was accomplished by the Mission Planning Cell (MPC), which was a contingent of 390th FS F-16CJ pilots borrowed from the 366th Wing at Mountain Home. The MPC took the ATO and broke it down, then planned and created briefing cards for the missions ahead. Alleviating this administrative workload allowed the pilots flying the missions to concentrate more on the fine details and the execution of the mission.

For a large number of Viper pilots deployed to *Iraqi Freedom*, this was their first operational tour in the F-16CJ. Some aircrew assigned to fly the night shift were so new to the jet that they were not even

## US Multi-Role Fighter Jets

# LOCKHEED MARTIN F-16

NVG qualified, forcing them to complete this upgrade program on the doorstep of Iraq. Flying combat for these young aviators was a sapping experience; not only did they have to maintain a visual formation with their flight lead, but they also had to spend a considerable time "heads down" in the cockpit looking at the information from the pod. Within days of the start of *Iraqi Freedom* it became readily apparent that the Iraqi IADS was not going to fight to its fullest capacity. More often than not the HTS detected only spurious transmissions, and the most potent threat came from mobile systems (the most prolific of which, it seems, was the Franco-German Roland). One pilot recalled that the HTS screen in his cockpit rarely showed any activity after the first few days, adding that a change of tactics and mission type became increasingly apparent as more and more jets returned home from sorties with a full weapons load onboard.

## ADAPTABLE WEASELS

The F-16CJs of the 52nd Wing and SCANG therefore rolled into a precision strike role, employing JDAM and WCMD against visually acquired threats, pre-planned targets and in support of FAC(A)s (forward air controller (airborne)) and Tactical Air Control (Party) (TAC(P)) groups. Pre-planned targets were often fixed SAM sites – on one sortie an F-16CJ dropped a JDAM on an SA-2 launcher and then rolled

Continued on page 104.

**Left:** Venice provides a splendid, peaceful setting for a formation of Aviano Vipers, but the Wing's F-16s have seen more troubled times. During the 1990s they worked with great effect to help resolve the many troubles of the Balkans.

**Overleaf:** A 422nd TES F-16CJ Block 52 leads a formation of the USAF's main MDS aircraft. While the testers at Eglin take care of technical test and evaluation, the "Green Bats" at Nellis AFB, Nevada, are responsible for operational test and evaluation.

in and released a WCMD on an SA-3 site while the JDAM was still in the air! On these missions pairs of Wild Weasels flew with mixed loads that saw one jet carry HARMs and the other GPS-guided weapons, typically a JDAM on one wing and a WCMD on the other.

When tasked to fly support in one of the many kill boxes across Iraq there was no telling exactly what they'd be called to do. Sometimes they struck hard targets such as ammunition bunkers, which were called out to them by F-15E Strike Eagles keen to preserve their own weapons; other times special forces troops would call that they were under fire and needed support; and occasionally a show of force was required, like the time that Coalition soldiers were handing out water to a throng of parched Iraqis. When the crowd grew impatient a riot threatened and F-16CJs flew low and fast over their heads to quell the unrest. On several other occasions the F-16CJ was called in to use its 20mm M61A1 gun to strafe soft mobile targets on the ground.

Limitations imposed by the lack of a TP became especially evident during *Iraqi Freedom*. The jet's inability to find and designate targets from altitudes that kept it away from lethal MANPADS (which home on the target's exhaust heat signature) was an inconvenience. Suffice it to say that F-16CJ pilots were dependent upon FAC(A)s and TAC(P)s for much of the war to find, positively identify (PID), and conduct collateral damage estimates (CDE) on their targets. Daytime operations saw exceptions to the rule, but it would seem that for those who flew at night, the addition of a target pod would have been most welcome.

Distinguished Flying Crosses were awarded to several F-16CJ pilots for their contribution to the war in Iraq, but one pilot in particular distinguished himself by receiving two such medals for missions flown within three days of each other. Capt Scott Ulmer, an instructor at the 16th Weapons Squadron, was providing force protection for Navy F/A-18 and F-14 strike aircraft when bad weather forced him to fly well below his normal tactical altitude. Receiving intense AAA and SAM fire, he had successfully provided protection to the strike aircraft when his flight was re-tasked to destroy a SAM radar that was covering southeastern Baghdad. Still flying below the same inclement weather system, he was once again fired upon by numerous AAA and SAM sites before successfully neutralizing the SAM site. Egressing the area at full speed, he jettisoned his wing tanks to allow him a faster escape. Two days later he was tasked as flight lead of a DEAD force protection sortie when he once again came under intense SAM and AAA fire. Ulmer and his wingman made multiple passes at four separate targets (two SAM launcher sites and two optical guidance systems) to ensure their destruction – an objective they achieved with just four munitions.

Interestingly, the F-16CJ was the only platform during *Iraqi Freedom* to carry a specialized form of WCMD that contained no exploding submunitions, but rather a payload of steel rods for puncturing tactical ballistic missiles suspected of containing warheads relating to the campaign against weapons of mass destruction. Only one of these weapons was released during the entire war, mostly because it was ineffective against anything other than its assigned target, but also because the pilots were under strict instructions to employ it only against TBMs. The release caused a stir within the community when it was learned that the pilot had deliberately employed the weapon against an unsuitable target.

With organized opposition thinning, the F-16CJs began flying DEAD and flexible tasking sorties. One of Carlton's DEAD missions was typical of the mixed-load two-ship flights that had been flown in the weeks prior. It, like many of the later missions, departed from the historical emphasis on striking IADS targets. Armed with two AGM-65 Mavericks and supported by a wingman with two JDAMs, he had taken his flight north of Baghdad when he called AWACS to ask for targets to expend his ordnance on prior to returning to base. AWACS passed him the details of a Marine FAC(A) that had located some ammunition storage bunkers. "The storage area was large enough to feature on our maps, so we got checked-in, got AWACS permission to drop and the Marine guy gave us a center point as said, 'You [Carlton] have the east side, you [Two] have the west side.' It was pretty much a fighter pilot's dream: he told us to pick anything we wanted to and didn't care what we hit, just so long as we hit something and then went on our way to let the next guys come in."

Coordinating with his wingman, Carlton discovered that the other man had never dropped JDAM before and was unfamiliar with working the switchology for a visual delivery. "So, I restricted him and got coordinates from the FAC to give to him. He went off and dropped on those coordinates. I then picked off a couple of ammo bunkers with my Mavericks." There were several visual deliveries of GBU-31 JDAM flown by the "Gamblers," but Sherer recalled that another useful delivery method was the lob: "You could lob that baby a long way. We'd get a call, 'Hey! We want you to DEAD at this SA-2 site,' and we'd simply type in the coordinates of the target, lob the bomb at the site and let the GPS take over and do its thing. That 2,000lb bomb was a real crowd pleaser."

The AGM-65 was a useful weapon for the F-16CJ community not only because of its excellent weapons effects, but because it was the closest they came to using an electro-optical or IR sensor system to find and attack targets. Manning said, "we were hampered during *Iraqi Freedom* for not having a [Litening II] pod. All of our weapons have large footprints – JDAM and CBU – so we were limited in the targets that we could strike. There were a couple of times when we checked in and were asked what we were carrying, only to be told that we couldn't be used and that new targets were being found for us." The problem stemmed from the obligation on all Coalition aircraft commanders to conduct a PID and CDE on all targets before rolling in and striking them. Doing so above the mandatory 10,000ft minimum altitude was nigh on impossible with the unaided eyeball, and even with a pod it still posed a challenge. Sherer added, "I'd have killed to have had a targeting pod back then, so that I could have worked more effectively with ground FACs. A pod would have made life 150 percent easier out there, and it would have allowed us to employ LGBs."

The 77th EFS had performed its duties with alacrity. Responsible for bedding down over 300 personnel and 16 combat aircraft, Manning was later awarded the Bronze Star for "his leadership, personal endeavor, and devotion to duty." In total, the 77th EFS employed 170 CBU-103, 105 AGM-88, 52 GBU-31, 16 AGM-65, and in excess of 7,000 rounds of 20mm PGU-28. The squadron had engaged 338 ground targets; destroyed 104 SAMs, radars and AAA pieces; and had also destroyed or disabled 20 tanks and APCs, 26 trucks, and 36 aircraft. Under the stewardship of Manning, Capt Walters and Chf MSgt Voigt, the maintainers and armorers from Shaw AFB had made it possible for the squadron's pilots to fly 676 sorties for a total of 3,803.5 combat flying hours. All the while the aircraft were maintained to a 75.3 percent full mission capable rate.

## BLOCK 40 AND BLOCK 30 EXPLOITS

At Ahmed Al Jaber AB, Kuwait, the 524th EFS was busy using its Block 40s to great effect, having already expended 176,500lb of munitions in Operation

Continued on page 107.

# F-16C FIGHTING FALCON BLOCK 50 SPECIFICATION

## Dimensions
Fuselage length: 49ft 4in
Wing span with tip-mounted AAMs: 32ft 9¾in
Wing area: 300sq ft
Wing aspect ratio: 3
Tailplane span: 18ft 3¾in
Vertical tail surface area: 54¾sq ft
Height: 16ft 8½in
Wheel track: 7ft 9in
Wheelbase: 13ft 1½in

## Powerplant
One General Electric F110-GE-129 turbofan rated at 28,984lb st (128.89kN) with afterburning, or one 29,160lb st (129.68kN) Pratt & Whitney F100-PW-229 in Block 52.

## Weights
Empty operating: 18,238lb
Normal take-off: 26,463lb
Maximum take-off, with maximum external load: 42,300lb

## Performance
Maximum level speed "clean" at 40,000ft: Mach 2.05
Maximum level speed at sea level: Mach 1.2
Maximum rate of climb at sea level: 50,000ft per minute
Service ceiling: more than 50,000ft
Combat radius: 295nm on a hi-lo-hi mission with six 500lb bombs

The image on the left shows the rear cockpit of the Block 40 F-16D, while the image above shows the rear cockpit of a Block 15 F-16B. The left MFD is set up to present radar data, with the picture from the AAQ-28 Litening II target pod being transmitted to the right MFD. Each display can be set to show a range of other data at the press of a button. Above the MFDs is a large TV screen, which acts as a HUD repeater. With the exception of the latter, the rear cockpit is almost identical to the front cockpit. By contrast, the F-16B cockpit has only one TV screen on the right (which can be switched between radar data or HUD repeater) and an LCD display on the left. This does nothing to help the pilot build situational awareness, but is instead a throwback to the days when the F-16 was intended to be a daytime, visual dogfighter.

## Armament

One internal M61A1 Vulcan 20mm cannon; maximum ordnance of 15,200lb on one fuselage and six underwing pylons. At 5.5$g$ maneuvering, the fuselage hardpoint is stressed for 2,200lb, inboard pylons for 4,500lb, center for 3,500lb and the outboard for 700lb. At 9$g$ maneuvering, these figures fall to 1,200lb, 2,500lb, 2,000lb, and 450lb respectively.

A wide variety of weapons can be carried, including unguided rockets and LDGP bombs; AIM-9M/X and AIM-120 AMRAAM; AGM-88 HARM; GBU-31, -38, -39, and -54 JDAMs; GBU-10, GBU-15, and GBU-12 guided bombs; and the CBU and WCMD series of cluster munitions. The AGM-65 Maverick is also carried.

*Southern Watch* strikes, before *Iraqi Freedom* had even begun. These were mainly some 87 2,000lb JDAMs, which the squadron, taking advantage of Iraqi threat reactions as an excuse to prosecute the *Iraqi Freedom* "battlefield preparation" phase, employed against Iraqi cable repeater sites, thus dismembering the enemy's communications network. Additionally, five GBU-12s had been used against Iraqi air defense assets.

1st Lt Russ "Spicoli" Piggott kept a journal of his 158 days at Al Jaber, and describes the first night of the war as NORRIS 28, the number four Viper in a formation of four:

> Our mission was to destroy communication sites about 50 miles west of Baghdad. The targets were small buildings that housed fiber optic switching equipment. It was a great night to fly, the moon was just past full, but there was a low-level haze from the dust. We were NORRIS 25, a flight of four F-16CG strikers; I took off at 1924Z [joined up] and headed to the west. New procedures were in effect for AAR [air-to-air refueling] and we were allowed to go into Saudi, something we were previously restricted from doing for political reasons. We hit the KC-135 and topped off with plenty of fuel for the rest of our mission to the north. The F-16CJs joined us on the tanker and pushed out just in front of us in order to get to their CAP point to support. It was about 200 miles from the tanker to the target area, a long way over Iraq on the first night of the war. As No. 4 it was my job as a wingman to clear for threats, and that's what I was doing [on the way] up to the target area. There was nothing coming towards us. About 40 miles to the north was Al Asad AB, housing MiG-25 "Foxbats" capable of chasing us down at Mach 2.8. I was expecting them to scramble those guys because we were past the 33rd parallel, unfortunately they didn't.
>
> We pressed to the target, which was just along the highway to Jordan. Snort [Piggott's wingman] was hitting a building just behind a rest stop with BLU-109s, the penetrators [JDAMs with BLU-109 warheads]. There was a Mosque about 500ft away, but the CDE was OK due to the fuse delay on the bomb. "Dewman" [Maj Wade Dewey, NORRIS 27] was hitting another building about half a mile to the north, and my building was about 1,000 yards away from his. We dropped our bombs on time for a 2106 TOT then turned to the south away from the threat. There were no threats seen during the whole flight and it was pretty uneventful. There was a worse haze layer when we returned and I had to [shoot an] approach down to minimums. It was really exciting to be out on the first night of the war dropping some of the first bombs.

At Azraq AB, Jordan, the Alabama ANG were similarly busy hunting "Scuds," but they had also been of considerable assistance to British, Australian, and American special forces operating under the moniker "TF20" in the western deserts of Iraq. As it turned out, despite their extensive counter-TBM planning, it was supporting the TF20 troops on the ground that ultimately became the most important mission that the ALANG Vipers would perform. The initial "standard" load-out was four "slant-loaded" GBU-12 laser-guided bombs, but soon moved to a mix of a single GBU-31 JDAM and two slant-loaded GBU-12s. As time progressed and GBU-12 stocks became critically low, Mk 82 500lb dumb bombs were used instead, typically with airburst FMU-14 fuses. Whatever the ordnance load out, the Alabama F-16s had a unique capability among the Viper community: their AAQ-28 Litening II target pods could be linked to their new SADL, allowing data from TF20's "BUG-E" vehicleborne datalinks to cue the Litening II pods directly onto targets.

But technology was not always the solution, as Lt Col William "Swapper" Sparrow's second *Iraqi Freedom* sortie on the early morning of March 21 showed. Flying as FLASH 13 – flight lead to FLASH 14, Capt Tony "Jaws" Simmons – Sparrow was flying as the second element of FLASH flight and was an hour into his vul time when:

> We get one of those calls from BONDO [AWACS] where you could just tell that something was going on. His voice was high and he was in a hurry: "Snap 320, contact immediately COBRA 25 on GREEN 17," and he gave us a secure frequency to go to. We went off at 320 degrees, tapped in the coordinates for the location of COBRA 25 and then headed the jet towards the green diamond in the HUD. We had about 80 miles to go, and we were making calls to COBRA 25, but no-one was talking to us, yet.

At 50 miles from the coordinates, Sparrow could tell that his steer point diamond was settling over some clouds:

… and I'm going, "son of a bitch!" because from 20,000ft we don't want to go below those clouds – we don't know how low they go. This was an event that we'd discussed in our meetings beforehand: the code name for guys on the ground whose lives were in danger was SPRINT. So, I'm thinking about this when the guys came over the radio; panicked and running. It went something like, "FLASH 13, this is COBRA 25 … brrrrp, brrrrp, brrrrp" as gunfire erupts in the background. "We're taking fire from four enemy trucks," then more gunfire and screaming. This is not supposed to be happening!

Taken by surprise, Sparrow took his flight lower and lower looking for a hole in the clouds. "I saw a little hole and shot through it. From 7,000ft to 3,500ft I was in cloud, but popped out into clear and blue sky. I was way too low to counter anyone shooting at me, and I'd thought for a minute looking down that I did not want to go through that cloud. It took me forever to find them, and they had been separated [into two groups] by the enemy."

COBRA 25 was a foot patrol made up of six or seven SF troops, and they had become separated from COBRA 25 Tango, which was a listening post/observation post. "COBRA 25T were forward of COBRA 25 by a couple of clicks, and when I showed up they were just two guys who were less than a kilometer from these four white pick-up trucks that were full of Iraqis shooting at them. I had to get my eyes onto both – 25 and 25T – before I could release, then I had to get eyes on the trucks, which blended into the desert so well that it really sucked to try and find them."

---

**Right:** Also based at Nellis is the 64th Aggressor Squadron, part of the 57th FW. Like the Alaskan Aggressors, the 64th AGRS provides realistic adversary threat training to participants in the Red Flag exercises. The 57th FW is also the parent of another F-16 operator, the USAF Air Demonstration Squadron, better known as the "Thunderbirds."

Sparrow spent 10 minutes over the non-descript desert at 3,000ft, but, fortuitously, the previous night's mission to hit a radio relay station gave him an advantage:

COBRA 25T starts telling me where he is in relation to what he describes as a stick-like figure in the distance. We need a ground point for reference, and SADL has stopped working because we're too far from our flight lead [FLASH 11, whose jet contains the lead SADL radio] and we've fallen off the SADL net. Finally it dawned on me that COBRA 25's voice sounds familiar – they were on the same frequency as us and I could hear them talking to each other. I think to myself, "that sounds like the guy from yesterday."

Quickly establishing that these were the same SF team that had directed them to drop on the radio relay station the night before, Sparrow established the remains of it as a point of reference and managed to get eyes onto COBRA 25 and 25T.

Having found the first vehicle I flew back, and then threw my pod at them. I got clearance from -25 and -25T and am now really nervous because I have to be straight and level. I think back to my days as an F-16 pilot in Germany and remember these visual lay-downs at 500ft we used to do. We had a six-second arming delay time, and I knew that if I went below 1,000ft my bomb would not arm. At the time we hadn't done the figures for dropping through the cloud so the guys on the ground could "lase" it to the target themselves, but it was the only option that I thought would work. If I knew then what I know now, I'd have gone up above the clouds and let COBRA 25 lase it in.

With the decision to drop from 1,000ft, Sparrow could either fly straight over the target, or execute a turning maneuver level turn (TMLT) to avoid the bomb blast. "But I don't want to pull $5g$s for a TMLT or the pod might lose track of the target and the bomb would miss. I made the pass and blew the truck up, but the delivery raised a few eyebrows when I got back and there were a lot of people who criticized me for my decision."

Following the direct hit:

They spotted some guys driving another truck behind a stone farmhouse in a compound. I maneuver to come in from a different direction – south to north – and I see the compound. I get clearance to re-attack and drop a bomb from 3,000ft on the south wall of the compound. The bad guys are behind the north wall, though. I should have taken my time, but I'm really keen to get my bombs off [and get some altitude]. Well, I blow the crap out of the south wall and the [bad] guys start running and the truck drives wildly out of the compound. There's one guy running after the truck, and he must be screaming, "wait for me!" I come back around for a 10-degree, low-angle, low-drag delivery, but I've lost the truck and come through the pass dry. I re-attack and this time I hit the truck directly and bug out to the east. Coming back in from the west I strafe the truck, and then I say, "OK, we've had enough of this." We know the threat to SPRINT is over and we're now really offensive.

Climbing back up to 20,000ft COBRA 25 called FLASH 13 and asked if he could neutralize one further truck. He agreed on the basis that it could be done from a safer altitude than before. "I start a 45-degree dive and am slaloming around these clouds, trying to find a clear spot to put the bomb through. The truck is locked in the pod, and I eventually get the bomb off at around 7,500ft traveling at what felt like Mach 2. It blew that truck up and I pulled out at about 3,000ft. Then we left. Back on the ground my wingman gave me a high five and said, 'that was awesome!' I said, 'Yep! And I'm going to be grounded!'" And so he was. Sparrow went straight to his commander and handed him his HUD tapes, resolved that he would have the tale straight from the source. Sparrow worked the scheduling shop for a few days before finally being allowed back into the jet.

While no F-16s were lost during the "shooting war" in mid-2003, two F-16s have been lost in Iraq to non-combat causes. A third mishap, which occurred during a 2007 mission in support of US troops in contact with an overwhelming enemy force, resulted in the loss of the pilot.

## MISSION SUCCESS

By 2009, the situation in Iraq had stabilized dramatically and the United States and Great Britain had withdrawn the majority of their ground troops, but even so, F-16s continued to maintain a constant presence in Iraq as part of the Air Expeditionary Forces tasking cycle into 2010. These Vipers based their operations out of Balad AB, Baghdad, their mission being NTISR and the engagement of insurgent fighters in a decidedly urban environment.

The 500lb GBU-38 JDAM, first used in combat in 2004 by the Block 30 F-16s of the ALANG during the battle for Falujah, is a tremendously useful weapon for such tasks. It has great precision, can be programmed to fly a trajectory to the target that allows for a specific impact angle, and has blast and fragmentation effects that are limited in their lethal range.

This Spangdahlem-based F-16DJ carries both the HTS (left intake) and Sniper XR target pod (right intake). Sniper allows the Wild Weasel Viper to be that much more effective at both SEAD and DEAD.

# HORNET & SUPER HORNET

## THE HORNET IS BORN

Designed from the start as a multi-role tactical fighter, the McDonnell Douglas F/A-18 Hornet was drawn up to meet a challenging requirement, and was based on an extensive redesign of the YF-17 from the LWF competition. The Hornet had to replace the Vought A-7 Corsair II in the light attack role, while also taking over from the McDonnell Douglas F-4 Phantom II in both air-defense and ground-attack roles. Finally, the aircraft had to act as a low-cost complement to the Grumman F-14 Tomcat. It had to be capable of fulfilling all of these roles with equal conviction, while operating from an aircraft carrier or from an austere forward airstrip for the US Marine Corps (USMC).

The US Navy began receiving its first Hornets in March 1979, with the Navy and Marine Corps Fleet Replacement Squadrons receiving airframes from 1982. The F/A-18A/B entered frontline service in 1983, and some 410 of the original version of the Hornet were built until production switched to the F/A-18C/D in 1987. A total of 371 production F/A-18As was built in Blocks 4 through 22. Of these aircraft, seven were given to NASA between 1984 and 1989. Additionally, two full-scale development two-seaters were followed by 39 production F/A-18Bs in Blocks 4 to 21.

Extremely capable in all of its roles, reliable and maintainable, the F/A-18 offers good "bang for the buck," yet the F/A-18 has had its critics. To carry bombs over the same range as the long-retired A-7 Corsair II or an A-6E Intruder, the F/A-18 must carry large amounts of external fuel, limiting the total payload available for offensive warload. This, some say, diminishes its utility. But range has come to be of less importance, because since the end of the Cold War an increasing emphasis has been placed on operations closer to the coastline.

With the retirement of the Grumman A-6E Intruder in 1997 and the F-14 Tomcat in 2006, the F/A-18 embarked on every US carrier is now a true multi-role fighter. It must fly an expanded selection of medium-range attack and air-defense missions, and will also be called upon to intercept threats and even perform "buddy" air-to-air refueling. The US Marine Corps replaced its Intruders with two-seat, night-attack F/A-18Ds from May 1990, expanding the role of their units to include FAC duties.

## VARIANTS

### F/A-18C HORNET

Despite early teething troubles, the F/A-18A/B evolved into the C/D models, which with their new avionics and weapons far surpassed their predecessors. Production of the F/A-18C for the USN and USMC ended in 1999.

By 1995, the US Navy had retired most of its A/B models from carrier-based service, the shortest first-line career of any modern fighter. The fact had been that the A/B Hornet was a somewhat inadequate aircraft that validated the old adage "Jack of all trades, master of none." It took a number of steps to produce a Hornet variant that could be called the master of most of its missions. This process started when the first of the F/A-18C/Ds were delivered from September 1987. Designed to accommodate new technologies and weapons, the first F/A-18C/Ds formed the basis of a series of Hornets whose exterior resemblance to the original A/B was entirely deceptive.

The F/A-18C/D airframe is not very different to that of the A/B, and did not change significantly in

---

**Previous page:** The F/A-18E/F Super Hornet represents the latest incarnation of the original F/A-18 design. These two F/A-18F Super Hornets belong to VFA-211 "Fighting Checkmates," stationed at NAS Oceana, Norfolk.

The Hornet first exercised its sting during the April 1986 raids on Libya. This F/A-18A, of VFA-132 "Privateers," readies for a "cat" shot off the bow of USS *Coral Sea* during the work-up phase prior to the mission. Although it is not the focus of this text, Adm John "Black" Nathman, skipper of the "Privateers" at the time, told the author that the A-model Hornet was still a phenomenal multi-role fighter.

production. The reason is not so much that the original design was perfect, as that it ran into a hard limit on its ability to grow.

The F/A-18 had been designed for an approach speed of 125 knots, but development problems raised this to 134 knots, a respectable speed for a land-based fighter but a little high for a carrier-based aircraft. This in turn set a cap on the Hornet's maximum landing weight which, coupled with the fact that the Navy requires its carrierborne aircraft to retain large fuel reserves for landings, meant that the Hornet could not undergo major airframe modifications without sacrificing the number of weapons carried or reducing the already limited range of its operations. In fact, the only visible outboard changes to the Hornet have been the addition of antennas and a pair of strakes or "billboards" above the LERX (leading-edge root extensions). These help to break up vortices at angles of attack above 45 degrees.

One significant change, though far from visible, is the addition of "stealthy" materials to the Hornet. During the 1970s and 1980s, new types of radar-absorbent material (RAM) were developed which were lighter and more durable than their predecessors. As a result, both the Navy and Air Force initiated programs to reduce the radar cross-section (RCS) of their aircraft. Under the Glass Hornet program, F/A-18s were given a gold-tinted canopy (the F-16 had received a similar modification under Have Glass II), coated with a thin layer of indium-tin oxide (ITO) in order to reflect radar signals away from the transmitter. RAM paint on the engines and engine inlets also helped to absorb radar signals. However, the price of this "stealthiness" was a weight gain of 250lb, which further reduced the Hornet's bring-back load.

Although the Hornet has changed little externally, one significant development has been the changes to its engines. General Electric's F404 had been free from handling limits and, by 1988, the basic F404-GE-400 engine had accumulated 700,000 flight hours, and reliability and maintainability statistics were good. However, some problems did surface at the million-hour mark. A number of fires broke out in these high-time engines, causing the loss of several aircraft. These fires were attributed to FOD (foreign object damage) eroding the coating on the compressor casing, which resulted in the titanium blades and any debris rubbing together and causing a fire. A number of new safety coatings were developed to cover these blades and to prevent any burning through friction, but the installation of a new engine was inevitable.

The F404-GE-402 enhanced performance engine (EPE) was developed to meet the Swiss Air Force's requirements for its SF/A-18C/D Hornets, but this motor would also become the standard powerplant on America's Hornets from 1992 onwards. Delivering 10 percent more static sea-level thrust than its predecessor, the EPE also offers 18 percent more excess power at Mach 0.9 and 10,000ft, and increased transonic acceleration. A typical runway-launched interception profile, from brake release to Mach 1.4 at 50,000ft, takes 31 percent less time than before.

The F/A-18 was the first true "digital aircraft," although the F-15E and F-16 had previously pioneered elements of the digital revolution, including the Viper's fly-by-wire control system. Many aspects of what the Hornet pilot sees on the cockpit displays are determined by a core mission computer, or by processors built into the other avionics subsystems. Because of this, the introduction of new software packages every couple of years has steadily improved the Hornet's capability. The center of the avionics suite is the mission computer. On the F/A-18C/D, this was the AN/AYK-14 XN-8 system, which was superseded by the XN-8+ system in the early 2000s.

The presence of the multi-sensor integration (MSI) system is another important aspect of the C/D-model Hornets. With the MSI, the computer receives inputs from different sensors, correlates them and displays them so that each target appears clearly on the pilot's display. This can be used in an air-to-air or air-to-ground role and is particularly useful in the suppression of enemy air defenses mission, where the AGM-88 HARM seeker, radar, and RWR can be integrated to locate threats and display them to the crew.

By 1994, all later-model F/A-18s were fitted with the new APG-73 radar, as opposed to the APG-65 of earlier variants. The APG-73 uses the same antenna and traveling-wave tube (TWT) transmitter as its predecessor, but the rest of the hardware is new. The receiver/exciter unit is more sophisticated and provides much faster analog-to-digital conversion, allowing the radar to cut the incoming signal into smaller fragments and therefore achieve better range resolution. What is more, air-to-air detection and tracking ranges are up by 7 to 20 percent. For air-to-ground mapping and bombing modes, the APG-73 also offers higher resolution than before.

Other systems fitted to the later Hornets include NITE (Navigation Infra-Red Targeting Equipment) Hawk FLIR, which can track moving targets on the ground and designate them for laser-guided bombs. A new, more reliable identification friend or foe (IFF) system was also incorporated after Kuwait decided upon it for its Hornets and, soon after, it was fitted to USN and USMC Hornets. The Advanced Tactical Airborne Reconnaissance System (ATARS) fits into the Hornet's nose and incorporates a low- and medium-altitude EO (electro-optical) sensor and an infra-red linescan imager. ATARS was used operationally for the first time in 2000, during Operation *Allied Force*.

The AIM-120 AMRAAM represents a massive leap forward in air-to-air capability over the AIM-7 Sparrow. AMRAAM has its own radar, datalink, and inertial navigation system. It is also lighter and faster (at Mach 4) than the Sparrow, and became operational on the F/A-18C/D from September 1993.

## F/A-18D – ATTACK DELTAS

The cancellation of the advanced A-6F Intruder II project and subsequent conclusion of Grumman A-6E Intruder production led the Marine Corps to adapt the two-seat Hornet for the night-attack role.

The F/A-18D is broadly similar to the single-seat F/A-18C, and 31 baseline aircraft were procured before production switched to the night attack-capable F/A-18D, which has the same avionics improvements as the night attack F/A-18C. The USMC received its first Night Attack Hornet in November 1989, and a total of 98 examples were ordered.

The F/A-18D replaced the Intruder with the USMC's VMFA(AW) units (Marine All-Weather Fighter Attack Squadrons). In November 1989 VMFA(AW)-121 became the first USMC "D" unit. By 2009, the six VMFA squadrons were divided into three units at Beaufort and three at Miramar, each tasked with the roles of FAC(A) and tactical air controller (airborne) (TAC(A)) as well as CAS. Each of the six squadrons has three aircraft equipped with the Advanced Tactical Airborne Reconnaissance System, giving a total of 18 ATARS-equipped aircraft altogether.

A US Marine Corps Hornet of VFMA-314 unleashes an AIM-9 Sidewinder during a weapons evaluation. The Hornet would later use the same missile to score its first ever kills, during the opening hours of the 1991 Gulf War.

## SUPER HORNET – F/A-18E/F

When the original F/A-18A (often referred to as the "Heritage Hornet") made its debut, it possessed a formidable beyond visual range (BVR) capability, but was also as agile as the leading lightweight air superiority fighters – and in the slow speed fight was practically indomitable. With the arrival of the C-model Hornet came the ability to "swing" from air-to-air to air-to-ground operations "at the flick of a switch." But the passage of more than two decades saw the emergence of new fighter prototypes, and while the F/A-18C "Legacy Hornet" remains a class leader, it was only ever a matter of time before it was supplanted by a newer model.

McDonnell Douglas had been working on advanced versions of the F/A-18A/B Hornet since 1986. In late 1987 the company outlined its Hornet 2000 proposals. The first phase – Design I – had more powerful engines and became the F/A-18C/D. Design II had more fuel in a dorsal hump, while Design III was a larger aircraft with a growth version of the F404 engine. Design III showed considerable promise, since its longer fuselage offered a major increase in fuel capacity without any aerodynamic penalties.

The Super Hornet originated from a 1987 requirement for an F/A-18C/D replacement for the US Navy and US Marine Corps, for service in the early years of the 21st century. At that time, it was envisaged that the new Hornet derivative would be augmented on US Navy carrier decks by the Naval ATF (replacing the F-14) and the General Dynamics A-12 (replacing the A-6E Intruder). Following the termination of advanced F-14 Tomcat versions, the Design III Super Hornet was left as the only ongoing carrierborne tactical aircraft program. Despite further attempts by Grumman to sell the Navy more Tomcats, it became rapidly clear that the Super Hornet really was the only game in town.

On May 12, 1992 McDonnell Douglas received an "intent to procure," followed by a $4.88-billion contract to develop the Super Hornet. The engineering, manufacturing, and development (EMD) award covered the construction of seven flying prototypes (five single-seaters and a pair of two-seaters), plus three ground test airframes for static test (ST-50), drop tests (DT-50) and fatigue tests (FT-50). Part of the money was given to General Electric to develop the F414 engine.

Under the original Design III the Super Hornet was to be little more than a scaled-up Hornet, but Navy requirements dictated major changes. The wing was made thicker to support an extra weapons pylon on each side. The taper and sweepback of the wings was increased to maintain performance, and a dogtooth was added to the leading edge.

The Super Hornet is known as the F/A-18E in single-seat form, and as the F/A-18F in two-seat guise, and is an evolutionary development of the earlier aircraft that looks superficially the same as its progenitor. But initial appearances are deceptive, and airframe commonality between the F/A-18A and the F/A-18E is put at only 10 percent. The F/A-18E/F is 25 percent larger, with massive rectangular-section, stealthy, raked intakes; bigger LERXes; and larger control surfaces, tailfins, and tailplanes. The new variants have a sawtooth wing leading edge and a lengthened fuselage, giving a one third boost in internal fuel capacity. But the imaginative use of advanced materials and modern manufacturing techniques has allowed this growth to occur without major weight penalty, and with a 42 percent reduction in parts count.

Continued on page 122.

---

An F/A-18C from Air TES Two Three (VX-23) releases 1,000lb Mk 83 bombs during a series of Advanced Targeting Forward-Looking Infra-Red (ATFLIR) adjacent stores release tests over the Atlantic Test Range.

# OPERATORS C/D

Once the major strike power of the US Navy at sea, the McDonnell Douglas F/A-18 Hornet served with more than 20 squadrons. Ordered from the late 1970s, the first of more than 1,000 Hornets destined for USN/USMC units were delivered to the Navy in May 1980. VFA-113 was the first operational Navy unit, forming in October 1983, and along with VFA-25 embarked aboard USS *Constellation* in February 1985.

A typical US Navy Strike Fighter Squadron is made up of between ten and 12 Hornets. With the exception of two squadrons based in Japan, the US Navy organizes its frontline Hornet units into West or East Coast Fleets, depending on whether they are based on the Pacific or Atlantic coasts, respectively.

US Navy Carrier Air Wings are divided between these two fleets, and each Strike Fighter Squadron (VFA) is assigned to a Carrier Air Wing (CVW), which is in turn attached to an aircraft carrier, and is stationed at a land base when not deployed. For example, the West Coast Fleet commands Carrier Air Wing 9 (CVW-9), which in turn boasts three Super Hornet Squadrons (VFA-146, VFA-147, and VFA-192). CVW-9 is attached to USS *John C. Stennis* (CVN 74), and, when not deployed, is based at Naval Air Station (NAS) Lemoore, California.

The East Coast operators of the F/A-18C/D are all based at NAS Oceana, Virginia, which is a Master Jet Base. VFA-106 is the East Coast Fleet Replacement Squadron (FRS), training new Hornet pilots, and those returning to the jet following a ground tour, on the F/A-18B/C/D/E/F. Most of the West Coast's Hornets are based at NAS Lemoore, California, where VFA-125 "Rough Raiders" are the West Coast's FRS.

Two squadrons are based overseas: VFA-115 "Eagles" and VFA-195 "Dambusters" are located at Naval Air Facility Atsugi, Japan, and both are attached to CVW-5, USS *George Washington*.

The USMC operates its Hornets in two distinct types of squadron: Marine Fighter Attack Squadrons (VMFAs) and Marine All Weather Fighter Attack Squadrons (VMFA(AW)). The squadrons report to a Marine Air Wing, and typically a Wing will have a mix of VFMA and VFMA(AW) squadrons. Marine Fighter Attack Training Squadron "Sharpshooters" (VMFAT-101) trains new naval aviators to fly the Hornet, and is based at MCAS Miramar.

As of spring 2010, the US Navy operated the Legacy Hornet in the following units:

The front office of the Super Hornet is well equipped. Not only does it have three color MFDs, but it also has a touch panel below the HUD. The stick grip is very similar to that in the front cockpit of the F-15E and provides the pilot with a range of switches with which to operate the jet's offensive and defensive systems.

## Ship Based

CVW-1 (USS *Enterprise* CVN 65): Tailcode "AB"
    VFA-86 "Sidewinders"    F/A-18C    (12)    MCAS Beaufort, SC

CVW-2 (USS *Abraham Lincoln* CVN 72): Tailcode "NE"
    VFA-34 "Blue Blasters"    F/A-18C    (12)    NAS Oceana, VA
    VFA-151 "Vigilantes"    F/A-18C    (12)    NAS Lemoore, CA

CVW-3 (USS *Harry S. Truman* CVN 75): Tailcode "AC"
    VFA-37 "Ragin' Bulls"    F/A-18C    (12)    NAS Oceana, VA

CVW-5 (USS *George Washington* CVN 73): Tailcode "NF"
    VFA-195 "Dambusters"    F/A-18C    (12)    NAF Atsugi, Japan
    VFA-115 "Eagles"    F/A-18C    (12)    NAF Atsugi, Japan

CVW-7 (USS *Dwight D. Eisenhower* CVN 69): Tailcode "AG"
    VFA-131 "Wildcats"    F/A-18C    (12)    NAS Oceana, VA
    VFA-83 "Rampagers"    F/A-18C    (12)    NAS Oceana, VA

CVW-8 (USS *George H. W. Bush* CVN 77): Tailcode "AJ"
    VFA-15 "Valions"    F/A-18C    (12)    NAS Oceana, VA
    VFA-87 "Golden Warriors"    F/A-18C    (12)    NAS Oceana, VA

CVW-9 (USS *John C. Stennis* CVN 74): Tailcode "NG"
    VFA-146 "Blue Diamonds"    F/A-18C    (12)    NAS Lemoore, CA
    VFA-147 "Argonauts"    F/A-18C    (12)    NAS Lemoore, CA
    VFA-192 "Golden Dragons"    F/A-18C    (12)    NAS Lemoore, CA

CVW-11 (USS *Nimitz* CVN 68): Tailcode "NH"
    VFA-97 "Warhawks"    F/A-18C    (12)    NAS Lemoore, CA

CVW-14 (USS *Ronald Reagan* CVN 76): Tailcode "NK"
    VFA-25 "Fist of the Fleet"    F/A-18C    (12)    NAS Lemoore, CA
    VFA-113 "Stingers"    F/A-18C    (12)    NAS Lemoore, CA

## Shore Based

Strike Fighter Wing Atlantic, NAS Oceana, VA
Fleet Replenishment Squadron: Tailcode "AD"
    VFA-106 "Gladiators"    F/A-18B/C/D    NAS Oceana, VA

Strike Fighter Wing Pacific, NAS Lemoore, CA
Fleet Replenishment Squadron: Tailcode "NJ"
    VFA-125 "Rough Raiders"    F/A-18A/B/C/D NAS Lemoore, CA

Western Pacific, Unit Deployment Program, MCAS Iwakuni, Japan
    VFA-94 "Mighty Shrikes"    F/A-18C/D    (12)    NAS Lemoore, CA

Test Wing Atlantic, Tailcode "SD"
    US Navy Test Pilot School    F/A-18A/B    NAWC Patuxent River, MD

Weapons Test Wing Pacific, Tailcode "AI"
    NWTS "Dust Devils"    F/A-18A/C/D    NAWS China Lake, CA

Test and Evaluation Squadron
    VX-9 "Vampires"    F/A-18C/D    (6)    NAWS China Lake, CA

Naval Strike and Air Warfare Center
    NSAWC    F/A-18    NAS Fallon, NV

## Naval Air Reserve Force

VFA-204 "River Rattlers"    F/A-18A+    (12)    NAS New Orleans, LA

VFC-12 "Fighting Omars"    F/A-18A    (12)    NAS Oceana, VA

## US Marine Corps

MAW-1, MAG-12, Iwakuni, Japan
    VMFA(AW)-242 "Batman": Tailcode "DT"    F/A-18D

MAW-2, MAG-31, Beaufort, SC
    VMFA-115 "Silver Eagles": Tailcode "VE"    F/A-18A
    VMFA-122 "Crusaders": Tailcode "DC"    F/A-18A
    VMFA-251 "Thunderbolts": Tailcode "DW"    F/A-18C
    VMFA-312 "Checkerboards": Taildcode "DR"    F/A-18C
    VMFA(AW)-224 "Bengals": Tailcode "WK"    F/A-18D
    VMFA(AW)-533 "Hawks": Tailcode "ED"    F/A-18D

MAW-3, MAG-11, MCAS Miramar
    VMFA-232 "Red Devils": Tailcode "WT"    F/A-18C
    VMFA-323 "Death Rattlers": Tailcode "WS"    F/A-18C
    VMFA(AW)-121 "Green Knights": Tailcode "VK"    F/A-18D
    VMFA(AW)-225 "Vikings": Tailcode "CE"    F/A-18D(R)
    VMFA(AW)-242 "Bats": Tailcode "DT"    F/A-18D
    VMFAT-101 "Shooters": Tailcode "SH"    F/A-18C/D, T-34C

## US Marine Corps Reserve

MAW-4 (Reserve)
    VMFA-112 "Cowboys": Tailcode "MA"    F/A-18A
    VMFA-134 "Smokes": Tailcode "MF"    F/A-18A
    VMFA-142 "Flying Gators": Tailcode "MB"    F/A-18A
    VMFA-321 "Hell's Angels": Tailcode "MG"    F/A-18A

The F/A-18E retains a high degree of avionics commonality with the original Hornet, resulting in a low unit cost (within 15 percent of the cost of the F/A-18C) and a smooth and swift transition of aircrew from one version to the other. The high commonality figure tends to mask the fact that the F/A-18E/F has a refined FBW flight control system, now without mechanical back-up, as well as a much improved cockpit.

The aircraft attracted some early controversy, much of it stirred up by those who favored the development of a longer-range strike aircraft based on the F-14, and there were some early technical difficulties with the aircraft's new F414 engines, even though these were derived from the original Hornet's F404. Wind tunnel tests prompted a minor redesign of the LERXes, while further minor modifications cured handling issues raised in early flight testing.

While retaining the agility of the original Hornet, the F/A-18E/F is less "draggy" and enjoys a lower approach speed, despite its higher maximum landing weight. This all helps the F/A-18E/F enjoy a much-improved bring-back capability, allowing the aircraft to land with unused ordnance that the original Hornet would have had to jettison before landing. Full-span slotted flaps bring carrier approach speeds in line with those of the F/A-18C, if not a little slower.

### Flight Test

Construction of the first EMD aircraft got under way in May 1994, just prior to the design passing its final critical review. On September 18, 1995, the first aircraft – F/A-18E1 – was rolled out at the St Louis factory. On November 19, 1995, at 1155 local time, Fred Madenwald took the aircraft aloft for a successful first flight. In February 1996 the aircraft left for the US Navy's principal test center at Patuxent River.

Testing was concluded on April 28, 1999. In all, the Super Hornet conducted more than 270 test flights during the course of its development phase.

In addition, more than 2,000 laboratory test hours were accrued at the F/A-18 Advanced Weapons Laboratory (AWL) at the Naval Air Warfare Center (NAWC) Weapons Division.

The process included the integration, through software development and subsequent testing, of the sensors, fire control systems, cockpit displays, and weapons that combine to make the Super Hornet a more capable aircraft than the soon to be named F/A-18C/D "Legacy Hornet."

### Operational Testing

With development testing complete in early 1999, Operational Test and Evaluation Squadron (TES) Nine (VX-9) at China Lake assumed the responsibility for putting the Super Hornet through a grueling six-month operational evaluation. This testing honed in on the operational capabilities of the aircraft, including a significant amount of air-to-air combat, air-to-ground strike, and evaluations aboard the aircraft carrier USS *John C. Stennis*. This testing differed from the development testing insofar as it was orientated towards the development of tactics, techniques, and procedures that naval aircrew would use when the Super Hornet became operational. By November 1999 the operational testing was complete, and the type officially entered service.

In all, the Super Hornet had been tested over the course of 3,100 test flights, amounting to some 4,600 flight hours.

The Pacific Fleet was the first to receive the Super Hornet when, in January 1999, VFA-122 "Flying Eagles" at NAS Lemoore, became the first Super Hornet squadron and was tasked with training the first operational Super Hornet pilots, using seven F/A-18E/Fs.

As they graduated the "Flying Eagles" conversion course, the new pilots reported to the first frontline unit, VFA-115 (then based at NAS Lemoore), which

A VFA-105 F/A-18C prepares to "tank" near Camp Sarafovo, Bulgaria, during Operation *Iraqi Freedom*. The aircraft is armed with AIM-9M Sidewinders, 500lb GBU-12 Paveway II laser-guided bombs, and the excellent AGM-154A Joint Stand-Off Weapon.

transitioned to the F/A-18E in December 2000. The squadron declared IOC in September 2001, having received its "safe for flight" certification in June 2001. The Super Hornet's operational debut followed in the summer of 2002, a deployment aboard USS *Abraham Lincoln* (CVN 72) as part of Carrier Air Wing 14. With an inventory of six Super Hornets, VFA-115 embarked aboard *Lincoln* on July 24, 2002, and within weeks was involved in punitive combat action over Southern Iraq as part of Operation *Southern Watch*.

With the ongoing "Global War on Terror," and the propensity for troops on the ground in Afghanistan and Iraq to call on close air support from FAC(A)s, the Navy's new Super Hornet squadron was in high demand, and the Navy worked with alacrity to convert more squadrons to what was quickly being called "the Rhino." Indeed, the first deployment of Super Hornets with two different squadrons was already taking place in March 2003, as VFA-14 "Top Hatters" and VFA-41 "Black Aces" deployed aboard

Continued on page 127.

**Overleaf:** The Hornet's nose wheel steering is designed to allow for maneuvering in exceptionally tight spaces, as this F/A-18C of Strike Fighter Attack Squadron One Nine Five demonstrated aboard the flight deck of USS *Kitty Hawk* (CV 63).

# OPERATORS E/F/G

By March 2009, Boeing had delivered 385 Super Hornets to the US Navy, consisting of 214 F/A-18F and 171 F/A-18E machines. These airframes equip nine operational US Navy CVWs, totaling 19 operational squadrons and four TESs. The USN planned to acquire an additional 75 examples by 2011.

Each Super Hornet squadron consists of between 12 and 14 aircraft, depending on whether the squadron comprises the single-seat F/A-18E or the two-seat F/A-18F. An Air Wing can mix the two types in order to achieve an overall balance, since the two-seat jet is ideally suited to ground-attack and FAC(A) roles, and there is a tendency for squadrons operating this type to specialize accordingly. For example, in 2005 VFA-102 "Diamondbacks" were operating their two-seat Super Hornets alone as part of CVW-5 at Naval Air Facility Atsugi, Japan. However, they were soon joined by a second squadron of Super Hornets in the form of VFA-27 "Royal Maces," which replaced their Legacy Hornets with the F/A-18E, thus complementing the "Diamondbacks" two-seaters.

There are ten operational West Coast Super Hornet squadrons. With the exception of CVW-5's two Super Hornet squadrons at Atsugi, all are based at NAS Lemoore.

With the transition to the Super Hornet firmly underway on the West Coast by 2002, the US Navy was preparing for the large-scale introduction of the F/A-18E/F to bases on the East Coast, intending originally to convert 11 operational squadrons to the Super Hornet, plus one FRS. This goal would have required 130 jets for the operational squadrons, and an additional 32 aircraft to train East Coast pilots and Naval Flight Officers (NFOs). This figure later changed to 11 squadrons total, including the FRS, due to the requirements for additional airframes by the West Coast Super Hornet community.

En masse introduction of the Super Hornet to the Atlantic Fleets was originally slated to run from 2004 through 2008, but the transition from the F-14 Tomcat to Super Hornet was already half complete in 2004. By 2006, the transition was still two years ahead of schedule.

By the end of 2010, 10 F/A-18E/F squadrons – five F/A-18E and five F/A-18F – are expected to be declared operational on aircraft carriers in the Atlantic Fleet, with crews trained through the East Coast Fleet Replacement Squadron, VFA-106 "Gladiators." In total, the Super Hornets operated by the East Coast squadrons have replaced 172 Hornets and Tomcats, comprising 24 F/A-18C/Ds and 148 F-14s. The East Coast Super Hornet squadrons are all based at NAS Oceana, Virginia, when not deployed at sea.

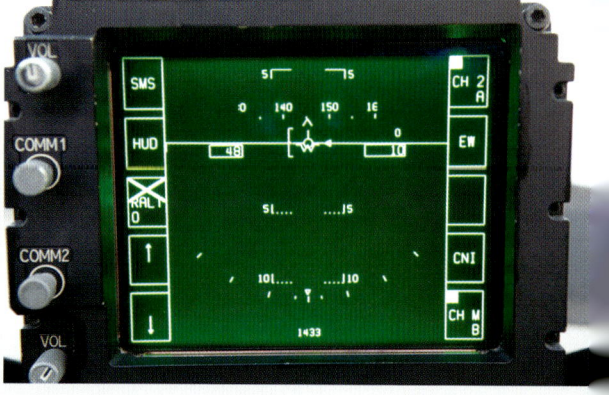

The Super Hornet's touch-sensitive display allows the crew to input a range of data into the aircraft's computers. As viewed from the back seat, the display is shown here in HUD repeater mode, but on each side are a range of options that change the displayed data, to show IFF, radio, stores management, radar altimeter, and electronic warfare information. The latter presents radar threats to the crew in a top-down format.

### Atlantic Fleet

| | |
|---|---|
| VFA-11 "Red Rippers" | F/A-18F |
| VFA-31 "Tomcatters" | F/A-18E |
| VFA-32 "Swordsmen" | F/A-18F |
| VFA-81 "Sunliners" | F/A-18E |
| VFA-103 "Jolly Rogers" | F/A-18F |
| VFA-105 "Gunslingers" | F/A-18E |
| VFA-106 "Gladiators" | F/A-18E/F (East Coast FRS) |
| VFA-136 "Knighthawks" | F/A-18E |
| VFA-143 "Pukin' Dogs" | F/A-18E |
| VFA-211 "Fighting Checkmates" | F/A-18F |
| VFA-213 "Black Lions" | F/A-18F |

### Pacific Fleet

| | |
|---|---|
| VFA-2 "Bounty Hunters" | F/A-18F |
| VFA-14 "Tophatters" | F/A-18E |
| VFA-22 "Fighting Redcocks" | F/A-18F |
| VFA-27 "Royal Maces" | F/A-18E |
| VFA-41 "Black Aces" | F/A-18F |
| VFA-102 "Diamondbacks" | F/A-18F |
| VFA-115 "Eagles" | F/A-18E |
| VFA-122 "Flying Eagles" | F/A-18E/F (West Coast FRS) |
| VFA-137 "Kestrels" | F/A-18E |
| VFA-147 "Argonauts" | F/A-18E |
| VFA-154 "Black Knights" | F/A-18F |

### Test and Evaluation Units

| | |
|---|---|
| VX-9 "Vampires" Air TES | F/A-18E/F |
| VX-23 "Salty Dogs" Air TES | F/A-18E/F |
| VX-31 "Dust Devils" Air TES | F/A-18E/F |
| NSAWC (Naval Strike and Air Warfare Center) | F/A-18F |

USS *Nimitz* (CVN 68) and were assigned a limited number of Super Hornets to supplement their Tomcats in the air-refueling and FAC(A) missions.

### Putting "Iron" On Target

While the Super Hornet's improvements over the Legacy Hornet include reduction in radar cross section, superior avionics, and an increased mission radius (520nm versus 369nm), the F/A-18E/F also boasts an improved weapons carriage capability and compatibility with all of the US Navy's "smart" weapons. Additional stores can be carried thanks to the inclusion of two more wing stations, and the jet's 1760 data bus allows communications between its computers and targeting systems, and a plethora of the world's most sophisticated air launched weapons.

The variety and depth of the F/A-18E/F's weapons loadout options allows the Super Hornet crew to fully harness the aircraft's diverse capabilities – it is truly a superb multi-role fighter. In the traditional interdiction and deep strike roles, the crew can elect to use stand-off weapons, such as the AGM-84 series, when the strength and sophistication of the enemy's defenses dictate; or may prosecute the attack at closer range using a selection of either unguided- or guided-freefall weapons.

The Super Hornet replaced the F-14 Tomcat as fleet defender, and is suitably equipped with the AIM-9, AIM-120, and AIM-7 families of air-to-air weapons. Indeed, the Super Hornet can carry a load of ten AIM-120 AMRAAM and two AIM-9 when tasked exclusively with the air-to-air mission. For visual engagements, and to aid in the visual acquisition of targets closing from beyond visual range, the jet is also suitably equipped to allow both pilot and WSO to use the JHMCS sight.

## GROWLER – E/A-18G

### Fighting with 'Trons

Electronic warfare (EW) is a key component in the toolbox of military commanders. It encompasses a myriad of disciplines, but for the purposes of air warfare it is best broken down into electronic attack (EA) in the form of electronic countermeasures (jamming) and electronic protection (EP) in the form

## US Multi-Role Fighter Jets

of counter-countermeasures and passive targeting against jamming sources. Additionally, EW plays a crucial role in SEAD. Indeed, the main goal of EW is to allow friendly forces to engage and destroy enemy forces without hindrance.

In recent history, the US Navy's Grumman EA-6B Prowler has fulfilled the fleet's EA function, but with the aircraft ageing rapidly – especially in light of the US Air Force's decision to retire the similarly roled Grumman EF-111A Raven in May 1998 – and with the need for an EW platform that could accompany a strike force deep into heavily defended airspace, the necessity for a replacement was clear.

In January 2000, the Department of Defense commissioned the Joint Airborne Electronic Attack Analysis of Alternatives study to suggest replacement options for the Prowler. Calling on recent experience in the Balkans, the study was concluded in late 2000. It looked at a range of options, but the most attractive to the Navy was a dedicated EW version of the Super Hornet, then designated F/A-18G.

It is true that the F/A-18G had minor shortcomings relative to the EA-6B ICAP-III (Improved Capability III), the improved Prowler also put forward by the Joint Airborne Electronic Attack Analysis of Alternatives study. However, these issues were easy to resolve through the inclusion of a digital receiver system, a complete communications electronic attack system, and a routable network information system. The study had already identified that the combat radius and time-on-station figures with typical SEAD weapon loads (AGM-88 HARM) were nearly identical between the

VMFA-533 deployed its F/A-18Ds to Al Asad AB, Iraq, during its deployment to Operation *Iraqi Freedom* in July 2006. These two "Knighthawks" carry laser-guided AGM-65E Maverick missiles, allowing them to very precisely strike moving or static targets from reasonable stand-off ranges.

two designs, and that the EA system components designed for the EA-6B ICAP-III were easily adaptable for use in the modified Super Hornet.

## Growler Development

Boeing had already started the engineering design phase on this, the fourth variant of the Hornet, in 1993, well before the Advanced Electronic Attack Analysis of Alternatives study took place. It took the Super Hornet design and modified it to form what is now officially known as the EA-18G Growler. The Growler is based on the two-seat F/A-18F, with Boeing using the basic airframe and combining it with Northrop Grumman's ICAP-III Airborne Electronic Attack (AEA) system. This approach creates an aircraft that retains 99 percent commonality with the Super Hornet, meaning that operational costs are minimized and logistical support is simplified for both land- and carrier-based operations.

In 2009, the Navy declared that the EA-18G had reached initial operating capability with VAQ-132 "Scorpions" at Whidbey Island NAS, Washington, meaning that it was ready for combat operations.

The EA-18 is based on the F/A-18F Block 2, including the APG-79 AESA radar and advanced rear crew station. The EA-18 costs US$7–9 million more than the nominal Super Hornet unit price of US$50 million, although the Growler retains its combat capabilities and can be reverted back to the F/A-18F specification with relative simplicity. Such flexibility ensures that the Navy can operate the type as efficiently and flexibly as threat conditions dictate. The key differences between the two-seat Super Hornet and the Growler are the latter's incorporation of ALQ-218 pods on the wingtip stations, and the replacement of the Vulcan cannon with avionics boxes containing an LR-700 receiver and satellite communications equipment.

The Growler is equipped with the ALQ-218 wideband receiver and ALQ-99 Tactical Jamming System to defeat any radar-guided surface-to-air threat. Combined, these systems allow the jet to undertake SEAD missions using both reactive and pre-emptive jamming techniques: stand-off and escort jamming; non-traditional electronic attack in coordination with ground forces, using the crew's enhanced situational awareness and uninterrupted communications to help troops on the ground counter hostile forces; and self-protection and time-critical strike support. Taking full advantage of the AESA radar, digital datalinks, AIM-120 AMRAAM, AGM-154 Joint Stand-Off Weapon (JSOW), ASQ-228 Advanced Targeting FLIR (ATFLIR), and Shared Reconnaissance Pod (SHARP), the Growler will be able to protect itself and aid strikers in finding, identifying and prosecuting time-sensitive targets.

Impressively, a Precision Airborne Electronic Attack option enables the EA-18G to rapidly sense and locate threats with a significantly higher degree of accuracy than was previously possible. In turn, this so-called "selective-reactive" technology enables the crew to concentrate jamming energy against threats in a much more effective manner.

Finally, an Advanced Communication Countermeasures set, in the form of the modular ALQ-227, allows it to counter a wide range of communication systems. This interfaces with an Interference Cancellation System (INCANS), which allows the crew to continue communication with other agencies even while the ALQ-227 is jamming.

With 12 Growlers delivered to the operational home of the type, NAS Whidbey Island, Washington in June 2009, it is anticipated that the fleet of 123 EA-6Bs will begin to be phased out of service by the end of 2010. A total of 57 EA-18Gs are being purchased as direct replacements for the Prowler with an additional 28 on order from Boeing to allow the Navy to equip a total of 11 squadrons.

## HORNET AND SUPER HORNET COMBAT OPERATIONS

The F/A-18 is widely regarded as being the most versatile and most capable tactical naval strike fighter of all time. It has earned an enviable combat record, starting with daring fighter-bomber raids on Khadaffi's Libya, then flying self-escorted "swing-role" missions in the Gulf War, adding to its laurels over the former Yugoslavia, and eventually performing superbly in Iraq and Afghanistan.

While concerns remained about its limited range in 1991, the Hornet, especially with the huge IFR assets available in theater, put in a stunning *Desert Storm* performance in US and Canadian hands.

Of eight carriers deployed during operations *Desert Shield* and *Desert Storm*, only *Ranger* and *John F. Kennedy* had air wings that did not include at least two squadrons of F/A-18s, while USS *Midway* embarked three squadrons. Nine squadrons of Hornets (VFA-15, -81, -82, -83, -86, -87, -151, -192, and -195) thus participated in *Desert Storm* from carrier decks, with four more squadrons participating in *Desert Shield*. Although this was a massive force of aircraft, six USMC squadrons of F/A-18As, F/A-18Cs, and two-seat F/A-18Ds, operating from Sheikh Isa, nevertheless augmented the USN's carrierborne Hornets. The F/A-18Ds operated mainly in the fast-FAC role. The USMC F/A-18s formed the backbone of the Corps' strike force in *Desert Storm*, a force that flew more ground-attack sorties than any other air arm involved in the war. The F/A-18 performed exceptionally well during *Desert Storm*, though warloads were often reduced by the need to carry two or three external fuel tanks.

Marine Corps jet assets, including the numerous F/A-18 squadrons, like VMFA-314 "Black Knights," gathered at Sheikh Isa AB, Bahrain, which inevitably became "Sharkey's Pizza" in USMC parlance.

Marine Corps Maj Steve Pomeroy of VMFA-333 described some of his *Desert Storm* experiences.

Our squadron's first mission actually took off before the first bombs hit Baghdad. That was a high-speed defense-suppression run, using HARMs in support of a strike package going into Iraq. My own first mission was the same thing, in support of a Navy carrier strike at Basra. I don't know the specific targets the Navy was going after, though being Basra the chances were that they were after petro-chemical complexes, airfields, air-defense sites or possibly bridges. We stood off from the target area before the strike package arrived, trying to locate and neutralize all of the radar-guided SAMs that we knew were there. I guess we were successful. Nobody was shot down.

Our mission was not quite the same as the Air Force's Wild Weasels. They went out to hunt SAMs. It didn't matter if they were accompanying a strike or they were preparing for one to come later. They considered a mission successful when they removed the radar. We'd actually be escorting a strike, and we went out with the intention of destroying an air defense site. In the second phase of the war we'd use HARMs to make sure that the missile radar was down and then go in with bombs to physically destroy the radar and missiles. The mission was known as a SEAD roll-back. Either the enemy air-defense system in Kuwait or southern Iraq would be destroyed or they would be moved back to safety, allowing us free rein in the theater of operations to go after significant military targets like artillery positions, infantry concentrations, and armor.

A typical strike would involve more than 12 aircraft, with HARM shooters, jamming aircraft, bombers, and maybe refueling support depending on how far you were going. If you are going to this effort to shut off a site, you might as well make sure you're going to destroy it. I saw as many as eight bombers used to take out a single site.

At night you could see the SAMs and AAA really well. I didn't see any SAMs fired during the day, but the folks

who did told me that the ignition signature was really intense. They'd see the smoke on the ground and pick up the missile in time to take evasive action. The shoulder-launched missiles were fairly easy to see. Some of the later versions didn't leave much of a trail, but any F-18s that were hit were not so seriously damaged that they couldn't get back. The Hornet could, and did, take some pretty serious hits and still get 200 miles or more back to base.

Missiles could be defeated by a combination of onboard expendables like flares or chaff, onboard jamming, and hard maneuvering. Any missile that stays in the same relative position to you is locked on. If you put a move on it, a sharp turn, and it doesn't follow, then you know that it either has broken lock, didn't have a lock in the first place, or is aimed at someone else.

My most memorable mission was a big strike. I'm a striker rather than one of the SEAD escort. My particular target was a railroad yard. Lousy weather, pitch black, low overcast so you can see all of the AAA and surface-to-air missiles coming up through it, but you can't physically see the target. We can acquire the target based on radar predictions. You're looking through the head-up display, showing slant range and elevation. You've told the computer where the target is, and weapons are released based on that information.

We are a four-plane mission, which is part of a much larger package of 30 or more aircraft all going to targets in the same vicinity. The guys shooting HARMs and the

Continued on page 137.

**Left:** Ready to fly another *Enduring Freedom* sortie, an F/A-18C of VMFA-232 goes to full power on the flight deck of USS *Nimitz*. The Hornet carries an asymmetric load of two fuel tanks, two GBU-38 JDAMs, one AIM-9X Sidewinder, and a single GBU-12 LGB.

**Overleaf:** The Legacy Hornet, so called because it has been supplanted by the Super Hornet, remains a vital ingredient in the United States' ability to project its foreign policy around the world. These two C-model Hornets carry a light load of precision munitions — one GBU-12 and one GBU-38 — as they fly over typical Afghan terrain.

guys providing the jamming are doing it for the whole package. Take off, get fuel from tankers in real bad visibility, climb back to altitude, in and out of clouds all the way. Approaching the coast the weather clears out some, except for the low overcast layer. As we get closer to the target I can see tracers from the AAA coming through the clouds. They are densely packed, although only one in five rounds fired is a tracer. There are a lot of shells in the air. I see four or five missile launches coming up through the overcast; a brief flash from the launch lighting up the underside of the cloud layer, then the missile itself climbing through. We all see SAMs detonate in the distance or burn out and fall away; at least they are not coming for me. The AAA is still going off above the canopy as I dive in to release my bombs, and it's there all the way to the coast on the way out.

We released bombs in a fairly steep dive. Delayed fuses were used to ensure penetration of hardened targets. We didn't hit everything we aimed at, but in general if an average F-18 pilot could see the target he could hit it. Something as small as a tank might not be destroyed by a single bomb, but it would almost certainly be rendered inoperable.

Ninety-nine percent of our targets were hard, where you either had to put a bomb through something like a bunker wall or hit something hard, like a tank. I won't say we weren't trying to kill people, because we were, but it was predominantly equipment or ground facilities that we were going for.

On the opening night of the war the Hornet community truly relied upon the multi-role capabilities of the Hornet, being required as they were to fight their way past MiGs into the target area. While this produced the US Navy's only air-to-air jet kills of the war (to the considerable chagrin of the far less flexible Tomcat community) in the form of two MiG-21 kills from AIM-9 shots at very short range, it also resulted in the loss of one of its own when the F/A-18C flown by Lt Cdr Scott Speicher was downed by what is widely believed to have been a short-range IR missile fired by an Iraqi MiG-25 "Foxbat."

## BALKANS

The Hornet's day and night, multi-role and precision-attack capability saw the aircraft being among the first to be used over the former Yugoslavia during Operation *Deny Flight* in 1993, and the type was again present during the opening rounds of Operation *Allied Force* in 1999.

Hornets were among the first NATO aircraft to become involved in the air war over the Balkans, since the Alliance's first action was to despatch naval forces to enforce a UN arms embargo imposed against the former elements of the Federal Socialist Republic of Yugoslavia in the summer of 1992. These forces naturally included USN carriers, which inevitably included F/A-18s in their air wings. In April 1993, when NATO began enforcing the No-Fly Zone originally imposed (but not enforced) the previous October, USMC F/A-18s based at Aviano were among the first aircraft to be involved. NATO operations over the former Yugoslavia required fighter aircraft to be supported by fighter-bombers and SEAD aircraft, while CAS aircraft began flying regular patrols over Bosnia from June 1993, ready to intervene if UN Protection Force troops on the ground came under attack.

Against this background the Hornet's multi-role/swing-role capabilities made it particularly

Left: The two-seat Super Hornet, the F/A-18F, is able to undertake a variety of missions. Armed with an array of air-to-ground and air-to-air munitions, and equipped with both AESA radar and a databus that ties its many sensors together via fiber-optic cables, it is a formidable adversary for America's enemies.

**Previous page:** The Super Hornet may be criticized as having shorter range than other contemporary fighters, but in fact the aircraft has shown itself to be capable of longer-range missions. The additional carry-back of the Super Hornet also gives its crews more options when planning strike missions from the "boat."

useful. An F/A-18D could simultaneously carry AIM-7 Sparrow BVR AAMs, close-range AIM-9s, external fuel, a Paveway LGB and targeting pod, and an AGM-88 HARM – an extremely useful warload for an aircraft operating over the former Yugoslavia, which might have to deal with enemy fighters, SAMs, or AAA positions. Pairs of F/A-18s made a number of small-scale attacks, and were destined to form the backbone of the first large NATO raid of the crisis.

F/A-18s were involved in the Udbina raid on November 21, 1994, when NATO fighters launched a major attack against Udbina airfield, which had been used by Serb aircraft attacking Bosnian positions in the Bihac pocket.

US Navy and US Marine Corps Hornets were destined to play a major part in Operation *Deliberate Force*, in 1995. This was a massive campaign of pre-planned air strikes against Serb military targets, which were triggered by a mortar attack on a market in Sarajevo, in which 38 civilians were killed. In reality, NATO had been waiting for a Serb provocation, ever since the Serb capture of the Muslim enclave of Srebrenica, which had nominally been under UN protection as a "safe area." A campaign of air strikes was felt to be the best way of protecting the remaining UN safe areas, and *Deliberate Force* began on August 30. The air campaign began with strikes against Serbia's integrated air defense system around Sarajevo. Under the codename *Dead Eye South East*, F-14s and F/A-18s from USS *Theodore Roosevelt* attacked targets with AGM-88 HARMs and Paveway LGBs, the three F/A-18 units being VFA-15, VFA-87, and VMFA-312. The campaign initially concentrated on targets in the Sarajevo area, but was widened from September 5, when it became clear that the Serbs would not pull back their heavy weapons. USS *America*, whose air wing also included three Hornet units, VFA-82, VFA-86, and VMFA-251, soon replaced *Roosevelt*. Land-based Hornets included those of VFMA(AW)-533, replaced by VFMA-224 from September 15, and the Spanish aircraft of 12/15 Ala. Weapons employed by the US Navy Hornets included the AGM-84 Stand-off Land Attack Missile (SLAM), while all operators made extensive use of HARM for defense suppression.

High intensity operations ended on September 14, when the Serbs agreed to pull back their heavy weapons, and the Dayton Peace Accords were finally signed in November 1995. NATO aircraft continued to fly regular sorties over the Balkans, monitoring Serb compliance with the Dayton accords, but no more bombs were dropped in anger.

For several years up to 1997, USMC F/A-18Ds were based at Aviano, Italy, to support UN and NATO missions in Bosnia. With their APG-73 radar, F404-GE-402 engines, laser designators, and (from the summer of 1995) ALQ-165 Airborne Self-Protection Jammer (ASPJ) systems, they represented the latest standard of the D-model Hornet.

Armament could often be mixed: two AIM-9s, one AIM-7 or AIM-120, two 500lb GBU-12 LGBs, a 500lb unguided bomb, and a FLIR/LTD-R (FLIR/Laser Target Designator-Ranging) pod. Weapons systems operators on Bosnian operations also carried digital cameras with zoom lenses for near real-time reconnaissance.

In a single mission, a pair of F/A-18Ds might "flex" among several missions. Using their radars, the aircraft would ensure that there were no aircraft violating *Deny Flight* restrictions. They would be available to provide CAS for UN forces on the ground, as requested by a ground forward air controller. They could also act as FACs for other aircraft, locating

The old and the new. In the foreground, a Marine VFA-106 F/A-18C Hornet taxis to its parking spot, while in the background a VFA-211 F/A-18F Super Hornet prepares to taxi to the "cat." Externally similar in appearance, the Legacy Hornet has several key differences to aid identification including its smaller, rounded engine intakes; smaller leading-edge route extensions; and an overall size difference that makes it about 25 percent smaller.

---

ground targets and talking incoming strike aircraft onto the target. Helicopters could be tracked and identified on the FLIR, and their landing sites could be photographed.

Marine F/A-18Ds flew more than 100 strike missions during Operation *Deliberate Force*, the raids against Serb military targets which began at the end of August 1995 and which are credited with persuading the Serbs to return to the bargaining table. Many of these operations were SEAD missions, mainly using GBU-16 1,000lb LGBs. The smaller GBU-12s were used where targets were located close to centers of population and where the risk of collateral damage was higher.

Poor weather prevented the successful use of LGBs from safe altitudes during daytime missions. As a result, more than half the missions were flown at night, when darkness concealed the fighters from ground fire and it was safe to fly at lower altitudes, under the weather. Eventually, the Hornets hit most of their designated targets.

Continued on page 144.

# TECHNOLOGY AND SPECIAL ROLES

## Super Hornet Special Roles

The Super Hornet was designed from the outset to offer flexibility in the number and type of roles that it can undertake. With space aboard the aircraft carrier at a premium, and with the retirement of stalwart naval jets like the A-6E Intruder and F-14B/D Tomcat, such flexibility is more important than ever.

Although it is tailored to the strike and interception roles, the F/A-18E/F is also capable of assuming responsibility for a variety of other important missions, including strike coordination and reconnaissance, buddy tanking, and reconnaissance.

The term strike coordination and reconnaissance (SCAR) was first coined in mid-2002 as the US geared up for its invasion of Iraq. It is closely related to the time-critical targeting work that the Super Hornet had been conducting over Afghanistan, and it also relates to the hunter-killer tactics that the Legacy Hornet and "Bombcat" communities had been flying for many years. SCAR enables all of the platforms in a given area to effectively and efficiently kill the enemy, and places the burden of responsibility on the Super Hornet crew for finding, identifying, evaluating for collateral damage, and handing off targets to other strike platforms as they enter the area. It is very similar to the FAC(A) role, although it is flown only when friendly troops are not in physical contact with the enemy. The big difference between SCAR and FAC(A) missions is that SCAR platforms cannot clear other aircraft "hot" to attack targets: they can only hand off a target and allow the other aircraft to conduct its own target and collateral damage assessments before releasing ordnance.

A number of strike fighters, including the Super Hornet, were assigned geographically defined "kill boxes" for SCAR patrol during the March 2003 invasion of Iraq. This had the advantage of concentrating the search for targets in a specific area, and of deconflicting the ongoing activities of hundreds of Coalition fighters as they criss-crossed the Iraqi landscape in search of targets. A two-ship of Super Hornets would arrive at its kill box, usually tasked primarily with kill box interdiction against fixed targets, or close air support to cover the rapid advance of the army northwards. They would then patrol 30 x 30 mile grids that defined a kill box, and having completed their primary mission, would then "re-role" to SCAR against other fixed targets or targets of opportunity.

SCAR tactics can vary depending on a number of conditions, but one option taken by Super Hornet crews over Iraq was to fly at medium altitude searching for targets using ATFLIR, radar, or eyeballs. Typically, before handing off targets to other fighters in the area, the Super Hornet crews would expend their own ordnance. When a target was found, the No. 2 aircraft was sometimes the first to release ordnance. The flight lead flew over the target and ensured both that it was hostile and that striking it would not result in civilian casualties; he would then clear No. 2 – who was usually flying three miles in trail – to drop his laser-guided or GPS-guided weapons. This SCAR tactic had the additional advantage of reducing No. 2's weapons load, allowing him to save fuel. This is important, since wingmen typically burn more fuel than the flight lead because they must manipulate the throttle more often to stay in formation.

## SHARP

Armed and unarmed reconnaissance can also be undertaken by Super Hornets equipped with SHARP. The Shared Reconnaissance Pod is a state-of-the-art, tactical digital reconnaissance system that boasts dual-band visible and IR imagery collection, and downlinking of images in real time via a common datalink to the Navy Input Station (NAVIS) ground station. This allows NAVIS analysts to perform real-time image screening and exploitation, seconds after the Super Hornet crew overflies the target. SHARP is

The rear cockpit in the Super Hornet is dominated by an 8 x 10in color tactical display that has almost no latency and can display a range of tactical symbols — navigation, threats, radar contacts, datalink information, and so on — as selected by the user. Either side are two MPDs, and to the bottom left is the engine and fuel digital data indicator (DDI) (the front cockpit also features a DDI).

mounted on the centerline station and has two sensors for stand-off oblique imagery: one for medium range (approximately 5 to 15nm) and one for long range (approximately 15 to 50nm).

## ATFLIR

Advanced Targeting Forward Looking Infra-Red (ATFLIR) is the Super Hornet's primary passive cueing sensor. It integrates advanced EO and IR sensors with one of the most powerful lasers on the market, allowing the location and designation of targets day or night at ranges exceeding 40nm and altitudes greater than 50,000ft.

The pod, which is attached to one of the flush-mounted fuselage pylons, has a laser spot tracker function that allows it to automatically spot the laser designation of other ground and airborne platforms. ATFLIR even has a built-in target identification system.

## AESA

The Super Hornet's APG-79 AESA radar represents the very latest in active electronically scanned array radar technology. Reaching far ahead of the jet, its detection range, multi-target track capabilities, and immunity from conventional electronic jamming techniques mean that it is a force to be reckoned with. Tying the radar, weapons, and sensors together is a very fast digital computer that uses fiber optic cables to receive huge volumes of data from each system, and which processes vast quantities of raw data before displaying it as digestible information to the pilot and WSO.

Finally, the F/A-18 played a pivotal role in Operation *Allied Force* in March 1999, NATO's response when Serb president Milosovic refused to withdraw his troops and special police units from Kosovo, where a tense situation had degenerated into open warfare between Serb forces and Albanian-backed separatist guerrillas.

A VFA-106 F/A-18C is propelled down the bow towards a waiting sky. The Hornet and Super Hornet are fully automated during the "cat" shot, and the pilot is required only to set the throttles to take-off power. Typically, this is accomplished without afterburner, but in this instance reheat has been selected to ensure a "good shot."

Hornets were already in theater and had been for many months, with USMC F/A-18D units taking it in turns to maintain a rotational detachment at Aviano, and with F/A-18Cs forming the backbone of every Sixth Fleet Carrier Air Wing deployed to the Adriatic, with USS *Theodore Roosevelt* being the principal carrier involved in *Allied Force*. Hornets from the USA, Canada, and Spain all started as they meant to go on and participated in the waves of attacks on the first day of the war, March 24, 1999.

Marine F/A-18Ds belonging to VMFAs-332/533, based at Taszar AB, Hungary, flew a total of 597 strike missions, dropping more than 303,500lb of ordnance

Equipped to deal with enemy SAMs and threat radars, this F/A-18C awaits its pilot in December 2001. During the very early stages of Operation *Enduring Freedom*, F/A-18C/D/E/F Hornets and Super Hornets flew missions in support of recce F-14 Tomcats. At that time, the Hornets carried AGM-88 HARMS (as in this case), because it could not be confirmed that the Taliban's radar missiles were either completely defunct or in a poor state of repair.

in the process. And it was during the conflict in Bosnia that the USMC introduced into service the Advanced Tactical Airborne Reconnaissance System, which gives the Marines a tactical reconnaissance ability superior to that even of the now-retired RF-4B Phantom II. The ATARS has a mix of three electro-optical and infra-red sensors, which provide near real-time tactical imagery via a datalink to a ground site. With clutches of unguided phosphorus rockets carried in four-round pods, the FAC(A) F/A-18Ds also undertook target-marking duties for other strike aircraft, or engaged hostile radar sites with their own AGM-88 HARMs. The Marines routinely used the two-seat F/A-18D for fast-FAC missions over the former Yugoslavia.

## MIDDLE EAST

Like the F-15E and F-16, the Hornet had already been patrolling the No-Fly Zone of Iraq's southern border for six years when, in December 1998, it took part in Operation *Desert Fox*. *Desert Fox* followed years of combat operations that had for the most part been limited to punitive response options (RO). ROs were typically pre-planned and very simple in nature, but *Desert Fox* would be a major bombing campaign that would rain down destruction on Iraqi military targets

## US Multi-Role Fighter Jets

over a four-day period. It was intended to curb Iraq's ability to create weapons of mass destruction, but was also politically driven in the wake of Saddam Hussein's refusal to cooperate with UN weapons inspectors. In what many saw as an attempt to actually target the leadership of Iraq, Hussein's palaces, security apparatus, and residences were all targeted.

In the Persian Gulf sat CVW-3's USS *Enterprise* (CVN 65) and CVW-11's USS *Carl Vinson* (CVN 70), each carrying two squadrons of Hornets that would take part in strikes against more than 25 targets in the four-day period. Of historical significance was that a handful of pilots belonging to VFA-37 "Ragin' Bulls" (aboard *Enterprise*) became the first female tactical naval aviators to go into combat. Charged with suppressing defenses, the Hornets launched AGM-88 HARMs to silence enemy radar sites, and carried out precision strikes against heavily defended targets, all without taking any losses

*Desert Fox* served only to irritate Hussein, and he instructed his air defense and interceptor forces to challenge the NFZs. As a result of a series of particularly audacious challenges – Coalition aircraft were fired upon by AAA and SAMs more than 60 times in a 60-day period – CVW-3 aboard USS *Harry S. Truman* (CVN 75) launched a large scale RO involving both Hornets and Tomcats in February 2001. Between them, they struck five command, control, and communications sites inside Iraq. Once again, they took no casualties. By September 2002, CVW-17 aboard USS *George Washington* (CVN 73) had been tasked to use its three F/A-18C squadrons to strike

AIRTEVRON Nine is the abbreviated name of VX-9, the Air Test and Evaluation Squadron. Nicknamed the "Vampires," the squadron is stationed at NAWS China Lake and operates a number of Hornets and, as depicted here, F/A-18E Super Hornets. The unit acts in a similar fashion to the USAF's 422nd TES, developing tactics and procedures for new weapons and attack systems.

Al Rutbah South AB in Iraq, as part of another expanded RO. VFA-34 "Blue Blasters," VFA-81 "Sunliners" and VFA-83 "Rampagers" did not need to be asked twice; all three squadrons struck the base with great enthusiasm.

By the time CVW-17 was attacking the Al Rutbah South AB in southern Iraq, America was already leading a Coalition force in a war against the Taliban in Afghanistan. As a result of US President George W. Bush's order to commit forces to the dilapidated country, the Hornets of the Fifth Fleet had been tasked to participate, and the carriers sailed east into the Arabian Sea and Indian Ocean to support Operation *Enduring Freedom*.

Flying missions that typically lasted up to eight hours, the Navy Hornet pilots initially flew combat air patrols over Pakistan, but when combat operations in Afghanistan commenced on October 7, VFA-15 "Valions" became the first Hornet operator to strike the Taliban. With no air threat and no air defense threat to speak of, the F/A-18s struck fixed targets associated with the Taliban's command and control apparatus. It was not long before the much despised extremists were retreating to the mountains – the same mountains in which they had granted Al Qaeda safe haven – and the Hornet pilots increasingly found themselves striking time-sensitive targets: mopeds, trucks, Taliban on foot, Taliban seeking refuge in the hills, and Taliban laying up in caves. For these missions, the AAS-38 NITE Hawk pod was instrumental in locating and tracking fleeting targets under cover of darkness, permitting the employment of 500lb GBU-12 laser-guided bombs with pinpoint accuracy.

By spring 2002 the Taliban had been ousted from power in Afghanistan and the air war had evolved to be orientated around supporting ground infantry operations, principally providing close air support.

## FREEDOM FOR IRAQ

As America led the Coalition force in the invasion of Afghanistan, by late 2003 it was about to do the same in Iraq, only this time the objective was to march into Baghdad and remove Saddam Hussein from power. The "Valions," who had already spent four weeks flying combat missions against the Taliban, returned to the Persian Gulf aboard *Roosevelt* in time for the launch of Operation *Iraqi Freedom*, on March 19, 2003. The same night, VFA-25 "Fists" and VFA-113 "Stingers" aboard USS *Abraham Lincoln* were tasked with first-night air strikes that took them over Baghdad as part of the "Shock and Awe" campaign. The "Fists" sustained an average of 20 daily combat sorties, and struck targets in Basra, An Nasiriya, Al Kut, Najaf, Al Hillah, and ultimately Baghdad. They flew 272 combat sorties in 18 days, attacking armored divisions, military airfields, facilities, and command and control infrastructures. By April 15, the "Valions" had employed more than 245,000lb of ordnance against Iraqi targets.

The "Fists," "Stingers," and "Valions" were just three components of a much larger Hornet contribution, however. VFA-137 and VFA-151 on USS *Constellation*; VFA-27, VFA-195, and VFA-192 on USS *Kitty Hawk*; VFA-82 and VFA-86 on USS *Enterprise*; and VFA-97 and VFA-94 on USS *Nimitz* were also flying combat sorties in their Legacy Hornets at a frenetic pace.

Over Iraq, the weapon of choice was the newly arrived GBU-38 500lb JDAM, along with the GBU-32 and GBU-31 (1,000lb and 2,000lb, respectively)

Continued on page 153.

---

**Right:** The APG-79 AESA radar in the latest Block 2 Super Hornets allows for exceptionally long-range search and track capabilities and boasts a fine ground mapping resolution via its SAR mode. Moreover, the AESA radar can work in air-to-air and air-to-ground modes simultaneously, allowing the WSO to concentrate on air-to-ground while the pilot looks for air-to-air threats.

# F/A-18E SUPER HORNET SPECIFICATION

## Dimensions

Length: 60ft 3½in
Wing span: 44ft 8½in
Wing span (folded): 30ft 7¼in
Wing area: 500sq ft
Height: 16ft
Wheel track: 17ft 9½in
Wheelbase: 10ft 2in

## Powerplant

Two General Electric F414-GE-400 turbofans each rated at 14,011lb st dry and 22,019lb with afterburning.

## Weight

Empty: 30,500lb
Maximum take-off: 66,000lb
Maximum payload for catapult launch: 34,000lb
Maximum carrier landing: 42,900lb

## Fuel and load

Internal fuel: 14,460lb
External fuel: approximately 6,290lb
Maximum ordnance: 17,747lb
F/A-18E maximum bring-back capacity: 9,900lb
F/A-18F maximum bring-back capacity: 9,000lb

## Performance

Maximum speed at 36,089ft: Mach 1.6
Approach speed: 144mph
Operational radius on a hi-lo-hi attack mission with four 1,000lb bombs, two AIM-9, two 400 Imp gal drop tanks: 390nm
Radius on a fighter escort mission with two AIM-120 AMRAAM and two AIM-9 Sidewinder AAMs: 410nm
CAP endurance at 150nm with six AIM-120 AMRAAM and three 400 Imp gal drop tanks: 2 hours 9 minutes
Service ceiling: 50,000ft
*g* limit: +7.6

## Armament

One internal M61A1 or -A2 20mm cannon, plus a wide range of stores carried on 11 hardpoints and including AIM-7, AIM-9, and AIM-120 AAMs; AGM-84 Harpoon anti-ship missiles, SLAM air-to-ground and SLAM-ER cruise missiles, AGM-65 Maverick AGMs (air-to-ground missiles), AGM-88 HARM anti-radiation missiles, AGM-154 JSOW cruise missiles, JDAM GPS-guided freefall bombs, Paveway LGBs, plus unguided bombs and rockets.

## Suppressing The Threat

The F/A-18 carries a specialist stand-off munition in the shape of the AGM-154 JSOW. During an Operation *Southern Watch* mission in January 1999, the Hornet became the first aircraft in history to employ the AGM-154A in combat. The weapon contains 145 BLU-97/B Combined Effects Bomblets. The F/A-18 community again employed the weapon with success during *Enduring Freedom* and *Iraqi Freedom*. It is a particularly devastating tool when used to incapacitate or destroy enemy air defense sites.

As the F/A-18 continued to expand its SEAD role in the 1990s, it became the Navy's main user of the AGM-88 High-speed Anti-Radiation Missile. Today, the AGM-88C, which has a more sensitive seeker, a better processor, and more onboard memory than the A-model, is the staple SEAD weapon for the Hornet. The AGM-65 Maverick, most commonly associated with the destruction of armored targets, is also a useful tool in the prosecution of SAM and AAA sites.

Another important, but little discussed store is the ADM-141 Tactical Air-Launched Decoy (TALD). This was used to great effect during *Desert Storm* and *Iraqi Freedom* when it was fired ahead of attacking aircraft, forcing enemy search and tracking radars to activate, thus increasing friendly anti-radiation missile kill probabilities. The Hornet can carry up to six of the 400lb decoys.

The EA-18G Growler employs the latest EW equipment and routines to jam threat systems, and can employ the full range of Super Hornet weapons. This example is operated by VX-31 TES.

One of the significant differences between the F/A-18E/F Super Hornet and the F/A-18C/D Hornet is the ability of the former to carry more weaponry. Combine that with its improved avionics and advanced ASQ-228 ATFLIR and its AESA radar, and you have an incredible capability to find a target, identify it and then prosecute it with great precision.

Of the Super Hornet's vast array of air-to-ground weapons, the AGM-84E Harpoon anti-ship missile, AGM-84H/K Stand-Off Land Attack Missile-Expanded Response (SLAM-ER), AGM-88 High Speed Anti-Radiation, and the AGM-65 Maverick are the cornerstones of its powered precision strike capability.

Each weapon achieves specific effects against specific targets, and each therefore plays an important role in giving the Super Hornet a well-rounded combat capability.

## AGM-84 Harpoon

The Block II AGM-84L Harpoon uses the software, mission computer, integrated global positioning system and inertial navigation system, and the GPS antenna and receiver from the SLAM-ER. Block III adds a datalink to allow the missile to be updated inflight via the Super Hornet's AN/AWW-14 datalink pod.

From a Super Hornet perceptive, Block II Harpoon can be fired at a pre-planned target, or at a target of opportunity (TOO). It can be utilized in both land-strike and anti-ship missions, and uses GPS to hit a designated target aim point that is pre-programmed before flight, or targeted in TOO mode via the Super Hornet's radar or ATFLIR.

With the Block III missile in the terminal phase of flight, the AWW-14 can be used to send it the latest coordinates of the target. Thus, if the pilot continues to monitor the target on radar or on the ATFLIR, he can periodically update the missile up until the moment of impact.

## AGM-84H/K SLAM-ER

Out of the very successful Block I Harpoon came the interim AGM-84E SLAM. SLAM used the seeker head from the AGM-65 Maverick missile and the datalink from the AGM-62 Walleye missile and was a great success.

From the interim SLAM came the AGM-84H SLAM-ER. SLAM-ER can strike targets more than 150 miles distant and is therefore an "over-the-horizon" precision strike weapon. The missile can be employed against sea and land targets, and even has the ability to strike moving ground targets.

Like Harpoon, SLAM-ER boasts both pre-planned and TOO modes of attack, and can be used in a fire-and-forget mode, or the tactically flexible "man-in-the-loop" mode.

GPS guides SLAM-ER into the target area (aided by mid-course updates generated by the Super Hornet's radar, if available) and ensures that its imaging infra-red seeker is pointed directly at the target. The missile then automatically computes target velocity and keeps the target within the missile seeker field of view. The pilot or WSO can now refine its aim point or leave the missile as it is.

SLAM-ER was actually the first missile ever to permit re-targeting after launch. For the Super Hornet crew this means that they can assess the state of the primary target through the missile imaging IR video display in the cockpit (transmitted to them via the AWW-14). If the primary target has already been destroyed or they receive information while the missile is airborne that makes them want to assign a new target to the weapon, they can use the datalink to re-target it at a secondary target.

This man-in-the-loop mode uses a software technique known as "Stop-Motion Aimpoint Update" that lets the Super Hornet crew freeze the target scene video on the cockpit display, and then use their "acquisition" cursors to designate a precise aim point.

## AGM-88 HARM

The radar-sniffing AGM-88 High Speed Anti-Radiation Missile is one of the Super Hornet's main weapons, primarily because the jet plays such an important part in the destruction and suppression of enemy air defenses (DEAD/SEAD) as part of the US Navy power projection force.

HARM is used to suppress and destroy surface-to-air emitters in order to allow strikers to ingress and destroy targets. It offers pre-briefed (PB), pre-emptive (PE), self-protection (SP) and TOO modes, and is a fire-and-forget missile.

In PB mode, the Super Hornet crew will program the missile with the known locations and frequencies of threat emitters in the target area. If the threat emitters are transmitting as the Super Hornet approaches launch time, the missile can refine its targeting solution prior to launch. Failing that, it will be fired regardless, but will keep "looking" for a radar source to guide on until it impacts the pre-programmed coordinates. PE mode offers a similar capability, but the missile is fired towards only a very general set of target coordinates. This mode leaves it with a slightly shorter range, since it must fly a less energy efficient route to the target.

SP mode gives the Super Hornet a short- to medium-range defensive capability that allows it to engage targets within 360 degrees. The HARM is slaved to the RWR and given a prioritized list of threats, and the pilot can either select the most pressing threat or allow the missile to decide which to engage immediately after launch. SP mode is similar to TOO mode, but TOO mode has a smaller search pattern that is limited to the field of view of the HARM's seeker and is better suited to the Super Hornet's self escort missions.

The flexibility of HARM means that Super Hornet crews on SEAD missions can fire pre-emptive and pre-briefed HARM shots that are timed to coincide with the timings of the main strike force. Similarly, the TOO and SP modes allow the crew to very quickly react to a pop-up threat emitter.

## AGM-65 Maverick

While the HARM, Harpoon, and SLAM-ER offer stand-off capability ranging from 50 to 150 miles, the AGM-65 Maverick is a more tactical weapon that is used within the confines of the battlefield and is particularly well suited to close air support and battlefield air interdiction missions.

The two-man crew of the F-model Super Hornet is ideal for both of these missions because they have extremely high task loadings: the pilot can dedicate more time to looking out for surface-to-air threats on the ground, while the WSO concentrates on sensors such as the radar, ATFLIR, and the Maverick seeker. The Maverick seeker, available in IR and EO TV variants, presents the WSO and pilot with an image of what the sensor sees in much the same way as SLAM and SLAM-ER. It too can be tied to the ATFLIR, radar, or the pilot's head up display.

The crew can either manually drive the Maverick sensor, so that the crosshairs overlay the target, and then fire the missile; or they can designate a target in the radar or ATFLIR and automatically hand-off to the missile. In HUD mode, the pilot can maneuver the aircraft so that a small box symbol in his HUD (representing the Maverick's seeker field of view) overlays the target, and then hit a switch to hand-off that target to the missile. Once the missile has been launched it becomes a fire-and-forget weapon and cannot be re-targeted or updated.

Maverick gives the Super Hornet crew an excellent weapon for taking care of battlefield threats such as armored vehicles. In addition, it is a useful DEAD weapon for taking-out pop-up radar-guided AAA, and for finishing-off surface-to-air missile sites following a successful HARM attack.

JDAMs. The GBU-12 LGB and AGM-65 Maverick were also relied on heavily. These weapons were particularly useful as the Hornets moved from interdictions and strike missions, to close air support and FAC(A) as the war progressed.

While taking a back seat to the JDAM and GBU-12, the AGM-145 JSOW was also employed in limited numbers – the three Hornet squadrons aboard the *Lincoln* launched only 65, for example – but its use tended to be limited to those targets where area suppression was desirable. Even less common was the AGM-84 SLAM-ER, of which Hornets fired only three in the entire war.

During *Iraqi Freedom*, the D-model was the USMC's workhorse Hornet, providing night attack and FAC(A) capabilities, the latter of which involved coordinating other strike platforms from the USAF, USN, and Coalition air forces. In both roles, the Marine "Deltas" were forward deployed to captured Iraqi airfields.

Only a single Hornet loss occurred, on April 2, when an American PAC-3 Patriot missile battery downed an F/A-18C. The pilot was killed.

Saddam's regime had rapidly capitulated and the "shooting war" in Iraq was over by the end of April 2003. From this point on, the Hornets supported US and Coalition troops as small contacts with enemy insurgents took on an increasingly urban feel.

In summer 2010, Navy and Marine Hornets continued to go to sea in support of operations *Enduring Freedom* and *Iraqi Freedom*, although the latter was winding down; July 2009 was the first month since the invasion where Coalition strikers did not drop a single weapon in anger.

## SUPER HORNET AT WAR

With the September 11 terrorist attacks on New York and the Pentagon, the floodgates for overwhelming US-led military response were opened, with major combat operations in Afghanistan commencing less than a month later. While the Super Hornet would soon play a crucial role in Afghanistan and what would later be termed the "Global War on Terror," its sting was first felt in a more sedate and long-standing combat operation: Operation *Southern Watch*.

*Southern Watch* had commenced following the cessation of the 1991 Gulf War with Iraq, and called for Coalition aircraft to patrol the NFZ covering Iraq's southern territory. With the US Navy's VFA-115 "Eagles," the first F/A-18 Super Hornet unit to declare combat readiness, deploying to the Middle East aboard USS *Abraham Lincoln* (CVN 72) in July 2002 as part of CVW-14, it was only a matter of time before the new jet would make its combat debut. That debut came on November 6, when two F/A-18Es conducted a *Southern Watch* RO strike on two SAM launchers at Al Kut, and an air defense command and control bunker at Tallil AB, Iraq. The Super Hornets dropped 2,000lb GBU-31 JDAM bombs on the two sets of targets.

VFA-115 made its presence felt throughout the *Southern Watch* deployment, expending twice the amount of ordnance compared to other squadrons deployed aboard *Lincoln*, recording a hit rate of 100 percent (22 JDAMs on 14 targets in Iraq), and exceeding all mission readiness requirements for the duration. This latter requirement is particularly crucial in combat, and thankfully the Super Hornet requires 75 percent fewer labor hours per flight hour than the Tomcat it replaced. More to the point, the Super Hornet's impressive combat capable rate was soon to prove even more important, as VFA-115's six jets were soon being tasked to support *Enduring Freedom*. The "Eagles" would eventually fly 214 combat missions in support of both operations *Enduring Freedom* and *Southern Watch*.

## OPERATION *IRAQI FREEDOM*

It was not yet over for VFA-115, however. By March 2003, the squadron had been tasked to participate in Operation *Iraqi Freedom*. On April 3 the "Eagles" flew the first operational flight of the Fast Tactical Imagery (FTI-II) photo-reconnaissance pod, but CVW-14 was largely tasked with CAS, strike, escort, SEAD, and aerial refueling. Sharing flight deck space with VFA-115 was a small detachment from VFA-14 "Top Hatters" and VFA-41 "Black Aces," both of which had also begun to transition to the Super Hornet. Two F/A-18Es from VFA-14 and two F/A-18Fs from VFA-41 were forward deployed from USS *Nimitz* to USS *Abraham Lincoln*; the former flew mostly as buddy tankers, and the latter as FAC(A)s.

Meanwhile, the remainder of the newly equipped VF-14 and VF-41 waited patiently aboard USS *Nimitz* as part of CVW-11, as it sailed quickly to the Persian Gulf. Eventually arriving and taking on combat responsibilities, both squadrons were soon in the thick of the action. They expended laser-guided bombs, JDAM and AGM-65 Maverick missiles and conducted numerous long-range missions that saw them patrol northern Baghdad and surrounding areas, including Tikrit.

Operation *Iraqi Freedom* was a clear success from a tactical air power perspective, and by the time President Bush had infamously declared major combat operations complete, *Lincoln*'s F/A-18E/Fs had dropped 380,000lb of ordnance and, while flying in the tanker support role, had passed 3½ million lb of aviation gas. This wartime performance earned the "Eagles" and the Lincoln Battle Group the Navy Unit Commendation. On April 6, 2003, the forward-deployed Hornets of VFA-14 and VFA-41 returned to USS *Nimitz*; leaving VFA-115 to return home aboard *Lincoln* to NAS Lemoore, California, on May 1.

While major combat operations in Iraq ceased as Iraq's regime crumbled and its military ceased its attempts at resistance, *Iraqi Freedom* would quickly deteriorate into an urban war in which the enemy looked just like any other person in the street. Coalition fast jets remained heavily tasked in support of troops on the ground, and the Super Hornet – of which more and more squadrons were coming online – was no exception. In fact, there are several F/A-18E/F squadrons that have deployed several times to support operations in Iraq or Afghanistan.

The "Top Hatters," VFA-14, is one such example. The unit had already contributed to the "real shooting war" in March/April 2003, but would once again participate in *Iraqi Freedom* in 2005, this time aboard USS *Ronald Reagan* (CVN 76), racking up more than 2,100 combat sorties and over 4,300 flight hours. And, on April 6, 2005, VFA-154's Super Hornets dropped two 500lb laser-guided bombs on enemy insurgents east of Baghdad. The "Black Knights" were

An F/A-18F of the "Red Rippers," Strike Fighter Squadron One One, is readied for flight aboard the flight deck of the Nimitz-class aircraft carrier USS *Harry S. Truman*. Red floodlights illuminate the deck and also help preserve valuable night vision.

executing their first Super Hornet cruise in the summer of 2005, aboard USS *Carl Vinson*, as part of CVW-9. They, too, would return to the conflict, in 2007. With *Carl Vinson* being overhauled, CVW-9 and VFA-154 were attached to USS *John C. Stennis* (CVN 74), and flew missions over both Iraq and Afghanistan.

In 2005 VF-143 "Pukin' Dogs" transitioned to the F/A-18E Super Hornet, deploying aboard USS *Eisenhower* in 2006 to support *Iraqi Freedom* and *Enduring Freedom*, their cruise ending in the spring of 2007. In January 2006, VFA-115 returned to *Iraqi Freedom*, deployed aboard USS *Ronald Reagan*. Once again, the "Eagles" flew hundreds of combat sorties providing close air support to Coalition troops. And, on September 8, VFA-211 "Fighting Checkmates" used its F/A-18Fs to employ GBU-12 and GBU-38 bombs against Taliban fighters and Taliban fortifications west and northwest of Kandahar, signaling the squadron's first combat actions as a Super Hornet operator. The "Fighting Checkmates" had also been active over Iraq, and returned to NAS Oceana on November 18 the same year, with hundreds of combat sorties under their belts. In the same timeframe, USS *Dwight D. Eisenhower* (CVN 69) carried VFA-103 "Jolly Rogers" to the Gulf, where the squadron conducted operations alongside Legacy Hornet squadrons, dropping 140 precision guided weapons and performing around 70 strafing runs in an increasingly urban setting.

Breaking away from an imaginary threat, two Super Hornets release flares in a bid to ruin their opponent's shot. At the merge, the F/A-18E/F retains the Legacy Hornet's much-revered "high-alpha" capability, which means that when the fight inevitably decays to a low-speed situation the pilot still has the pitch authority required to raise the nose; he can either shoot his opponent with the gun, or intimidate him with nose position. In such a scenario the F/A-18 is even more of a threat than the F-16 Viper.

Finally, the East Coast's VFA-11 "Red Rippers" deployed with CVW-3 aboard USS *Harry S. Truman* in November 2007, conducting ongoing combat operations until their eventual return to NAS Oceana in June 2008.

Although the majority of F/A-18E/F squadrons deployed to the Persian Gulf have been tasked to fly and fight over Iraq and Afghanistan, there have been a handful of notable deployments where the emphasis has been firmly on the destruction of the Taliban and rooting out Al Qaeda. On September 8, 2008, VFA-31 "Felix" and the rest of CVW-8 deployed onboard USS *Theodore Roosevelt*. The Air Wing went on to fly more than 3,100 sorties and drop more than 59,500lb of ordnance while providing close air support for International Security Assistance Forces in Afghanistan. On March 21, 2009, USS *Dwight D. Eisenhower*, with more Super Hornets aboard, relieved *Roosevelt*.

**Left:** Two Super Hornets of VFA-211 go "feet dry" as they cross the sand of Virginia Beach on their way home to NAS Oceana. For particularly bad weather conditions and when operating at sea, all Hornets have a fully automated landing system.

This VFA-125 "Rough Raiders" F/A-18C lands at NAS Lemoore. In October 2010, the squadron was merged into VFA-122 "Flying Eagles" as a cost-reducing measure in anticipation of the replacement of the Legacy Hornet with the Super Hornet.

RAPTOR

# US Multi-Role Fighter Jets

The F-22A Raptor is the first fifth-generation fighter to enter service, and represents the very best in design and technology that money can buy. Against both air and ground targets, the F-22A Raptor's dominance over its adversaries gives it a fighting edge that is unassailable. Having spent two decades in development, in December 2005 it was declared operational at Langley AFB, Virginia.

The driving force behind the F-22's design was the need to operate over a densely packed field of interlocking SAM sites, anti-aircraft artillery and early warning radars – the integrated air defense system (IADS) – and all of this in the face of advanced "Flanker-plus" air defense fighters. To survive and dominate in such an environment, the F-22 had to be both stealthy and a superb performer in air combat.

In the post-Cold War world, the fighter threat from advanced Soviet fighters has receded, but that from the IADS remains very real. This is especially true today, when Russia continues to export its most capable IADS components to nations with which the United States has poor relationships or is ideologically opposed. The F-22 is ideally equipped to function as part of the USAF's Global Strike Force. In this concept, the Raptor protects the bombers by providing protection against both air and ground threats. Against enemy fighters the F-22 has little to worry about, and for the defense suppression mission the F-22 uses GPS-guided bombs such as the JDAM or SDB (small diameter bomb) to take on the IADS, not using brute force in abandon, but instead carefully hitting network nodes and the most threatening SAM sites and in doing so "breaking down the door" for others to follow.

More than 15 years elapsed between the first flight of the YF-22 technology demonstrator and the Raptor's first operations, a period characterized by shrinking budgets and decreasing requirements. Along the way the F-22 program has come under intense scrutiny from the politicians, with the result that the once-planned mighty force of 750 aircraft has been slashed to a withered force of just 187.

This is through no fault of the aircraft's design, but is rather a reflection of the times into which it has been developed. The end of the Cold War signaled an end to massive levels of expenditure on defense-related programs. With no short-term threats to the United States, successive administrations took the opportunity to cut deeper and deeper into the defense acquisition budget. In the 21st century the war against global terrorism has become the main preoccupation, and equipment geared towards counterinsurgency warfare is seen as the most deserving of budgetary allocations. Unsurprisingly, the F-22 has no part to play in Afghanistan or Iraq, where all political eyes are focused, and the bill for ongoing operations and research and development for equipment better suited to America's long-term commitment to Afghanistan places a further squeeze on procurement. Finally, the need to bail out large financial institutions with public money following the 2009 global financial collapse has emptied the coffers still further, and any hope that F-22 procurement could be extended was dashed in 2009 when the limit was set at the paltry figure of 187 Raptors, and the next-generation multi-role Lockheed Martin F-35 began flight testing in earnest with operational software loads.

## ATF

The startling dwindle in procurement numbers would have seemed highly unlikely when the Advanced Tactical Fighter (ATF) project was launched in 1971

---

**Previous page:** The F-22A Raptor is the first operational fifth-generation fighter in the world. This example, flown by Royal Australian Air Force exchange pilot Flt Lt Matthew Harper, belongs to the 525th FS "Bulldogs," based at Elmendorf AFB, Alaska.

Pitching back into the fight, two Raptors of the 422nd TES, based at Nellis, show off the F-22's clean lines. The ability to carry weapons internally is a key facet in reducing the aircraft's radar cross section.

The ATF program slowly evolved at a time when the F-15 was just entering service, and then gained additional momentum in the late 1970s when US intelligence analysts detected important developments in Soviet aviation and technology.

ATF moved forwards through a series of requests for proposals in the first half of the 1980s, resulting in teams led by Lockheed and Northrop being awarded contracts for demonstration/validation (dem/val) technology demonstrators. Lockheed teamed with Boeing and General Dynamics, the former later buying the latter's fighter business, along with its world-famous F-16.

It was not until September 29, 1990 that the YF-22 demonstration/evaluation aircraft took to the air. Nearly seven years later the first F-22A Raptor flew. The intervening period saw the first in several dramatic cuts in planned numbers, and also the cancellation of the proposed F-22B two-seater. Initial operating capability was not declared until December 15, 2005, when the F-22 began taking its part in Operation *Noble Eagle* air defense missions over the United States.

Thus, it was 15 years after the YF-22's first flight that the Raptor eventually entered service, reaching IOC on December 15, 2005. The 27th FS, 1st FW, at Langley AFB, Virginia, accomplished this milestone; declaring IOC meant that the 27th FS was able to deploy 12 Raptors to any conflict in the world, where they would then be ready and able to fly air-to-air or air-to-ground missions. The ability came following extensive and

exhaustive testing of the Raptor's Block 3.0 software – the first combat ready version – by the 422nd TES at Nellis AFB from 2001.

The Raptors have taken the reins from the F-15 Eagle, but so incontrovertible is the F-22's capability that the mission is no longer called air superiority, but air dominance. The subtle difference alludes not only to the Raptor's ability to dominate the air, but also to its limited air-to-ground ability to strike the most sophisticated air defense systems with near impunity. Of course, the Raptor's 144:0 kill ratio against US fighters during the Northern Edge exercise in late 2006 showed the title change to be most fitting.

In February 2007, the US Air Force sent the Raptor on its first temporary duty (TDY) assignment. The TDY was intended to test the 1st Wing's ability to deploy, and also represented an opportunity for the US government to flex its muscles for the benefit of international neighbors. The TDY was to Kadena AB, Japan, and included 12 Raptors from the 27th FS at Langley. However, it resulted in some embarrassment as navigation and communications computers on the first two aircraft crashed as they crossed the international dateline west of Hawaii. The glitch was corrected in short order and all 12 aircraft spent 120 days in Japan without further incident. The second F-22 TDY occurred in October 2008, when eight Raptors from the 90th FS deployed to Andersen AB on the Pacific island of Guam. They were later replaced by six jets from their sister squadron, the 525th FS.

The F-22 was built to have a structural life of 8,000 flight hours, and the USAF has projected a usage rate in the region of 335 hours per year, giving the Raptor an approximate service life of about 24 years. As such, Lockheed Martin is currently investigating the possibility of extending the aircraft's fatigue life to 10,000 hours.

Interestingly, whereas all other fighters are designed with planned depot maintenance (PDM) inspections to occur throughout their fatigue lives, the F-22 was built to fly the full 8,000 hours without requiring PDM. (PDM is an exhaustive "strip down" of the aircraft that takes several weeks.) However, it does require depot level maintenance to rebuild its low-observable (LO) skin. In fact, the F-22's LO coatings have proven to be a weak link in its armor, since they have been shown to be the cause of a low mission capable (MC) rate in the operational fleet. In 2009, the USAF released data showing that the Raptor requires 30 maintenance man-hours per flight hour, half of which is spent working on LO issues, leaving the F-22 with an MC rate of around 62 percent.

## MIXED FORCE TTPS

Looking beyond the Raptor's MC rate, the real issue that exists in 2010 lies with being able to use the comparatively small F-22 fleet in coordination with the less capable fourth-generation fighters in US service. Making this possible is the role of the "Green Bats," the 422nd TES at Nellis AFB, Nevada.

In 2009, the "Green Bats" commander was Lt Col James Vogel, a high-time Eagle and Raptor pilot. Of the 38 jets on his ramp, 13 were F-22As.

The F-22 is a fifth-generation fighter that is employed completely differently to anything else, and so we need to work out how to employ it in a mixed force... The question we have to answer is this: "How do you use two F-22s alongside a four-ship of F-15s or F-16s?" Our goal is to let the F-15 and F-16 guys know what to expect

**Left:** The Boeing YF-22 Advanced Tactical Fighter fought off competition from Northrop's YF-23 design to win the competition. The F-22A features a slightly redesigned nose and canopy, and is somewhat more refined in planform, but is otherwise externally similar to the YF-22.

## US Multi-Role Fighter Jets

# Raptor

from us, where we are going to be, what radio calls we are going to make, and the way in which we work... We do this by getting that information into the classified tactics manuals for each MDS [Mission Design Series]. We are really trying to help each community understand what the tactical considerations are when employing with the F-22.

These manuals will stop short of revealing exactly how the Raptor is accomplishing its goals, but will provide enough information to make cohesion possible through the execution of well-defined tactics, techniques, and procedures (TTPs).

The F-22A integration test, development, and evaluation (TD&E) process has involved some outside help from other Air Force and US Navy units. "We're a big enough unit that we can normally do all of our testing in-house – we use our own F-16s and F-15s as Red Air [simulated enemy forces]. But for the F-22 integration testing, we have almost exclusively used the Aggressors from down the road [at Nellis] to fly against. We also, fairly recently, had some visiting Navy F/A-18 Hornets that flew as part of a mixed force so we could do some additional integration TD&E work."

## "DICEMEN"

Since IOC, the Raptor community has quickly developed tactics, techniques, and procedures in concert with the work of the "Green Bats" in order to allow it to take full advantage of the jet's unrivaled

Lt Col Jeffrey "Cobra" Harrigian, Commander, 43rd FS, 325th FW, Tyndall AFB, Florida, flies Raptor 01-018, the first of 48 new F/A-22 Raptors assigned to the 325th FW. Air Education and Training Command owns the Wing, which trains new Raptor pilots. This flight took place on September 26, 2003 and enabled the 43rd FS to commence training on type.

capabilities. Nowhere has this been demonstrated better than in Alaska, where the 3rd Wing has for decades been responsible for protecting America from the snooping of Russian aircraft and the threat of airborne nuclear attack.

On Friday September 3, 2008, the 90th FS declared it had reached IOC with the F-22A Raptor at Elmendorf AFB, Alaska. Situated adjacent to the city of Anchorage, Elmendorf AFB is home to the 3rd Wing, Pacific Air Forces (PACAF). The Wing boasts a complement of three fighter squadrons, the 90th FS and the 525th FS, operating the F-22 Raptor; and the 19th FS, the sole remaining F-15C/D Eagle operator at the base. Additionally, the 525th FS is part of the 477th Fighter Group, AFRC, and is one of two reserve F-22 units (the other being at Langley AFB, Virginia).

While PACAF's operations at Elmendorf have often been associated with sovereignty operations, and specifically protecting Alaska from the threat of Soviet and now-Russian incursions, the F-22's *raison d'être* in Alaska is much broader, according to Maj Mike Cabral, an F-22 pilot with the 90th FS.

> Our mission is air dominance. I would not say that we are dedicated to executing sovereignty operations – that's certainly not our primary role. Here at Elmendorf, our mission is not much different than it is for the F-22 as a system in the entire US Air Force and Coalition air environment. In other words, our job is to kick the door down for follow-on forces. We are going to use our stealth, our advanced sensors, precision targeting capability, and our integrated avionics to go places that other people cannot.

Elmendorf's northerly location is ideally situated to allow the Wing's F-22s to support combat operations anywhere north of the equator via a quick hop over the North Pole. Once in situ, Cabral continues, "We will take out the threats that are going to be a challenge to other platforms. That might be advanced fighters, or highly advanced surface-to-air missile threats."

Even prior to attaining IOC, the 3rd Wing's F-22s were active in defense of the continental United States. When the 19th FS's F-15s were grounded in late 2007 as part of a fleet-wide stand-down due to structural concerns, it was the 90th FS that filled the gap, manning PACAF's quick reaction alert facility at Elmendorf. "It was a big move for us, and a stressful affair for the squadron. We had very few combat-ready pilots at the time of the grounding, but we did have the assets and the resources to step up to and man the quick reaction alert facility," Cabral acknowledged. This no-notice period of sovereignty operations resulted in the first ever F-22 intercept of a Russian Tu-95MS "Bear-H," on Thanksgiving Day, 2007. The "Bear-H," which is capable of employing the Raduga Kh-55 cruise missile, had approached Alaskan airspace and was silently intercepted by two F-22s as it neared the Aleutian Islands. Of note in the intercept photographs subsequently released by the USAF was the use of drop tanks on the F-22s. Cabral commented, "They are absolutely vital for that mission. One of the things we always talk about when operating in the Pacific theater of operations is the 'tyranny of distance.' Well, that applies to Alaska as well – just from Elmendorf to the western coastline is a very significant distance, and with the weather being as bad and unpredictable as it can be up here, we certainly want that extra gas."

---

**Right:** An 168th Air Refueling Wing, Alaska Air National Guard, KC-135R Stratotanker refuels an F-22A of the 27th FS, 1st FW, Langley AFB. A long way from home, the Langley Raptors had deployed to Alaska in June 2006 to participate in Exercise Northern Edge.

## BLOCK 30

To be the world's premier air dominance fighter, and to kick down the doors that Cabral talked about, the Raptor incorporates stealthy features with cutting edge avionics and sensors. Indeed, the USAF maintains that there is unlikely to be any other aircraft capable of matching it for decades to come. Significantly, the Raptors assigned to the two Elmendorf squadrons are Block 30 models. This denotes that they are the most advanced of all the operational Raptors, and are the beneficiaries of improved and enhanced avionics and capabilities. In the case of the F-22, there are currently three main Blocks.

Block 10 F-22s are those delivered with an IOC configuration, conferring a multi-role capability that is analogous to the deep-strike capability of the F-117A, but more survivable. The Block 20 configuration is the baseline for the so-called "Global Strike Task Force" (GSTF) fleet, and features such improvements as a dedicated high-speed radar processor, and common integrated processors (CIPs) that can carry out 10.5 billion instructions per second. This additional computing power, coupled with improved software code, gives the Block 20 high-resolution synthetic aperture radar modes, improved radar electronic counter-countermeasures, two-way voice and datalink capability, and improved electronic countermeasures. The RTU's Raptors at Tyndall AFB and a portion of those at Nellis AFB, are early Block 20 models, comprising around 34 aircraft in total.

Some 63 aircraft were built to early Block 30 configuration, and build on those enhancements already made to the Block 20: compatibility with side-looking passive radar arrays provide a significant information, surveillance, reconnaissance (ISR) capability; a satellite communications terminal provides continuous network connectivity during deep-strike profiles, and allows the jet to relay electronic intelligence (Elint) data to commanders on the ground. Likewise, this increased ISR and Elint capability gives the Block 30 a greatly enhanced ability to attack ground targets, and enemy air defenses in particular. Indeed, the new Raptor's sensitivity to electronic emissions is so finely tuned that it can even detect the discrete transmissions that individual components of IADSs use to communicate with one another. No one is safe from the Raptor, it would seem.

At Elmendorf, the 90th and 525th FSs work closely with the F-15s of the 19th FS, as Cabral explains:

> One of the great things about Elmendorf, with having the F-15s and the AWACS right here on base, is that we have a self-contained air dominance team. We are simply never going to have enough Raptors to be able to cover the type of air-to-air engagements we might encounter globally, so having the Eagles here and being able to work with them to integrate together is a huge advantage. Add the AWACS, and the 3rd Wing has an awesome set of resources to be able to train for war, and to go to war together.

Getting to that stage has taken time. Raptor flying operations at Elmendorf began in August 2007, at which time all of the base's Raptor pilots were assigned to the 90th FS. "We then broke off the individuals that were going to go and flesh out the 525th [FS]," Cabral says.

With the F-22 capable of executing the multi-role mission, daily training in the 525th and 90th FS is carefully balanced. Cabral continues:

> We have been directed to concentrate on the air-to-air mission, so most of our time is spent practicing that. However, part of being an air dominance fighter is all about being able to operate inside the range of highly

Continued on page 173.

# OPERATORS

By May 2010, the Air Force had acquired and placed 168 Raptors into its inventory, with the vast majority going to the operational world: the 27th and 94th FS, 1st FW, Langley AFB, Virginia; 7th and 8th FSs, 49th FW, Holloman AFB, New Mexico; and the 90th and 525th FSs, 3rd Wing, Elmendorf AFB, Alaska. The 19th FS, 15th Wing, Hickam AFB, Hawaii, received its first Raptors in July 2010, and is expected to be re-activated later in the year.

In addition, there are two AFRC and two Air National Guard Associate Squadrons that operate as associates of the Active Duty Air Force. The AFRC units are the 302nd FS, 477th Fighter Group at Elmendorf and the 301st FS, 44th Fighter Group at Holloman. The ANG units are the 149th FS, 192nd FW, at Langley and 199th FS, 154th Wing, Hawaii.

Training of new Raptor pilots is provided by Air Education and Training Command's 43rd FS, 325th FW at Tyndall AFB, Florida. Test and evaluation continues to be conducted by both Air Combat Command's 422nd TES at Nellis, and Air Force Materiel Command's 412th FTS, 412th Test Wing, Edwards AFB, California.

## Air Education and Training Command

325th Fighter Wing, Tyndall AFB, FL
   43rd Fighter Squadron (Formal Training Unit)

## Air Combat Command

1st Fighter Wing, Langley AFB, VA
   27th Fighter Squadron
   94th Fighter Squadron
49th Fighter Wing, Holloman AFB, NM
   7th Fighter Squadron
   8th Fighter Squadron
44th Fighter Group, Holloman AFB, NM; AFRC
   301st Fighter Squadron (associate AFRC squadron to the 49th FW)
53rd Wing, Eglin AFB, FL
   422nd Test and Evaluation Squadron ("owned" by the Eglin-based 53rd Wing, but actually stationed at Nellis AFB, NV)
57th Wing, Nellis AFB, NV
   433rd Weapons Squadron

## Air Force Materiel Command

412th Test Wing, Edwards AFB, CA
411th Flight Test Squadron

## Pacific Air Forces

3rd Wing, Elmendorf AFB, AK
   90th Fighter Squadron
   525th Fighter Squadron

## Air Force Reserve Command

477th Fighter Group, Elmendorf AFB, AK
   301st Fighter Squadron
   302nd Fighter Squadron (associate AFRC)

## Air National Guard

192nd Fighter Wing, Langley AFB, VA
   149th Fighter Squadron (associate ANG squadron to the 1st FW)
154th Wing, Hickam AFB, HI
   199th Fighter Squadron

## US Multi-Role Fighter Jets

sophisticated threat systems, while simultaneously being able to employ ordnance against high value targets on the ground. That's a unique attribute that we train to, so we certainly can and are very capable of employing in that regime – it's a pretty important subset mission to us. The good news is that the smart weapons and the precision capabilities of the JDAM have taken out a lot of the old school weaponeering and attack planning. So, it simplifies the process for us a lot.

We have a set of F-22 tactical standards for Elmendorf – 3rd Wing tactical standards – and that makes us slightly different from other F-22 squadrons, some of which have their own squadron standards. So we talk to the guys at the 525th a lot, we have lots in common, and we attend the same WATTs (weapons and tactics talks) so that there is a unified vision as to where we are going to go. As for training, there is a greater RATP (ready aircrew training program) message that dictates how much of our training is air-to-air and air-to-ground. It breaks everything down for us, and our training syllabus is therefore designed to get all of our pilots to the same level.

With the Raptor so dominant in the air-to-air role, one wonders how the F-22 community is able to extract positive learning outcomes from training sorties that, according to one F-22 pilot, can be so one-sided that a single Raptor can kill eight F-15s before they even see him:

Continued on page 177.

**Left:** The 94th FS became the second squadron at Langley to receive the F-22A, when two Raptors arrived on March 3, 2006. The massive leap in capability between the F-22 and previous multi-role fighters means that, while the Raptor is not difficult to fly, learning to exploit its "capes" takes new pilots a little time.

**Overleaf:** Powered down, the Raptor's control surfaces droop as hydraulic pressure decays, running the jet's svelte lines but offering an interesting subject for the photographer nonetheless. The thrust-vectoring nozzles of the two Pratt & Whitney F119 engines are clearly visible on this 90th FS "Dicemen" jet.

# US Multi-Role Fighter Jets

It is sometimes hard for us to get great training, but don't make any mistake about it, there is not a fighter pilot out that likes to lose. So, the longer the F-15 and F-16 guys fight against us, the more of our sneaky tricks they tend to learn. In time, their tactics become more creative and they find ways to exploit. The other aspect to this is that because we want them to be part of our team, we work closely with them; and they start asking themselves, "I wonder if this tactic will work?" or, "I wonder if that tactic will work?," and they start trying all kinds of things. The real answer lies in numbers: the more of them there are out there, the more they can stress our flow. One of the big things that we strive to do is create very complex scenarios, to up the numbers and stress our pilots as much as we can. That can be difficult, as it takes a lot of resources – lots of "enemy" fighters – to give us a challenge. To that end, you also have to think about the F-15 and F-16 guys, who may not be getting the full benefit out of their own training against us.

While the pilots of the legacy F-15 and F-16 struggle to simply survive when pitted against the Raptor, the challenge for the F-22 pilot lies less with the operation of the jet's sophisticated avionics systems, which are almost completely automated and seamless to the pilot, and more with being a battle manager. That involves looking at the synthesized "big picture"

**Left:** Any surface that sits perpendicular to a radar transmitter makes for an excellent reflector, so the F-22 has been designed to minimize such angles. Particular attention has been paid to designing non-reflecting gaps between the flight control surfaces, as can be seen on the leading-edge slats of these two unidentified Langley-based Raptors.

**Overleaf:** The F-22 cants its rudders outwards to act as speed brakes, creating two almost unreal condensation streamers in humid air. This Raptor, flown by Lt Col James Hecker, Commander of the 27th FS, demonstrates the phenomenon well during the delivery flight of the first operational F-22A Raptor to its permanent home at Langley AFB, in May 2005.

The F-22A's vertical stabilizers are deceptively large, although the term itself is something of a misnomer since the surfaces cant outwards in order to reduce radar reflections. The large "AK" stencil identifies this as an Elmendorf, Alaska-based machine.

of information being presented on the large color displays in his cockpit, fed by an array of sensors, and then deciding how and when to execute the correct tactic. Having all of this information is known as situational awareness (SA) and comes as a result of the Raptor's ability to fuse together a wide array of data from a host of sensors. Speaking in 2008, Fl Lt Matthew Harper, then a new member of the 90th FS, agreed: "I have about 40 hours in the jet, and am totally comfortable with flying it, but what I am nowhere near comfortable with is being the tactician who has all this information and has to know how to use it. Lockheed Martin have built a jet that is so good that the pilot really is the weak link in the entire package." And Harper is no novice; he arrived at Elmendorf in mid-2008 on exchange from the Royal Australian Air Force, having already accrued almost 1,100 hours flying the F/A-18 Hornet in the air-to-air and air-to-ground roles.

Thanks to the F-22's exceptional stealth properties and sensor fusion, plus its ability to fly very fast and high, the pilot is able to get inside the decision-making cycle of his opponent before his opponent even knows he is there; and that is a crucial goal for any fighter pilot. For Cabral, who was an experienced F-15 pilot before coming to the jet, sensor fusion, and the simplicity of the man-machine interface, are among the most breathtaking aspects of the F-22:

> I am much less concerned with the mechanics of operating the radar, or looking to make sure my wingman is in the right position, or the mechanics of having to execute a very complex weapons delivery. These are all greatly simplified. Now, the pilot is free to make tactical flow decisions: where does my formation have to be to protect or kill what I am going after on today's mission? And that is the crux of it – in other airplanes, we have wingmen who spend three, four, five years just trying to understand the mission before they step up to be a four-ship flight lead or an instructor pilot. In the Raptor, we almost expect our brand new wingmen to have the same type of flow and decision making capability as our flight leads in other platforms.

The F-22 presents the overall battlespace picture to the pilot via four primary screens in the cockpit. Harper notes:

The displays are very well laid out, and after a few hours in the simulator it becomes intuitive to know where to look and when… Your eyes get trained on where to look. Everything is color-based: a bad guy is red, an unknown is yellow, and a friendly is green. The system is laid out so that if you are defensive you have a display for that, if you are attacking someone you have a display for that, and then there is the largest display that is used to locate all the information that is coming in from the sensors. This is the display – the situational display [SD] – that we use to make all of our main tactical decisions. You no longer control the radar as you would do in a traditional aircraft; the jet is very smart in its ability to prioritize which sensors it uses for a particular task. It will go ahead and do that, and then present you with what it determines is the optimum solution for the situation at hand.

Cabral, who called this color- and shape-coding a "cartoon for fighter pilots," further explains: "The SD gives us a fused picture, rather than showing you what each individual sensor is seeing. The picture it gives us is a fusion of everything the jet knows about everything." Harper continues, "the information is always there, it's just a question of being able to use it to make tactical decisions. We know where the other formations are, where we are, and where the threat is."

Cabral, an instructor pilot in the Raptor with some 500 hours in the aircraft by late 2008, says that the most challenging aspect of teaching new F-22 pilots is getting them to learn how to do display management. The information is all there, but you have to know which

Continued on page 186.

Rounded "humps" on the underside of the wings and empennage of the Raptor hide the mechanics of the F-22's hydraulic actuators and control rods from radar. Note the small cylindrical radar transponder in the center of the fuselage, a must for a stealth fighter operating in civilian airspace.

# TECHNOLOGY, WEAPONS, AND SENSORS

While the F-22 Raptor's shape and radar absorbent coatings allow the jet to close undetected to within killing range of its foe, it is its clever suite of avionics that contributes significantly to its ability to do so. Moreover, these same avionics, and the weapons that they cue to multiple targets, are what really give the Raptor a potency that is unmatched today.

## Active Systems

The F-22's avionics are built with two main operational principles in mind: the ability to operate with a low probability of enemy interception (LPI), and the importance of being able to "fuse" the active and passive signals collected by the jet, and other friendly assets, to form a single picture for display to the pilot. Three main sensors, each comprised of subcomponents, work together to achieve both aims.

In the nose, the Northrop Grumman APG-77 AESA radar can passively detect enemy transmissions, but is most useful when actively transmitting. Making extensive use of LPI techniques, and capitalizing on the inherently stealthy modes of operation AESA provides, it changes frequencies more than 1,000 times per second to reduce the chance of being detected. In doing so, the F-22 pilot can drive into the heart of his weapons envelope, simultaneously engage six targets with a single AIM-120 AMRAAM each, and then leave the fight, all the while remaining undetected.

Alternatively, he can engage with AIM-120, and then clean up stragglers with his two AIM-9M Sidewinders, or 480 rounds of 20mm ammunition fired by the M61A2 Vulcan gun. However, given the limited number of Raptors available and the fact that, despite superb maneuverability, the aircraft is optimized for beyond visual range, the tactical situation would have to be permissive for a Raptor pilot to choose to do so.

When a quiet approach will not work, the Raptor pilot can dispense with LPI techniques and use the APG-77's superior power and steerable electronic beams to focus emissions on enemy radars and passive detection devices to overload and overwhelm them. For an opposing pilot this would have the effect of causing both his radar and electronic sensors to behave erratically, or to physically shut them down outright.

The APG-77 can provide weapons-grade tracking of numerous targets; maintain a long-range surveillance for new threats; electronically "scan" targets to create a synthetic picture of them, allowing non-cooperative target recognition (NCTR); "break out" very close formations of individual aircraft at long range through the use of pencil-thin radar beams; and perform basic ground mapping, all at the same time. Unsurprisingly, therefore, it can operate well in coordination with other US fighters. This is a critical facet, and interoperations between F-22s and F-15s give the Raptor pilot the task of delegating "low-risk" targets or "stragglers" to the Eagles, while the Raptors themselves pursue those that pose the greatest lethality or are best protected by other layers of the IADS. The radar is being developed to transmit and receive data at 548 megabits and one gigabit per second, respectively. This is a speed increase of 500 and 1,000 times that of Link 16, and will further enhance the Raptor's ability to operate as a mini AWACS, broadcasting a detailed battlespace picture to other friendly forces.

## Passive Systems

The importance of reducing and controlling emission output from within the F-22 is born not only out of the need to prevent enemy detection (which would negate the Raptor's stealthy radar cross section), but also out of the doctrinal differences between America and potential adversaries. In short, the air forces of China, Russia, India, and others, employ electronic attack (active electronic systems) in their primary game plan, whereas America is increasingly focusing on passive systems ("electronic protection") to identify and prosecute the enemy through the identification and tracking of its electronic signatures.

To enable this, the F-22 is equipped with the ALR-94 RWR and the AAR-56 IR and UV missile approach warning system (MAWS). The two systems integrate with the APG-77 to detect, classify, and then alert the pilot to threats in the battlespace. The RWR in particular contributes to the jet's electronic protection as it sniffs the air for radio-frequency (RF) transmissions and then creates a set of geographical coordinates that are accurate enough for the pilot to engage the threat with AMRAAM (or JDAM, if the radar is ground-based) without any targeting support from the APG-77. Indeed, the RWR is the key passive component used to create a picture of the battlespace while non-cooperatively identifying the friendly and threat systems that occupy it.

In the cockpit, the pilot sees all of this information as a series of colored, synthetic symbols on large screens; the data from all the onboard sensors already analyzed, coded, and then fused together thanks to two common integrated processors (computers) that are variously reported as being able to process between 700 million and 1.5 billion instructions per second. Tying the systems together is a 1394B databus known to most civilians as the "FireWire" system.

The CIPs provide the processing power for the RWR, MAWS, and radar, and also for the communication, navigation, identification (CNI) system, which completes the avionics suite by adding secure communications, GPS navigation, and NCTR. Also included in the CNI is the all-important inter/intra-flight datalink (IFDL). This allows the Raptor to share information with its flight and to send and receive information to and from other suitably equipped aircraft in the region. Naturally, the CNI system is optimized for LPI operations.

Development of the CNI system, expected with "Increment 3.2" updates in 2015, will see the installation of the Multi-function Advanced Data Link (MADL), allowing the Raptor to communicate with the F-35 Lightning II and UAVs. In the meantime, the USAF has equipped three business jets as interim Battlefield Airborne Communications Node aircraft, to allow communication between F-22s and other manned and unmanned aircraft.

### Ground Attack

When attacking ground targets, the pilot currently relies on coordinates supplied before flight to strike pre-planned static targets, but in June 2009 the Air Force began testing the Increment 3.1 software that will endow the APG-77 with SAR modes. This followed 2008 tests demonstrating the capability to generate high-resolution SAR maps using the improved APG-77(V)1. Increment 3.1 also incorporates the 500lb GBU-39 SDB

A 1,000lb GBU-32 JDAM is loaded into one of the two main weapons bays of an F-22A. Two of these weapons would be carried on an air-to-ground sortie in addition to two AIM-9M/X missiles in the fuselage bays (one next to each JDAM) and two AIM-120C AMRAAMs in the side fuselage bays.

and new electronic attack capabilities. The (V)1 and Increment 3.1 combination are expected to be tested by the "Green Bats" at Nellis in 2011, with rollout to the fleet soon thereafter.

Into the mid-term future, Increment 3.2 will take full advantage of the SDB's flexible targeting capabilities, add an automated ground collision avoidance system and add support for the AIM-9X Sidewinder and AIM-120D AMRAAM. Subsequent increments are expected to add automatic target tracking and information warfare capabilities, further relieving the pilot's workload and enhancing his ability to operate less as a fighter pilot and more as a battle manager. Increment 3.2, which should be in test on the 422nd TES's Raptors by 2013, will also add the MADL developed initially for the F-35 JSF.

## Block Increment Limitations

However, since MADL will require new hardware, a question mark exists over whether it will be retrofitted to the Block 20 Raptors operated at the F-22 RTU at Tyndall using Increment 2 software loads.

On a similar note, while the 63 early Block 30 jets will receive the full Increment 3.1 upgrades, they will probably not benefit from the full Increment 3.2 modifications, again because of the need for hardware changes that may not be affordable. Certainly, some capabilities from 3.2 will be ported over, but only those that are software-driven (EP radar modes, Combat ID, and Link 16 improvements). Regarding the addition of AIM-9X and AIM-120D to these jets, the Air Force is currently evaluating whether it can afford to do so.

It will only be the newest 87 Block 30 models, and those others that are delivered before the production line closes in 2011, that will get the full Increment 3.2 update. When the update is installed, these Raptors will become Block 35 Raptors.

## Advanced Cockpit

The F-22's cockpit is obviously a key ingredient in allowing the pilot to get the most from the Raptor's sensors, and in doing so maximize the potential that the jet has to offer. Lt Col Shower, who has flown F-15s and flown in F-16s and F/A-18s, had this to say:

> The cockpit is fairly roomy for a fighter and overall it's well designed with a lot of human factors engineering inputs, and very importantly, pilot inputs during the design and development phases. It's night compatible and is essentially an all-glass cockpit. So there is very little for the pilot to do after starting up the jet and loading all the critical mission data. Overall, I find it a little more comfortable than the Eagle cockpit and seat because it has a slightly better seat designed to alleviate stress on the body.
>
> The Raptor start-up sequence is very easy: it has a battery; you turn it on, start the APU [auxiliary power unit – a small turbine engine] and then push the throttles over the cut off. The start sequence is automatic after that, to include loading of the mission data required to make the Raptor come alive. After you close the [weapons bay] doors and do a flight control system check, you're pretty much ready to go. There's normally some manual data you might program for your mission, but that takes a minute or two and then you're ready to taxi.

The Raptor also boasts a pilot aid unique to any Air Force jet fighter – a series of electronic checklists displayed to the pilot on one of his screens at various times. "The electronic checklist is a great addition that helps the pilots out a great deal, and not just during emergencies. It also has most of the normal checklist items such as start-up, refueling, etc," Shower explains. And if the jet has a problem?

> It's announced via an electronic message to the pilot and he can select the checklist which tells him what is wrong with the airplane and what actions need to be taken to fix the problem or get the jet safely on the ground. The Raptor has multiple back-up systems for virtually everything, so it's very robust in that sense. And the aircraft constantly monitors thousands of system inputs so it's very "self" aware of what is going on inside itself. Incidentally, this is a great help to maintenance, who can quickly narrow down the problem to fix any issues with the jet.

The displays have a ton of information, but it's filtered and presented well, so after just a few flights it's easy to interpret everything the jet is telling you – and that's a lot of information!

## ATAGS

In addition to the Combat Edge anti-*g* vest and Combat Edge helmet and oxygen mask worn by fastjet aircrew in the USAF, the F-22A pilot also wears a CSU-23/P Advanced Technology Anti-G Suit (ATAGS). This garment, which completely wraps around the pilot's legs and buttocks, sits lower on the torso than previous *g*-suits, preventing it from pushing against the chest when it inflates. Because of these two design features, it provides increased protection from the effects of prolonged high-*g* environments. On its own, ATAGS provides a 60 percent increase in aircrew endurance. Combined with Combat Edge, it increases aircrew endurance by 350 percent over the level currently achieved by F-15 and F-16 pilots.

Shower says, "The new *g*-suit, combined with a better seat design, seems to allow us to pull *g*s better than previous jets. Nine plus *g*s still hurts, but not as bad as it did in an Eagle and I do not feel as fatigued as I used to." He adds, "we are allowed to operate above 50,000ft without having to wear a partial pressure suit so we're not artificially restricted from operating where we need to."

## Information Sharing

When F-22A Raptors from Langley AFB, Virginia deployed to Alaska for a joint exercise with the F-16s and F-15s of the 3rd Wing, called Northern Edge, it was to be expected that they would fare extremely well. They didn't disappoint. Within the first week alone the Raptors had racked up no fewer than 140 simulated air-to-air kills for not a single loss, and had scored direct hits using satellite-guided bombs against 26 targets without a single miss.

In order to achieve such overbearing dominance, the Raptor relies on its stealth and advanced avionics systems to give its pilot a previously unattainable level of situational awareness. With the F-22A pilot able to know exactly what is happening in the battlespace around him, where his adversaries are, where his wingmen are, where the ground threats are, he can use this superior SA to make the best decisions about how to engage the enemy. This kind of warfare, this ability to "fuse" data from multiple sensors and to remain undetected until it's already too late for the enemy, is what makes the Raptor unique. It is called "netcentric" warfare. Such warfare will be the key to fighting and winning future battles, since it maximizes the usefulness of information already available (but previously unshared), enhances SA by an order of magnitude, and allows jet fighters like the Raptor to collaborate with other airborne assets. Equally, it allows the F-22A to operate autonomously to its own strengths.

Using the information passed to it via datalink from an E-3 AWACS or RC-135 Rivet Joint electronic spyplane, its own radar and onboard radar warning sensors, other F-22As, or datalinked UAVs in the region, the Raptor uses onboard computer processors to combine the information into a single picture of the battlespace, displayed on one of the large liquid crystal displays in the cockpit.

It is as much the Raptor's ability to display to the pilot this massive array of information in a clear and concise format, as it is to fuse it all together in the first place, that allows the pilot to manage the battle effectively. To do this, the F-22A uses two powerful computers that form the brain of its avionics systems. Each can perform more than 700 million instructions per second, receiving all of the raw data from the jet's advanced electronic scanned array radar, EW system, and the CNI system, which it then processes and analyzes. When it has finished crunching and filtering the raw data, it displays it in the cockpit.

## Datalink

The large cockpit display uses distinct symbols and colors to help the pilot interpret what he's seeing: red for hostile contacts, green for friendly; green circles for friendly aircraft and red triangles for hostile aircraft, etc. The pilot can choose to add or remove symbology and information to help de-clutter the display and keep it clear at times when there are multiple symbols in view. Similarly, he can instruct the computer to overlay the radar footprint of his own APG-77, as well as those of his wingman. As such, he can see a visual representation of the radar coverage of his flight, allowing him to more quickly issue his wingman with commands on which contacts to engage. And that's not all. Assuming he has two hostile aircraft ahead of him, he can drag his cursor over one and use the datalink to request his wingman to attack, and then turn his attention to killing the other himself. The datalink broadcasts the message in nanoseconds, and the wingman can use his own display to see which target his leader wants him to attack. He can even send a message back accepting the tasking or rejecting it.

In addition, the IFDL automatically lets the pilot see how many weapons his wingman has remaining, who his wingman has his radar locked onto, how much fuel he has remaining, and a host of other information that would normally require radio conversation to acquire. Because anyone on the datalink network can send information about targets on the ground and in the air, it helps to fill gaps in the battlespace picture that fall outside the range of the Raptor's onboard sensors.

Stealth depends on more than having low visual, radar and infra-red characteristics. In today's age of advanced electronics capable of detecting even the faintest signal, it is also heavily dependent on reduced electronic emissions, something known in the Raptor community as EMCON (emission control). To assist the datalink in operating discretely, the F-22A uses transmissions that not only "hop" many hundreds of frequencies per second, but are also sent in very short bursts, using a reduced power output to lessen the chances of detection. Equally, the Raptor pilot may choose to be very selective about using his radar, relying instead on the air picture created by AWACS and other fighters in the area. When he does wish to use it, the APG-77 features highly advanced frequency-hopping capabilities that diminish the probability of it being detected by hostile electronic listening equipment.

displays to be on at any given time in order to find the information you need. If you are on an incorrect display, it's very easy to have an overwhelming amount of information that you simply cannot process. In previous airplanes, you spent a lot of time "housekeeping" all of your sensors; now, it's much more about display and information management. Which display do I want to see to derive the information I need right now? The goal of the airplane was to free you up to be a tactical manager. In the F-15, I spent 80 percent of my time gathering information, and 20 percent making decisions. In the Raptor, it's almost the exact opposite."

The physical mechanics of using the displays and creating and employing ordnance "takes the best of the F-15, F-16, and F/A-18," Harper acknowledges. "We use buttons on the stick to select the display of interest and to manage what information we want to see. On the throttle, a switch allows us to move the display cursor around." Cabral adds:

> We call the process "cursor capturing," and it takes about 30 minutes of practice to become used to moving the cursor around the various displays and understanding the symbology. After that, guys who are brand new to the jet will be able to add a target to the shoot list and employ ordnance. By way of example, cursor-capturing an object of interest on the SD display will cause a data block to appear in the bottom left corner of the display, and that will tell you everything

that the jet knows about that target: what its range is, its bearing, heading, true airspeed, Mach number, everything the jet knows. That information is repeated on the other displays.

## SIMULATIONS

Perhaps the most effective way to become a great tactician in the Raptor is to use highly advanced flight simulators, providing a more capable threat to engage in a virtual world. The most interesting simulator is the advanced combat simulator [ACS] located in Marietta, Georgia, which Lockheed Martin owns. "Their advanced combat simulators offer us some great training capabilities," Cabral volunteers, adding, "It is purely designed to be a tactical training device – it's not focused on the procedural portions of flying the jet, but it allows you to jump in and fly for a 30-minute mission, and repeat the same tactical problem over, and over and over. We don't have to take off and fly to the airspace or come home." Harper concurs: "Jumping in the ACS allows you to immerse yourself

Continued on page 191.

Entering the pattern at Elmendorf, a "Bulldogs" F-22A flies downwind amid a smattering of cloud. The lack of external aerials and antennas is noteworthy. These are all built into the fuselage, as well as the leading and trailing edges of the wings and stabilizers.

**Overleaf:** With the Raptor's peculiar streamers once more in evidence, this 525th FS F-22A crests the mountains north of Elmendorf, neatly dissecting a meandering glacier.

in as real a simulation as you can get anywhere in the world. If you spend a couple of days there doing simulation after simulation you will get better training than you can get by actually flying for real. You come away having learned things at a rate that would have been impossible in the actual aircraft. Why? Because you have not been worried about fuel, diverts and minimizing your risk when executing a real life training mission."

ACS is a networked simulator that allows up to four F-22 pilots to train in concert with one another, and which goes even further, according to Cabral.

> The other advantage to it is that it has Red Air simulators linked in to replicate the bad guys. Instead of flying against computer-programmed threats flying scripted routines, we are flying against humans thinking like a real adversary. The Red Air "domes" are configurable to replicate whatever threat we need, but are typically set up to be a Su-27 "Flanker" or Su-30 "Advanced Flanker" sort of threat. They simulate, to the best of our knowledge, a "Flanker" or "Advanced Flanker" cockpit, systems, and avionics – they even have a helmet-mounted sight that is used to replicate high off-boresight weapons.

While the ACS will not be brought to Elmendorf, a distributed mission operations (DMO) simulator will

Continued on page 194.

**Left:** Viewed in the correct light, the Raptor's smooth paneling and saw-tooth edges are clear to see. A minimum of removable panels ensures that RCS is reduced, while many of the panels or joints feature saw-tooth edges to dissipate radar reflections by bouncing the radar echoes back and forth until they are too weak to be detected.

**Overleaf:** The 422nd TES at Nellis operates examples of all of the USAF's tactical fighters. Here, a "Green Bats" Raptor leads an F-15C, A-10C, F-15E, and F-16C over the Nellis ranges north of the base.

be installed in the future. "The DMO allows us to link up with units who have their own DMO simulators," Cabral clarifies. "Tinker AFB with their AWACS, F-15C bases, F-16CJ locations; we'll be able to link up with them all. That will have its own unique training benefits. Although we will lose the ability to have a real, thinking, breathing Red Air component, the ability to get all those platforms together will mean we can get the entire war package together without burning fuel."

## STEALTH, SPEED, AND ALTITUDE

From the outset, the Raptor was built to harness as many low observable technologies as possible without compromising on its ability to find, identify and kill the best enemy fighters for decades to come.

Lt Col Mike "Dozer" Shower, who commanded the 90th FS, cites the F-22's stealth as being, "by far the aircraft's greatest strength and most revolutionary characteristic." This, he says, is because, "if I can see my adversary, track and shoot him well before he can see or shoot me, then I have an incredible advantage in combat. It would be the same as stepping into the ring to fight the world boxing champion ... but with a twist: he's invisible. You're on the floor before you even know what hit you."

So effective is the Raptor's stealth, Shower quips, "that one of our challenges is convincing other units to come fly with us for training – it's hard to train and fight against something you don't see."

Like the ability to remain undetected, the Raptor was also designed to operate at very high altitudes and at supersonic speeds for the majority of the time that it is airborne. Shower, who shot down a Federal Yugoslavian Air Force MiG-29 "Fulcrum" during Operation *Allied Force* in March, 1999, explains why speed and height are key:

Speed is probably not far behind stealth in terms of its importance. You can imagine that the faster we are the more complicated the problem for our adversary becomes. Imagine that same boxing match, already an incredibly tough problem, but now the invisible guy can move nearly twice as fast as you in his "combat" configuration – it makes a significant difference. Altitude is important, too. The higher we are and the faster we are, the more we are able to neutralize most threats by simply avoiding the areas where they can shoot us. This is especially true of anti-aircraft artillery and most surface-to-air missile systems. Another advantage is range. The higher you are the less fuel you burn for a given speed (generally), so in supercruise we do very well at high altitude. And, quite honestly, the jet was built for, and loves to be, high and fast.

## FLYING THE F-22A

Air show performances have left few observers with any doubt that the Raptor has the ability to out-fly any other jet fighter in the world. Naturally, Shower concurs.

It's the fighter aircraft fighter pilots have been dreaming about. There were so few compromises made for the aircraft's performance that it excels in virtually every arena. We lose virtually none of that performance when loaded for combat like you do in every other aircraft because all our weapons are carried internally. It's an absolute thoroughbred for raw power and speed, it turns as tight as anything out there (or better), and has all of the super maneuverability you see other thrust-vectored aircraft performing.

Continued on page 198.

**Right:** Rocketing skyward, two Raptors in full afterburner blast through 35,000ft above the Nellis ranges. The photo chase, an F-15D, followed into the near-vertical, but soon petered out. The photographer could only watch in amazement as the two "OT"-tailcoded F-22As didn't miss a beat and simply kept going.

# F-22A SPECIFICATION

**Powerplant**
Two Pratt & Whitney F119-PW-100 pitch thrust-vectoring turbofans each rated at more than 35,000lb st with afterburning.

**Performance**
Maximum speed Mach 2.25 at altitude, with a five-minute supercruise capability in the region of Mach 1.78

**Weights**
Empty: 43,340lb
Loaded: 64,595lb

Maximum take-off weight: 83,500lb

**Dimensions**
Wing span: 44ft 6in
Length: 62ft 1in
Height: 16ft 8in

**Armament**
One internal 20mm M61A2 Vulcan cannon and up to six AIM-120 AMRAAM and two AIM-9 Sidewinder. Air-to-ground weapons may be carried in place of the bay-installed AIM-120s, including GBU-32 JDAM and GBU-39 SDB.

---

Of the Raptor's ability to fly at very low speeds – which is sometimes necessary when a dogfight has gone on for a while and each aircraft has used up all of its airspeed and altitude trying to outmaneuver the other, Shower grades the Raptor as "phenomenal," adding, "as is its acceleration from post stall to its maximum speed." He's quick to qualify these remarks, though: "But that's all just window dressing. We hope to never need the maneuvering capability, the goal is to destroy our adversaries long before we ever hit a visual merge by taking advantage of its stealth and speed. And, so far, we're doing really good in our training and test [programs]."

The F-22A will replace the stalwart F-15 as America's premier air superiority fighter and interceptor, so how does it compare to the Eagle? Shower answers, but not before prefacing his comments first.

*Previous page:* The black and gray symbol shown here behind the canopy and the center of the fuselage provides visual cues for the "Boomer" of KC-135 and KC-10 refueling aircraft. A large scuff or heavy brush with the boom receptacle, which are common during inflight-refueling operations, might otherwise damage the radar absorbent coating on the fuselage, diminishing overall RCS in the process.

I love the Eagle, so I will never say a bad word about it. In my opinion it might very well be written in history as the best overall fighter ever produced, it certainly has the combat record to prove it as the only aircraft to never be shot down in aerial combat. But, it can't hold a candle to the F-22, nor was it meant to. The whole point of designing a superfighter is to make it absolutely dominant over everything else out there – and I believe the F-22 has achieved that goal. The F-22 is a revolutionary, not evolutionary leap, very, very far forward.

## INTO THE FUTURE

The F-22's reduced numbers mean that it will always be regarded as something of a "silver bullet," to be used sparingly on missions where its unique capabilities offer a game-changing influence.

With the Raptor's limited air-to-ground capability promising to be shored up in the future, Lockheed Martin and the Air Force are further enhancing the utility of the APG-77 AESA radar for SAR mapping static ground targets and tracking moving ground targets. In a bid to curry favour with policy makers in Washington, the USAF has already revealed that the

Left: An F-22A drops an inert, concrete-filled GBU-32 on a target near Edwards AFB, California. Released from the heights and airspeeds that the Raptor can reach, the weapon has a significant glide range. Right: A single GBU-38 SDB is released against another target on the range. The 250lb weapon uses a combination of kinetic energy and explosive power to give it similar destructive punch to a 500lb weapon. The F-22 will be able to carry eight of the little bombs.

APG-77 has phenomenal electronic warfare capabilities that can be used to jam or even physically disable enemy IADS components, and it is reasonable to conclude that these capabilities are also subject to development and expansion.

Despite the tremendous capabilities of the Block 30 F-22, there are notable omissions in the box of tricks that the aircraft has to offer. Most obvious among these is the lack of helmet-mounted sight (HMS), an essential tool for launching the AIM-9X Sidewinder missile at high off-boresight angles, and a system heavily utilized in legacy fighters from both East and West.

For Harper, the Australian exchange pilot, the acquisition of a HMS would offer "significant" benefits: "Trying to get long-range tally [visual acquisition] on long-range threats; looking down at the threat environment below; being able to slave sensors; being able to take advantage of forthcoming improvements in the F-22's ability to fly the air-to-ground role and employ the SDB; and so on. These would all be benefits. Is it essential? Not for the mission we are tasked with right now, but certainly in the future."

F-22 instructor pilot Maj Cabral, who flew with the Joint Helmet Mounted Cueing System (JHMCS) in the F-15, admits that he greatly misses the device:

> but the reality is that, based on a finite amount of money available to us, the path has been picked as to what is going to come out in the future, and what type of upgrades we are going to get. The majority of those upgrades are designed to help us defeat anti-access [double-digit surface-to-air missile] threats. The SDB is a perfect example of that: do we want to get JHMCS, or do we want to get SDB so that we can take out these systems in greater numbers and at greater ranges? Right now, the ability to carry eight SDBs has won out."

The JHMCS helmet sight is much desired, but is a luxury that current budget constraints prohibit.

In addition to the impending arrival of the 250lb GBU-39 SDB, the F-22 will also eventually be cleared to carry the improved AIM-120D AMRAAM and the AIM-9X Sidewinder. "Each one of those will bring a very significant change to how we do business, and to our tactics. We are looking forward to receiving every single one of them," says Cabral.

# F-35 LIGHTNING II

The second of the so-called fifth-generation fighters, the F-35 Lightning II combines exceptional stealth qualities with the latest suite of sensors to provide a strike capability that will remain unmatched for many years.

Still often referred to by its original name, Joint Strike Fighter (JSF), the F-35 is the result of more than a decade of collaboration between the governments and defense contractors of Britain and America. While America's primary contractor Lockheed Martin has provided the bulk of the technical know-how required to build this stealthy multi-role fighter, Britain's BAE Systems and America's Northrop Grumman have also been major partners. The F-35 is actually the result of a multi-national collaboration that also includes the financial contributions of Australia, Canada, Denmark, Italy, the Netherlands, Norway, and Turkey, with Israel and Singapore as "security cooperation participants" in the program.

The American-led JSF was conceived in the mid-1990s, with a view to replacing a number of ageing aircraft in the British and American air forces. From the outset, three different variants of the F-35 were planned, each offering unique capabilities tailored to specific customer requirements, while retaining at least 80 percent parts commonality. The F-35A offers conventional take-off and landing (CTOL) capabilities, and is intended to equip land-based customers like the USAF, and the air forces of Italy, the Netherlands, Turkey, and others. By contrast, the F-35B is heavily modified to allow short take-off and vertical landing (STOVL) capability, making it ideally suited to the likes of the US Marine Corps and the Royal Navy. Finally, the F-35C is a carrier-based (CV) variant that will equip the US Navy.

The basic design specifications behind the JSF were that it had to be four times as effective in air-to-air combat as legacy fighters like the F-15 and F-16; that it had to be eight times more effective in the air-to-ground role; that it had to be three times more effective in the reconnaissance role, and in suppressing enemy air defense systems; and that it had to be all of this while being able to fly further than any legacy fighter, while all the time remaining less maintenance intensive.

The X-35 demonstrator flew in 2000, following which it competed against the Boeing X-32 for the JSF contract. Lockheed Martin won the competition in October 2001 and the first F-35A flew on February 19, 2006. Unsurprisingly, the more complex F-35B STOVL variant took much longer to make its maiden flight, but on June 11, 2008 it finally did so. At the controls was the lead STOVL test pilot, Graham "GT" Tomlinson of BAE Systems.

Tomlinson, a veteran pilot of the vertical take-off and landing Harrier "jump jet," has more than 5,000 hours of flying experience, much of it on the Harrier with the Royal Air Force. Explaining the philosophy behind the three different F-35 variants in early 2008, he says:

> They are designed to be easy for a pilot to be able to flit between. It is a bit like the Airbus family of airliners, where it is simple to convert a pilot of an A320 to an A330, in that the cockpits of the three types are almost identical. A pilot can go from one version to another and require very little retraining, accordingly.
>
> I have to say that retaining this familiarity for the F-35B STOVL variant is something of a miracle. If you look at the cockpit of a Harrier, it is like no other cockpit you will see.

---

**Previous page:** Critics of the F-35 program argue that the aircraft will carry too few weapons to make the required impact on the battlefield, but proponents of the aircraft argue that this will not be the case, because while a stealthy internal carriage will be required for the first few days of any war, external carriage will be permissible once the enemy's air defense systems have been knocked out. Note the saw-tooth edges on the exhaust petals of this pre-production F-35.

F-35 Joint Strike Fighter Lightning II test aircraft AA-1 undergoes flight test over Fort Worth, Texas. The F-35 program is rife with controversy, not least of all about the eventual capabilities of the aircraft.

There are three main controls in the form of the stick, throttle, and nozzle lever. Well, the Harrier was great for the 1960s, when we all had black and white TV and there were no computers around!

The F-35 cockpit is also very different from what one would expect, albeit for very different reasons. Tomlinson continues:

We have a very large 20 x 8in display that is touch sensitive and can be divided up into a number of "pages" according to what the pilot wants. The rest of the cockpit looks remarkably blank, and we don't have rows of switches. We just have a battery, engine start, IPP [integrated power package] start switch and a few others.

We call the display a "chin up" display, and it combines with our HOTAS and our direct voice input [DVI] system. The left and right half of the display have independent computers controlling them, so there is redundancy built in, and if one computer fails we can still control the other half of the screen. To be even safer, there is also what you might call a "get you home" flight display that is activated following serious failures, and this gives basic information on attitude, airspeed, and altitude so that the pilot can make a safe landing.

These highly configurable displays, and the overall intuitiveness of programming them, amounts to much more than just "eye candy." Tomlinson reveals:

In the Harrier … you had 10 percent spare capacity to do a mission, with 90 percent spent on not crashing. "Fly the aircraft. Don't crash. Fly the aircraft. Don't crash. Here are some golden rules, make sure you remember them. And don't crash," was what they told us. "And by the way, with

Lightning II will be the largest military aircraft procurement program of modern times. On July 7, 2006 the F-35 Joint Strike Fighter program was inaugurated at Lockheed Martin's Fort Worth plant.

what little spare capacity you have left, we want you to complete a difficult and demanding mission," they would add. Well, this aircraft reverses that situation. I would actually go as far as to say that it's trivial to fly this aircraft. I tell people that it's akin to hiring and driving a rental car: you turn the key and drive away without really even thinking about it. So, the focus for a pilot flying the F-35 will be on the mission, the bad guys, where the target is, where the threats are, and so on.

But can too much information lead to cognitive saturation – a "helmet fire," as fighter pilots call it?

"That's always a possibility. It's not enough to just display this information," Tomlinson concedes.

We have to ensure that the information is presented sensibly. Getting the balance right is not always easy. Test pilots will often instruct the software engineers to take some information away from the displays, arguing that it will confuse the operational pilots who fly it. When we do this, the operational pilots invariably turn around and ask that we give them more information – in fact, the guys just seem to want more and more data. Another advancement that we have made with the F-35 is the quality of our simulations and training tools. We also now have excellent desktop simulations that an F-35 pilot can "fly" in order to improve the quality of his training, and his understanding of the aircraft.

# F-35 VARIANTS

The F-35A will be purchased by the USAF, and is the CTOL variant that uses standard runways for take-offs and landings. Internal fuel capacity is nine tons, providing an unrefueled range of more than 1,200 miles without external tanks. The F-35A carries a 25mm GAU-22/A cannon internally and has a standard internal weapons load of two AIM-120C air-to-air missiles and two 2,000lb GBU-31 JDAM guided bombs. When stealth is no longer required, external pylons can be added, giving the aircraft a weapons payload of more than 18,000lb.

The F-35B is "the first aircraft in history to combine stealth with short take-off/vertical landing capability and supersonic speed," Lockheed Martin states. The F-35B will be purchased by the US Marine Corps for deployment near combat zones, dramatically shrinking the distance from base to target, increasing sortie rates, and decreasing the need for logistics support. Internal fuel capacity is seven tons, providing an unrefueled range of more than 900 miles without external tanks. Standard weapons load is two AIM-120C AMRAAMs and two 1,000lb GBU-32 JDAMs. The F-35B's external pylons can carry more than 15,000lb of stores.

F-35C boasts larger wings and control surfaces and the addition of wingtip ailerons to allow improved control and precision during carrier approaches. It first flew in June 2010 and will be operated by the US Navy. The aircraft incorporates larger landing gear and a stronger internal structure to withstand the forces of carrier launches and recoveries. "Ruggedized exterior materials mean low maintenance requirements for preserving the aircraft's very low observable radar signature, even in harsh shipboard conditions," according to Lockheed Martin. F-35C internal fuel capacity is almost 10 tons, providing an unrefueled range of well over 1,200 miles without external tanks. Like the F-35A, the C-model Lightning II has external pylons rated to carry more than 18,000lb of weapons.

Unique to the F-35 is a fully integrated HMS that replaces the ubiquitous HUD, says Tomlinson: "We don't have a HUD, and this is the first aircraft not to have one for a long time. The first generation of our HMS has been flying for a year, and our second generation is coming later in 2008. One of the symbols on the display is a symbol called 'flight path,' and it is used all the time." While not an innovation new to the F-35, its integration with the HMS does make life simpler for the pilot.

> You put it where you want it to go, and it always displays where the aircraft is going. It's very useful and on recovery to the ship, for example. All the clever sensors around the aeroplane will be displayed on this visor, allowing the pilot to look "through" the aircraft... It's a bit like a video game or like flying with night vision goggles. It's a green world, and one that is uses electro-optical, infra-red and RF sensors that have very high resolutions and can be used for targeting.

The technology for the HMS is continually being refined and Tomlinson reveals that one key area of continued development is in reducing the system's "latency"; that is increasing its ability to update several times per second. "The important thing is to get the update rate on the display good enough to sense where your head is and do the calculations, even when the aircraft and the pilot are vibrating. The challenge is to be able to do this without any latency. We have also changed the visor for the next display; our existing display has

## US Multi-Role Fighter Jets

# F-35 Lightning II

a crease down the middle of it, but the new one will be totally smooth."

Completing the F-35's cockpit interface will be the DVI system. "We will use the DVI to do altimeter changes, radio changes, input waypoint information, etc. It's a tool that we will tend to use for what I call 'domestic issues.' We have a five-way switch on the throttle, one position of which allows you to talk to the aeroplane. You could say 'Comm A, one-two-three-decimal-five. Go!' and the Comm A radios will change to a new frequency of 123.5. DVI is not in the jet at the moment, but it is planned for operational service."

## STOVL FLIGHT

As the lead STOVL pilot for the F-35B, Tomlinson was the first person to fly this variant. He also worked extensively on the pilot interface and control laws that govern the jet's STOVL capability.

The magic with the F-35 is that when you get down to the STOVL flight parameters the throttle seamlessly transitions to an "acceleration controller." Our system means that there will be initial training for those pilots who fly the STOVL variant, but nothing like that required for the Harrier, for which there was a tremendous amount of training because of the complexity. With the F-35, your left hand on the throttle controls thrust to make the jet go faster or slower, but the acceleration controller will now hold airspeed in the neutral position, decelerate when pulled back, and accelerate when pushed forward. Sitting in the hover, you push the stick forward to descend at zero airspeed, or pull back to climb. We enter this "blending" mode at about 50 knots – above that the wing is still

AF-01, the first USAF specification CTOL F-35A, takes to the air for the first time on November 14, 2009, with Dave "Doc" Nelson at the controls. The A-model F-35 is the only variant equipped with the internal GAU-22/A 25mm cannon.

## US Multi-Role Fighter Jets

generating lift and the pilot can still control the flight path by moving the stick back and forward.

Naturally, computers control the process from start to finish. "There's 40,000lb of thrust squirting out of the bottom of the aircraft," says Tomlinson, "so there's lots of induced airflow moving us around. In the hover, the airplane corrects its attitude to keep it at an ideal pitch. There are some very sophisticated control laws governing the process."

## MOTOR

The F-35B's Pratt & Whitney F135 (or General Electric/Rolls-Royce F136) uses Lockheed Martin's LiftSystem® that is comprised of a lift fan, driveshaft, clutch, two "roll posts," and a 3 Bearing Swivel Module (3BSM) thrust-vectoring nozzle. "When we want to enter STOVL mode, the pilot hits a button that initiates conversion. It is a complex process that starts by opening up a bunch of doors for the lift fan and auxiliary intakes for the main engine. Roll post doors open under the wing to maintain roll control, and this entire process takes about six seconds," Tomlinson elucidates. He adds:

> The motor simultaneously repositions a clutch that drives a lift fan just behind the cockpit, taking about seven seconds. The next stage is for the lift fan to spool up, then the clutch is engaged by bolts to take the torque, and then the lift fan is spun up to maximum thrust – 18,000lb. The main engine, meanwhile, is generating 17,000lb, and the roll posts are generating about 4,000lb from bleed air taken from the main

AF-01, freshly painted, was one of two F-35A Lightning II JSF that flew non-stop to Edwards AFB, CA, for extended testing in May 2010. It forms part of the F-35 flight test operations expansion, which includes ground- and flight-test activities for propulsion, aerial refueling, logistical support, weapons integration, and flight-envelope expansion. The arrival of these two A-models brought the Edwards AFB F-35 test fleet to eight aircraft.

# F-35 WEAPONS AND AVIONICS

The brain of the F-35's sensor suite is the integrated core processor (ICP), a digital processor that integrates all of the jet's sensors and weapons systems, crunches the numbers, and then presents the pilot with a clear picture of the battlespace. The ICP is so powerful that it can be used simultaneously to execute operations such as the automatic recognition and classification of targets.

Raytheon's APG-81 Multi-function Integrated Radio Frequency System (MIRFS), based on the AN/APG-77 radar found in the F-22 Raptor, will be the electronic eyes of the F-35. This multi-mode radar will be capable of undertaking active jamming of threat radar systems, passively sniffing out radar emissions from other sources and acting as a communications system. Although MIRFS will use improved technology compared to the AN/APG-77, the fact that the fixed antenna is physically smaller than that of the APG-77 means that it will be limited to about two-thirds the range (around 90 miles against a target with a $1m^2$ radar signature).

The APG-81 will work in tandem with the electro-optical targeting system (EOTS) and a multitude of electro-optical sensors belonging to the AAS-37 missile warning system, to find, identify, and target the enemy. EOTS is the overall term for a FLIR imager, a digital TV camera, a targeting laser, and a laser spot tracker. EOTS is blended into the aircraft's nose contours and covered by a window that is opaque to radar. It remains operational through the entire mission.

The F-35 is also fitted with an infra-red search and track (IRST) system for defense and air-to-air combat, and a targeting system for precision attack on ground targets. The IRST is known as the Distributed Aperture Infra-Red System (DAIRS), which consists of six IR sensors mounted on different points of the fuselage to provide full-sphere IR detection and tracking. It can identify and pinpoint both incoming missiles and airborne targets.

Once found, the enemy can be engaged by a wide range of weapons, including the four-barreled GAU-22/A cannon. The F-35A is the only variant to carry this weapon internally, along with 180 rounds, the B- and C-models featuring an external cannon pod, with 220 rounds, as required.

Two weapons bays, one either side of the jet, can carry up to two air-to-air missiles and two air-to-ground weapons: two 2,000lb bombs in A- and C-models, two 1,000lb bombs in the B-model. These weapons include AIM-120 AMRAAM, AIM-132 advanced short-range air-to-air missile (ASRAAM), JDAM, JSOW, SDB, the Brimstone anti-armor missile, WCMD, and HARM. The European MBDA Meteor air-to-air missile is currently under evaluation for carriage.

Four wing pylons and two wingtip pylons increase payload for sorties when stealth is not the priority. The two wingtip pylons carry only AIM-9X Sidewinder, while the AIM-120 AMRAAM, Storm Shadow cruise missile, Joint Air-to-Surface Stand-off Missile (JASSM), and 480 US gal drop tanks can be carried in addition to the stores in the internal bays.

engine. Underneath the lift fan, a variable area guide vane exchange box changes the vector angle of the thrust. In total, it takes about 15 seconds for all of these changes to complete.

Continued on page 212.

**Overleaf:** Graham Tomlinson completes a hover landing during flight 41 of the F-35B variant on March 17, 2010. As is clear, numerous doors must open in order to allow the lift fan to operate, but Tomlinson reports that the process is entirely seamless to the pilot.

The F135 is an evolution of the highly successful F119 engine installed in the F-22 Raptor and it is rated at more than 40,000lb thrust in afterburner, making it the most powerful fighter engine built. The F135 powered three Lightning II flight tests in two days in April 2007, marking the first time the F-35 completed more than one flight test in 24 hours, and three flight tests in less than 48 hours. Two of the flights required only a 90-minute turnaround time for routine inspections.

In addition to these flight test accomplishments, there have been relatively few hiccups along the way. A loss of primary electrical power in the first pre-production F-35A forced test pilot Jeff Knowles to cut short the 19th test flight in May 2007, although the aircraft's electrical system recognized the failure and automatically reconfigured and restored power to the flight controls by reconfiguring its architecture to provide alternative pathways. And, during a ground test of the Rolls-Royce lift fan that will enable the F-35 to hover, the fan was stalled deliberately and in a particularly aggressive manner, resulting in a fractured shaft connecting the lift fan to the main engine. Although this sounds severe, the test exaggerated by 300 percent the kind of airflow restrictions that would be encountered in real life.

Tomlinson is highly impressed with the F-35 so far, and shrugs off the comparisons between it and the Lockheed Martin F-22A Raptor.

> It's at least as good as the F-22 in many of the mission systems, but of course it was designed to be a jack of all trades, and is not going to be better than the F-22 in dogfighting. That said, the F-35 is a 9*g* fighter with a good post-stall maneuvering capability, and we have a 50-degree angle of attack limit.
>
> The F-35 is going to be by far the best choice of aircraft for the first few days of any future war, when we will need to stealthily destroy the enemy's air defenses. From days five or six onwards, we are going to be able to add pylons to the wings and use the F-35 as a bomb truck, because by then we won't need the jet to be at its stealthiest any more. The beauty of the F-35's stealth is that you can see and kill the enemy before he sees you; it's very difficult to kill a JSF when you cannot see it.

## F-35A / F-35B / F-35C SPECIFICATION

### Performance
Maximum speed: Mach 1.6 (all three variants)
Range (nm): >1,200/*c.*900/>1,200
Engine thrust, dry (lb): 24,960
Engine thrust, with afterburner (lb): 40,027
Vertical thrust (F-35B only) (lb): 39,712

### Weights
Empty weight (lb): *c.*26,500/*c.*29,983/*c.*29,983
Maximum weight (lb): 60,000-class (all three variants)

### Dimensions
Wing span (ft): 35/35/43
Wing area (sq ft): 460/460/668
Height (ft): 15.09/15.09/15.42
Length (ft): 51.40/51.40/51.51

### Fuel and load
Internal fuel (lb): 18,250/13,500/19,750

The aircraft is able to perform air-to-air and air-to-ground missions that include SEAD/DEAD, close air support, strategic pinpoint attack, fighter sweep and escort (offensive counter air), and defensive counter-air against fighters, bombers, and low-RCS targets, such as unmanned aerial vehicles and cruise missiles.

## INTO SERVICE

To date, the JSF program continues to attract criticism and controversy. The US RAND Corporation think-tank has conducted simulations that depict the F-35 being defeated by "Advanced Flankers" (the Sukhoi Su-30 family of fighters) simply by interfering with the air refueling tankers that will top up its fuel tanks before it pushes into enemy territory. Others argue that the F-35 carries too little ordnance and is range-limited, meaning that it represents poor value for money. Yet the US Air Force remains resolute that these observations and studies are specious insofar as they fail to take into account the full capabilities of the jet, or are otherwise based on inaccurate or incomplete data.

With this in mind, the US still intends to buy a total of 2,443 F-35s at an estimated total program cost of US$323 billion, although Lockheed Martin is resolved to reduce these costs by some 20 percent. Of these, 1,735 will be purchased by the USAF at a forecast "fly away" cost of US$89 million apiece. Despite these projections, the F-35 was valued at US$113 million per aircraft in July 2010, with signs that the price could rise further still.

Current plans see the F-35 being introduced to service from 2012 with a software suite that will allow the jet to achieve a great deal of its potential, but it will only be through subsequent software updates that the JSF will achieve full combat capability. The Air Force revealed in late July 2010 that Luke AFB, Arizona, is the favorite choice as the home of the RTU, but that Eglin AFB, Florida, which had originally been earmarked as the RTU home, will still receive 59 jets. In additional, Hill AFB, Utah, and Burlington Air Guard Station, Vermont, will also be home to its F-35s. These plans are far from set in stone and may well change – as with everything F-35, there is nothing simple or predictable about what will happen in the future.

The F-35's cockpit is revolutionary, consisting as it does of almost nothing but a large flat-panel display. The pilot may configure this to display a range of information, or may rely on pre-set configurations that change automatically as he manipulates the aircraft and its weapon/sensor systems.

# CONCLUSION

The United States continues to be heavily dependent on the tenacity, inventiveness, and consistent high performance of the multi-role fighter as it continues to battle in irregular warfare with the Taliban and Al Qaeda in Afghanistan. For some, like the current Secretary of Defense, Robert Gates, the focus on irregular warfare has resulted in a target fixation that in 2010 drives the funding and acquisition policies of the military. The US defines irregular warfare as: "A violent struggle among state and non-state actors for legitimacy and influence over the relevant population(s) [which] favors indirect and asymmetric approaches … to erode an adversary's power, influence, and will."

In 2008, a policy directive was introduced that compelled Pentagon planners to increase their capabilities in unconventional warfare to the same level as for conventional warfare. For many senior military leaders this target fixation is as dangerous in the formation of policy and spending as it is in the cockpit of a jet fighter. With Gates allegedly having already fired one Chief of Staff of the Air Force (Gen Michael "Buzz" Mosely) for failing to support his cull in F-22 procurement, there is resentment that the government is complacent in its belief that conventional threats have waned, despite the increasing threat that some of the world's largest nation states will almost certainly pose in the future.

For detractors of conventional warfare, the retort commonly heard is, "Who is the enemy? Why do we need the Raptor at all?" The question is somewhat moot as the military learned long ago that one trains for the worst case scenario. That scenario could be a Chinese crossing of the Taiwan Strait, or it could be an attempt by Russia in the decades ahead, using its new fifth-generation fighter, PAK-FA, to forcibly lay claim to oil under the Arctic Sea. Aggressor F-16 instructor pilot Lt Col "Popeye" Hansen handles such questions this way:

> Answering that question requires long-distance planning. You could look at China, a growing powerhouse that is not necessarily a threat, but is an important power. At a strategic and tactical level, what can they do militarily? You have to forecast who the threat is and who is most likely to be equal to, or potentially more powerful than, the United States, in both the near-term and the decades to come. Is it going to be the sabre-rattling North Koreans, or are you going to look at more capable nations like India or China? How are these countries posturing themselves? My personal opinion is that you have to kick the can down the road and imagine that there is a war: who can match or beat us? How do we combat their threats?

The point is not whether there is a credible or immediate threat today, it is whether there will be one in 10, 20, or 30 years time.

The gradual erosion of war-fighting abilities against state nations who have real capabilities – netcentric capabilities, space warfare capabilities, sensor fusion, properly integrated IADS featuring "double digit" SAMs, numerical advantage, sophisticated electronic attack, AESA radars, and fourth, four-point-five and fifth generation fighters – will seriously undermine America's political and military options. While Gates

**Previous page:** The introduction of the CCIP upgrade to the F-16 gives it capabilities more analogous in the air-to-ground role with contemporaries such as the F-15E and F/A-18E/F. But it is the most recent model, the F-16E/F Block 60 which the USAF has declined to purchase, that offers the greatest potential, far outstripping the utility of these Block 40 Vipers from Aviano.

**Right:** The latest Super Hornet update – Block 2 – makes the F/A-18E/F what some call a 4.75-generation fighter. It adds the ALQ-214 internal jammer and APG-79 AESA radar, giving the Super Hornet even more autonomy amidst the densest of air defense networks.

**Previous page:** The F-15E Strike Eagle is, at time of writing, beginning to receive the APG-82(V)1 AESA radar as part of a radar modernization program. The new radar will bring the jet back in line with the Block 2 Super Hornet in terms of capabilities, thus increasing survivability in any future conventional war.

talks about developing irregular warfare capabilities in the short- to mid-term, the negative effect on conventional capabilities will have far reaching long-term implications for which there will be no quick fix.

There is no question that irregular warfare capabilities must be bolstered and developed to combat insurgent and terrorist actions now and in the future, but to neglect the conventional capabilities, and in doing so to scale back the "overmatch in considerable capabilities" that the US government has identified that it currently has, could lead to it being vulnerable when the next big war breaks out. That considerable overmatch in capabilities depends on who you are comparing it to, after all. The balance between the two competing demands is a fine one, but for many who have built their careers as master tacticians and planners, the current emphasis is too heavily weighted to unconventional warfare.

For those in the multi-role fighter business, this means that more must be done with less, since funding is more limited than ever. Lateral thinking and innovative approaches must be taken to solve new problems. It means that in order to stand any chance against a foe of the type that China may one day be, for example, the mixed force concept of "silver bullet" Raptors and cheaper, more expendable F-15s, F-16s, and F/A-18s, must prevail over the sheer weight of numbers that the enemy will be able to field.

Such an approach is overly simplified in this text, however. China and Russia both operate on the basis of using overwhelming numbers in conjunction with extensive electronic attack (EA), using jamming and other techniques to overwhelm and disrupt the radars, sensors, and communications systems of their adversaries. In contrast, the United States relies more heavily on passive capabilities, detecting these emissions and targeting its quarry based on this very "visible" electronic signature. There is evidence, however, that the EA technique is currently a problem, especially with the recent development of digital radio frequency modulation (DRFM) jammers, which can be made cheaply, are highly effective, and can be carried by many different platforms in abundance. In one test, a DRFM jammer was even able to physically shut down the APG-70 radar of an F-15E Strike Eagle.

Moreover, the United States is increasingly reliant on its netcentric capabilities, but these (coupled with its cyber and space systems) would be a, if not the, primary target for an adversary like China. Without them the cohesion of a mixed force of US fighters could be compromised. In short, there may appear to be a significant mismatch in capabilities, but ask any tactical fighter pilot or WSO how close even a limited war against China would be, and the chances are that they will admit that it is difficult to call.

Of course, the arrival of the newest fifth-generation fighter should improve those odds dramatically, but it really does remain to be seen whether the F-35 Lightning II will be all that its advocates say that it will, or whether its detractors are correct. Will it have the ability to survive against a dominant "Advanced Flanker" threat at a time when, in the first few days of a war, its limited payload will in any case have a correspondingly limited effect on the enemy's ability to wage war? As always, time will tell.

**Right:** The Raptor community has been forced to make difficult decisions about which upgrades and improvements it requests. The JHMCS, for example, has been forgone in favor of integration of AIM-9X and the GBU-39 SDB. It is hoped that JHMCS will follow soon.

# ABBREVIATIONS

| | |
|---|---|
| AAA | anti-aircraft artillery |
| AAI | air-to-air interrogator |
| AAR | air-to-air refueling |
| AB | Air Base |
| ACC | Air Combat Command |
| ACO | Airspace Coordination Order |
| ACS | advanced combat simulator |
| AD | active duty |
| AEA | Airborne Electronic Attack |
| AEF | Aerospace Expeditionary Forces |
| AEG | Air Expeditionary Group |
| AESA | Advanced Electronically Scanned Array |
| AEW | Air Expeditionary Wing |
| AFB | Air Force Base |
| AFMC | Air Force Materiel Command |
| AFRC | Air Force Reserve Command |
| AGL | above ground level |
| AGM | air-to-ground missiles |
| AGRS | Aggressor Squadron |
| ALANG | Alabama Air National Guard |
| ALICS | Avionics Launcher Interface Computer |
| AMRAAM | advanced medium-range air-to-air missiles |
| ANG | Air National Guard |
| AOR | area of operations |
| ASPJ | Airborne Self-Protection Jammer |
| ASRAAM | advanced short-range air-to-air missiles |
| ATAGS | Advanced Technology Anti-G Suit |
| ATARS | Advanced Tactical Airborne Reconnaissance System |
| ATF | Advanced Tactical Fighter |
| ATFLIR | Advanced Targeting Forward-Looking Infra-Red |
| ATO | Air Tasking Order |
| AWACS | Airborne Warning and Control System |
| AWL | Advanced Weapons Laboratory |
| BVR | beyond visual range |

# Abbreviations

| | |
|---|---|
| CAOC | Combined Air Operations Center |
| CAS | close air support |
| CBUs | cluster bomb units |
| CCIP | Common Configuration Implementation Program |
| CDE | collateral damage estimates |
| CEM | Combined Effects Munition |
| CEP | circular error probability |
| CFT | conformal fuel tank |
| CIPs | common integrated processors |
| CNI | communication, navigation, identification system |
| CTOL | conventional take-off and landing |
| CV | carrier based |
| CVN | aircraft carrier |
| CVW | Carrier Air Wing |
| DAIRS | Distributed Aperture Infra-Red System |
| DDI | digital data indicator |
| DEAD | destruction of enemy air defenses |
| DMO | distributed mission operations |
| DOD | Department of Defense (United States) |
| DRFM | digital radio frequency modulation |
| DVI | direct voice input |
| EA | electronic attack |
| ECCM | electronic counter-countermeasures |
| ECM | electronic countermeasures |
| EFS | Expeditionary Fighter Squadron |
| EGBU | Enhanced Guided Bomb Unit |
| ELINT | electronic intelligence |
| EMCON | emission control |
| EMD | engineering, manufacturing, and development |
| EO | electro-optical |
| EOTS | electro-optical targeting system |
| EP | electronic protection |
| EPE | enhanced performance engine |
| EW | electronic warfare |
| FAC | forward air controller |
| FAC(A) | forward air controller (airborne) |
| FBW | fly-by-wire |
| FCC | Fire Control Computer |
| FDL | fighter datalink |

| | |
|---|---|
| FLIR | Forward-Looking Infra-Red |
| FOD | foreign object damage |
| FRS | Fleet Replacement Squadron |
| FS | Fighter Squadron |
| FSD | full-scale development |
| FTS | Flight Test Squadron |
| FW | Fighter Wing |
| GMT | ground moving target |
| GSTF | Global Strike Task Force |
| GWOT | Global War on Terror |
| HARM | High-speed Anti-Radiation Missile |
| HAS | hardened aircraft shelters |
| HMS | helmet-mounted sight |
| HOTAS | hands on throttle and stick |
| HSD | horizontal situation display |
| HTS | HARM Targeting System |
| HUD | head-up display |
| IADS | integrated air defense system |
| ICAP-III | Improved Capability III |
| ICP | integrated core processor |
| IFDL | inter/intra-flight datalink |
| IFF | identification friend or foe |
| IFR | in flight refueling |
| INCANS | Interference Cancellation System |
| intel | intelligence |
| IOC | initial operating capability |
| IPE | Improved Performance Engine [program] |
| IR | infra-red |
| IRST | infra-red search and track |
| ISR | information, surveillance, reconnaissance |
| JASSM | Joint Air-to-Surface Stand Off Missile |
| JDAM | Joint Direct Attack Munition |
| JHMCS | Joint Helmet Mounted Cueing System |
| JSF | Joint Strike Fighter |
| JSOW | Joint Stand-Off Weapon |
| J-STARS | Joint-Surveillance Target Attack Radar System |
| LANTRIN | low altitude navigation targeting infra-red for night |
| LDGP | low drag general purpose |
| LGB | laser-guided bomb |

| | |
|---|---|
| LIT | Look Into Turn |
| LO | low-observable (in relation to skin of the Raptor) |
| LPI | low probability of enemy interception |
| LWF | lightweight fighter |
| MADL | Multi-function Advanced Data Link |
| MANPADS | man-portable air defense systems |
| MAW | Marine Aircraft Wing |
| MAWS | missile approach warning system |
| MC | mission capable |
| MDS | Mission Design Series |
| MDSP | Manned Destruction Suppression Program |
| MEZ | missile engagement zone |
| MFD | multi-function display |
| MIRFS | Multi-function Integrated Radio Frequency System |
| MN | Mission Navigator |
| MPC | Mission Planning Cell |
| MPCD | multi-purpose color display |
| MPD | multi-purpose display |
| MR | mission ready |
| MSI | multi-sensor integration |
| NAS | Naval Air Station |
| NAVIS | Navy Input Station |
| NAWC | Naval Air Warfare Centre |
| NAWS | Naval Air Weapons Station |
| NCTR | non-cooperative target recognition |
| NFZ | no-fly zone |
| NITE | Navigation Infra-Red Targeting Equipment |
| NSAWC | Naval Strike and Air Warfare Center |
| NTISR | non-traditional information, surveillance, and reconnaissance |
| NVG | night vision goggles |
| OFPs | Operational Flight Programs |
| ORE | Operational Readiness Exercise |
| PACAF | Pacific Air Forces |
| PDM | planned depot maintenance |
| PGM | precision-guided munitions |
| PID | positively identify |
| RAF | Royal Air Force |
| RAM | radar absorbent material |
| RCS | radar cross-section |

| | |
|---|---|
| RF | radio frequency |
| RLG INS | ring laser gyro inertial navigation system |
| RMP | Radar Modernization Program |
| RO | response options |
| ROE | rules of engagement |
| RTU | replacement training unit |
| RWR | radar warning receiver |
| SA | situational awareness |
| SADL | Situational Awareness Data Link |
| SAM | surface-to-air missile |
| SAR | synthetic aperture radar |
| SCAR | strike coordination and reconnaissance |
| SD | situational display |
| SDB | small diameter bomb |
| SEAD | suppression of enemy air defenses |
| SF | Special Forces |
| SHARP | Shared Reconnaissance Pod |
| SLAM | Stand-off Land Attack Missile |
| SLAM-ER | Stand-off Land Attack Missile-Expanded Response |
| STOVL | short take-off and vertical landing |
| TAC | Tactical Air Command [later became ACC] |
| TAC(A) | tactical air controller (airborne) |
| TACC | Tactical Air Control Center |
| TAC(P) | Tactical Air Control (Party) |
| TALD | Tactical Air-Launched Decoy |
| TBM | Theater Ballistic Missile |
| TD&E | test, development, and evaluation |
| TDY | temporary duty |
| TES | Test and Evaluation Squadron (USAF) |
| TEWS | Tactical Electronic Warfare Suite |
| TFR | terrain following radar |
| TFS | Tactical Fighter Squadron |
| TFW | Tactical Fighter Wing |
| TFW (P) | Tactical Fighter Wing (Provisional) |
| TLAM | Tomahawk Land Attack Missile |
| TMLT | turning maneuver level turn |
| TOO | target of opportunity |
| TOT | time on target |
| TP | target pod |

| | |
|---|---|
| TST | time-sensitive tasking |
| TTPs | tactics, techniques and procedures |
| UAV | unmanned aerial vehicles |
| UFC | up-front controller |
| USAF | United States Air Force |
| USAFE | United States Air Forces Europe |
| USMC | United States Marine Corps |
| USN | United States Navy |
| VFA | Strike Fighter Squadron |
| VMFA | Marine Fighter Attack Squadron |
| VMFA(AW) | Marine All Weather Fighter Attack Squadron |
| VMFAT | Marine Fighter Attack Training Squadron |
| WATTS | weapons and tactics talks |
| WCMD | Wind Corrected Munitions Dispenser |
| WFOV | wide field-of-view |
| WMD | weapons of mass destruction |
| WSO | weapons systems officer |

# SELECTED READING

The vast majority of the content of this book has been drawn from first-hand accounts and primary research conducted by the author or close associates of the author. Some of this research is available in the titles below, while other titles are listed because the reader may want to turn his/her attention to them in order to learn more about US-operated multi-role fighters. As such, the author recommends the following titles and resources:

## BOOKS

Davies, S., *Boeing F-15E Strike Eagle, All-Weather Attack Aircraft*, Crowood Press, 2001
Davies, S., *Combat Aircraft 47: F-15C/E Eagle Units in Operation Iraqi Freedom*, Osprey Publishing, 2004
Davies, S., *Combat Aircraft 59: F-15E Strike Eagle Units in Combat 1990–2005*, Osprey Publishing, 2005
Davies, S., & Dildy, D., *Combat Aircraft 61: F-16 Fighting Falcon Units of Operation Iraqi Freedom*, Osprey Publishing, 2006
Donald, D., ed., *Gulf Air War Debrief, Aerospace Publishing*, 1991
Holmes, T., *Combat Aircraft 46: US Navy Hornet Units of Operation Iraqi Freedom (Part One)*, Osprey Publishing, 2004
Holmes, T., *Combat Aircraft 58: US Navy Hornet Units of Operation Iraqi Freedom (Part Two)*, Osprey Publishing, 2005
Holmes, T., *Combat Aircraft 52: US Navy F-14 Tomcat Units of Operation Iraqi Freedom*, Osprey Publishing, 2005
Holmes, T., *Combat Aircraft 56: US Marine Corps and RAAF Hornet Units of Operation Iraqi Freedom*, Osprey Publishing, 2006
Holmes, T., *Combat Aircraft 70: US Navy F-14 Tomcat Units of Operation Enduring Freedom*, Osprey Publishing, 2008
Newdick, T., ed,, *Air Warfare: From WWI to the Present Day*, Thunder Bay Press, 2008
Rosenkranz, K., *Vipers in the Storm: Diary of a Gulf War Fighter Pilot*, McGraw-Hill Professional, 2002
Smallwood, W., *Strike Eagle: Flying the F-15E in the Gulf War*, Potomac Books, 1994

## PARTWORKS

World Aircraft Information Files, Aerospace Publishing
Fighting Aircraft, Amber Publishing / DeAgostini

## WEBSITES

F-16.net: www.f-16.net
F-15E Strike Eagle.info: www.f-15estrikeeagle.info

# PICTURE CREDITS

**Front cover**
Lockheed Martin F-16 (Getty Images)

**Angel DelCueto via Lockheed Martin**
p.208

**Steve Davies (www.FJPhotography.com)**
p.7; pp.8–9; pp.12–13; pp.16–17; pp.18–19; p.20; p.21; pp.22–23; pp.28–29; p.31; p.32 (all images); pp.34–35; p.37; pp.38–39; pp.40–41; p.43 (both images); p.47; pp.50–51; pp.62–63; p.65; p.66; pp.68–69; pp.72–73; pp.74–75; p.77; pp.78–79; pp.82–83; p.85; p.87; pp.88–93; p.95; pp.96–97; pp.100–101; pp.102–103; p.106 (all images); pp.112–113; p.120; p.126; p.136; pp.138–139; p.143; p.149; pp.156–157; p.158; pp.160–161; p.163; pp.174–175; p.180; p.181; p.187; pp.188–189; pp.190–191; pp.192–193; p.195; pp.196–197; p.198; pp.214–215; p.217; pp.218–219; p.221; back cover and endpapers

**Jamie Hunter (www.Aviacom.co.uk)**
title page; pp.4–5; p.14; p.27; p.109; p.146–147; p.151

**Lockheed Martin (www.lockheedmartin.com)**
pp.200–201; p.203; pp.206–207; pp.210–211; p.213

**Randall Haskin**
p.15; pp.24–25; p.52; pp.54–55

**Ty Rogoway**
p.11; p.61; p.111; p.159; p.229

**United States Air Force (www.af.mil)**
p.49; p.81; p.164; p.166–167; p.169; pp.172–173; pp.176–177; pp.178–179; p.183; p.199 (both images); p.204

**United States Navy (www.navy.mil)**
p.115; p.117; p.118; p.123; pp.124–125; pp.128–129; pp.132–133; pp.134–135; p.141; p.144; p.145; pp.154–155

**US Department of Defense**
p.59 (all images)

# INDEX

References to illustrations are shown in **bold**.

*Abraham Lincoln*, USS (CVN 72) 121, 123, 148, 153, 154, 155
Advanced Tactical Airborne Reconnaissance System (ATARS) 117, 145
Advanced Tactical Fighter (ATF) program 162–163, 165
Afghanistan operations 26, 33, **52**, 83, **133**, 148, 153, 159, 216 *see also* Operation *Enduring Freedom*
air defense system, integrated (IADS) 98, 162
Air Tasking Order (ATO –"frag") 33, 36, 56, 99
Airbus airliners 202
Al Qaeda **20**, 53, 56, 57, 148, 159, 216
*America*, USS (CV 66) 140
Angelella, Col 98
ATARS (Advanced Tactical Airborne Reconnaissance System) 117, 145
ATF (Advanced Tactical Fighter) program 162–163, 165
ATO (Air Tasking Order –"frag") 33, 36, 56, 99

BAE Systems 202
    Harrier 202–204
Baghdad 98, 148
Bakke, Capt Dan B. 51
Balkans operations 52 *see also* Operation: *Allied Force*; *Deliberate Force*; *Deny Flight*
    F-16 77, 79, 81
    F/A-18 131, 137, 140–141, 144–145
bases
    US Air Force
        Ahmed Al Jaber AB, Kuwait 53, 83, 84, 105
        Al Kharj AB, Saudi Arabia 33
        Al Udeid AB, Qatar 61, 85, 98
        Ali al Salem AB, Kuwait **39**
        Andersen AB, Guam 165
        Aviano AB, Italy 77, 81, **98**, **101**, **216**
        Azraq AB, Jordan 84, 107
        Bagram AB, Afghanistan **26**, 33, 53
        Balad AB, Baghdad 111
        Dhahran AB, Saudi Arabia 30
        Edwards AFB, California 33, 171, **208**
        Eglin AFB, Florida 33, **83**, 213
        Elmenford AFB, Alaska 168, 170, **180**, 180, **187**
        Hickam AFB, Hawaii 171
        Hill AFB, Utah 213
        Holloman AFB, New Mexico 171
        Kadena AB, Japan 165
        Langley AFB, Virginia 162, 171, **177**, 185
        Luke AFB, Arizona 213
        McDill AFB, Florida: Combined Air Operations Center (CAOC) 56–57
        Mountain Home AFB, Idaho **29**, 32, 33
        Nellis AFB, Nevada 33, 165, 167, 170, 171, 184, **191**, **194**
        Prince Sultan AB, Saudi Arabia 83, 84, 94
        RAF Lakenheath 26, 32, **33**, 33
        Seymour Johnson AFB, North Carolina 30, 32, 33, **47**
        Spangdahlem AB, Germany 69, 81, 85, **111**
        Thumrait AB, Oman 30
        Tyndall AFB, Florida 170, 171, 184
    US Air National Guard
        Burlington Air Guard station, Vermont 213
    US Marine Corps
        Al Asad AB, Iraq **129**
        Aviano AB, Italy 137, 140, 144
        Sheikh Isa AB, Bahrain 131
        Taszar AB, Hungary 144
    US Navy
        NAF Atsugi, Japan 120
        NAS Lemoore, California 120, 126, 155, **159**
        NAS Oceana, Virginia 120, 126, 157, 159
        NAS Whidbey Island, Washington 130
Beamer, Tod **20**
Beletic, Col Bob "Surf" 98
Bennett, Capt Richard T. 51–52
Bin Laden, Osama 53
Boeing
    B-52 Stratofortress 36
    E-3 AWACS (Airborne Warning and Control System) 36, 37, 45, 60, 105, 108, 170
    E/A-18G Growler **14**, 127, 129–130
        development 130
        operators 126–127
        VX-31 **151**
    F-15E Strike Eagle **20**, **26**, 26–27, **27**, 29–33, 36–37, **37**, 39, 42–48, 51–53, 56–61, **61**, 76, **101**, 104, 116
        86-0183 (prototype) 30
        86-0184 and 86-0185 30
        88-1689 48
        88-1692 51

333rd FS  47
335th FS  **31**, **39**
366th Wing  29
391st FS  **39**
492nd FS  **15**, **33**
cockpit  29, **32**
electronics  26–27, 29
engines, General Electric F110-GE-129  30, 58
engines, Pratt & Whitney F100-PW-220  29, 58
engines, Pratt & Whitney F100-PW-229  30, 58
head-up display (HUD)  27, 42, **43**, 45, 48
LANTIRN (low altitude navigation targeting infra-red for night) pod, AAQ-13 navigation  27, 42–43, 48, **59**
LANTIRN pod, AAQ-14 target  27, 42, 43, 44, 48, 60
Litening II Advanced Target Pod, AAQ-28  42, 43–44
and Operation *Desert Shield*  30–31, 33
and Operation *Desert Storm*  see Operation *Desert Storm* and F-15E Strike Eagle
and Operation *Enduring Freedom*  53, **56**, 56–61, **61**
operators  32–33
pivotal role  52–53
radar, Raytheon APG-70  26–27, 29, 42, 46, 220
radar, terrain-following (TFR)  26, 42, 43, 48
Radar Modernization Program (RMP), APG-82(V)1  42, **220**
Sniper XR target pod, AAQ-33  42, 44
specification  58
technology  42–44
F/A-18E Super Hornet  **21**, **26**, **147**
F/A-18E/F Super Hornet  119, 122–123, 127, 130, **157**
VFA-211  **114**
armament  150–152
ATFLIR  143
cockpit  **120**
engines, General Electric F414-GE-400  122, 150
flight test  122
Operation *Iraqi Freedom*  154–155, 157, 159
operational testing  122–123, 127
operators  126–127
putting "iron" on target  127
radar, APG-79 AESA  143, **148**
SHARP (Shared Reconnaissance Pod)  142–143
special roles  142
specification  150–152
technology  142–143
touch-sensitive display  **126**
at war  153–155, 157, 159
F/A-18E/F Block 2:  **216**
F/A-18E1  122
F/A-18F  **21**, **26**, **137**, **140**
VFA-11  **155**

VFA-121  **141**
VFA-211  **158**
rear cockpit  **143**
tactical display  **143**
KC-135 Stratotanker  107
KC-135R  **168**
X-32  202
Boeing/Northrop Grumman
E-8 J-STARS (Joint-Surveillance Target Attack Radar System)  47, 52
E-8C J-STARS  60
Bolt, Col Russell "Rusty"  31
bombing, "Dive Toss"  45
Bosnia  137, 145
Bosnia-Herzegovina  77
Britschgi, Lt Col Andrew "AJ"  53, 56, 57, 58
"Bud" (weapons school instructor WSO)  61
Burbach, Capt Christian  44
Bush, President George H. W.  36
Bush, President George W.  148, 155
"Buzzer" (F-15E WSO)  60

Cabral, Maj Mike  168, 170, 173, 177, 180, 181, 186–187, 191, 194, 199
*Carl Vinson*, USS (CVN 70)  147, 157
Carlton III, Capt Paul K. "Zero"  86, 94, 99, 104–105
China  216, 220
Clinton, President Bill  83
*Constellation*, USS (CV 64)  120, 148
*Coral Sea*, USS (CV 43)  **115**
Crandall, Rich  45
Creech, Gen Wilbur  26

Dayton Peace Accords (1995)  140
DEAD (destruction of enemy air defenses) role  71, 104–105, 152
Decoy, ADM-141 Tactical Air-Launched (TALD)  150
Department of Defense: Joint Airborne Attack Analysis of Alternatives  129
Dewey, Maj Wade "Dewman"  107
*Dwight D. Eisenhower*, USS (CVN 69)  121, 157

Eberly, Col David  51
electronic warfare (EW)  127, 129–130
*Enterprise*, USS (CVN 65)  121, 147, 148
Exercise Northern Edge  165, **168**, 185
exercises, Red Flag  **94**, **108**

Fairchild A-10 Thunderbolt II "Warthog"  46, 47
Fairchild A-10C  **101**, **191**
"Fang" (F-15E WSO)  56, 57, 59, 60

# INDEX

forward air controllers (FACs)  53, 57, 58, 59, 60
forward air controllers (airborne) (FAC(A)s)  44, 76, 101, 104, 105, 123, 140–141, 142, 145, 153, 154
fuel tanks, conformal (CFTs)  27

Gale, Al  39, 45, 48
Gates, Robert  216, 220
General Dynamics  64 see also Lockheed Martin
    A-12  119
    F-16XL  30
    F-111 Aardvark  26
    F-111E  26
    F-111F  26, 27, 36, 76
    YF-16A  64
General Electric engines
    exhaust tunnel "turkey louvres"  **77**
    F110-GE-129  30, 58, 65, 70, 106
    F404-GE-400  116
    F404-GE-402  116
    F414-GE-400  122, 150
General Electric/Rolls Royce F136 engine  208–209, 212
*George H. W. Bush*, USS (CVN 77)  121
*George Washington*, USS (CVN 73)  120, 121, 147
Georgia State University satellite imagery  56
"Global War on Terror"  153
Goldfein, Maj Gen Dave  **66**
Gordon, Capt Jeremy "Mount"  99
Griffiths Jr, Maj Thomas E.  51
Grumman  see also Northrop Grumman
    A-6E Intruder  36, 114, 117
    EA-6B Prowler  84, 99, 129, 130
    EF-111 Raven  33, 36, 76
    EF-111A  129
    F-14 Tomcat  36, 104, 114, 126, 127, 153
        advanced versions  119
    F-14D  44
Gulf War (1991)  see Operation *Desert Storm*

Hansen, Lt Col "Popeye"  216
Harper, Flt Lt Matthew  **162**, 180–181, 186, 187, 191, 199
Harrigan, Lt Col Jeffrey "Cobra"  **167**
*Harry S. Truman*, USS (CVN 75)  121, 147, **155**, 159
Haskin, Maj Randy "Hacker"  **56**
Hecker, Lt Col James  **173**
Helmet Mounted Cueing System, Joint (JHMCS)  71, 199, **220**
Holland, Maj Donnie "Chief Dimpled Balls"  48
HTS (HARM Targeting System) pod, AN/ASQ-213  **65**, 70–71, 75, 80, 101, **111**
    R7 upgrade  80
Hughes  26
Hussein, Saddam  30, 31, 76, 83, 86, 94, 147, 148, 153

IADS (integrated air defense system)  98, 162
Iraq
    Al Taqaddam airfield  98
    Baghdad  98, 148
    H-2 air base  36, 45
    Operation *Desert Storm*  see Operation *Desert Storm*
    Operation *Iraqi Freedom*  see Operation *Iraqi Freedom*
    Republican Guard  31
    "Super MEZ" (missile engagement zone)  76, 94, 98, 99

jammers, digital radio frequency modulation (DRFM)  220
jamming pod, ALQ-131  **75**
JHMCS (Joint Helmet Mounted Cueing System)  71, 199, **220**
*John C. Stennis*, USS (CVN 74)  120, 121, 122, 157
*John F. Kennedy*, USS (CV 67)  131

Kitty Hawk, North Carolina  **31**
*Kitty Hawk*, USS (CV 63)  **123**, 148
Knowles, Jeff  212
Koritz, Maj Thomas F. "Teek"  48
Kosovo  144
Kosovo Liberation Army  79
Kuwait invasion (1991)  30, 36, 75–76
Kwast, Col Steve  36–37, 39

LANTIRN (low altitude navigation targeting infra-red for night) pod, AAQ-13 navigation  27, 42–43, 48, **59**, 76
LANTIRN pod, AAQ-14 target  27, 42, 43, 44, 48, 60, 76
leaflet dispensers, M129  84
Libya raids (1986)  **115**, 131
Lightweight Fighter (LWF) competition  64
Litening II Advanced Target Pod, AAQ-28  42, 43–44, 71, 80, 108
Lockheed Martin
    F-16 Fighting Falcon/"Viper"  36, 56, 64–67, 69–71, 75–77, 79–81, 83–86, 94, 98–99, 101, 104–108, 110–111, 116, 163, 167, 177
        52nd FW  **66**
        64th AGRS  **108**
        Aggressor aircraft  **86**, **94**
        Air Intake Duct, Modular Common ("big mouth" inlet)  65
        Balkans campaigns  77, 79, 81
        cockpit  80–81, **81**
        cockpit, rear  **106**
        development  64–65
        engine, Pratt & Whitney F100  64
        F-16C/D  65–66, 69
        fly-by-wire (FBW) control system  80, 116
        freeing Kuwait  75–77
        HOTAS (hands on throttle and stick)  80–81
        Manned Destructive Suppression Program (MDSP)  80

Operation *Desert Fox* 83–84
Operation *Iraqi Freedom* see Operation *Iraqi Freedom* and F-16
operators (Block 30 and above) 67
prototype (YF-16A) 64
radar, AN/APG-68(V) 65, **79**
radar, Westinghouse AN/APG-66 64
technology 80–81
Wild Weasel development 69–71
Wild Weasel roles 71, 75
YF-16A (prototype) 64
F-16A 64, 65
F-16A/B Block 15/20/25: 67
F-16AM 81
F-16B 64, 67
F-16B Block 15: rear cockpit **106**
F-16C **20**, 65
 18th AGRS **64**
 40th FTS **83**
 engine, Pratt & Whitney PW-220E **85**
F-16C Block 25: 64
F-16C Block 30: **75**, 84
F-16C Block 32: **85**
F-16C Block 40: **15**, 69, 84, **101**
 Aviano-based **216**
F-16C Block 50
 armament 107
 engine, General Electric F110-GE-129 106
 engine, Pratt & Whitney F100-PW-229 106
 specification 106–107
F-16C/D 65–66, 69, 83
F-16C/D Block 30: 67
 engine exhaust tunnel "turkey louvres" **77**
F-16C/D Block 30/32 65–66
 engine, General Electric F110-GE-129 65
 engine, Pratt & Whitney F100-PW-220 65–66
F-16C/D Block 30B/Block 30D 66
F-16C/D Block 32: 67, **79**
F-16C/D Block 40: 66, 67, 69, 76, 105, 107
F-16C/D Block 42: 66, 67, 69, 76
F-16C/D Block 50/52 see Lockheed Martin F-16CJ/DJ
F-16C/D Block 60: 67
F-16CG 107
F-16CG Block 40: 77, 79, 84
 31st FW **98**
F-16CJ (F-16C Block 50/52) "Wild Weasel" 53, 99, 101, 104–105, 107
 52nd FW **69**, **75**
F-16CJ Block 50: 84
F-16CJ Block 50/52: **65**
F-16CJ Block 50D/52D 70

F-16CJ Block 52: **101**, **191**
F-16CJ/DJ (F-16C/D Block 50/52) "Wild Weasel" 67, 69, 70–71, 75, 77, 79, 81, 83, 84, 85, 86, 94, 131
 Avionics Launcher Interface Computer (ALICS) 70, 75
 engine, General Electric F-110-GE-129 70
 engine, Pratt & Whitney F-100-PW-229 70
 HTS (HARM Targeting System) pod, AN/ASQ-213 70–71, 75, **111**
 HTS pod, AN/ASQ-213, R7 upgrade 80
F-16D 65
F-16D Block 25: 64
F-16D Block 40 rear cockpit **106**
F-16DJ (F-16C/D Block 50/52) "Wild Weasel" **111**
F-22A Raptor **14**, 162–163, 165, 167–168, 170–171, 173, 177, 180–187, **181**, 191, 194, 198–199, **199**, 212, **220**
 01-018 **167**
 05-107 **191**
 27th FS **168**
 43rd FS **167**
 90th FS **173**
 94th FS **173**
 422nd TES **101**, **163**
 525th FS **162**, **187**
 and altitude 194
 Anti-G Suit, Advanced Technology (ATAGS) 185
 ATF (Advanced Tactical Fighter) program 162–163, 165
 block increment limitations 184
 CNI (communication, navigation, identification) system 183
 cockpit 180–181, 184–187
 datalink 185–186
 "Dicemen" (90th FS) 167–168, **173**
 engines, Pratt & Whitney F119-PW-100 **173**, 198
 flying 194, 198
 future plans 198–199
 ground attack 183–184
 inflight-refueling operations **198**
 information sharing 185
 Langley AFB-based **173**
 mixed force TTPS (tactics, techniques, and procedures) 165, 167
 Nellis AFB-based **194**
 operators 171
 radar, AESA APG-77 182, 183, 186, 198–199
 sensors 182–183
 simulations 187, 191, 194
 specification 198
 and speed 194
 stealth 165, 194, **198**
 technology 182–186
 vertical stabilisers **177**, **180**

# Index

weapons 183–184, 198
weapons bay **183**
F-22A Block 10/20: 170
F-22A Block 30: 170, 173, 177, 180–181, 184, 199
F-35 Lightning II (Joint Strike Fighter – JSF) 162, 202–205, 207–209, 212–213, 220
   AA-1 test aircraft **202**, **203**, **204**
   avionics 209
   cockpit 202–203, 207, **213**
   helmet-mounted sight (HMS) 205, 207
   into service 213
   specification 212
   variants 205
   weapons 205, **207**, 209
F-35A (CTOL – conventional take-off and landing) 202, 205, 212
   AF-01 **207**, **208**
F-35B (STOVL – short take-off and vertical landing) 202, 205, 207–208, **209**
   engine, General Electric/Rolls Royce F136 208–209, 212
   engine, Pratt & Whitney F135 208–209, 212
F-35C (CV – carrier variant) 202, 205
F-117 Nighthawk 61, 86, 94
X-35 202
YF-22 Advanced Tactical Fighter 162, 163, **165**
LWF (Lightweight Fighter) competition 64

Madenwald, Fred 122
Manning, Lt Col Scott "Zing" 98, 105
Martin Marietta LANTIRN (low altitude navigation targeting infra-red for night) pods
   AAQ-13 navigation 27, 42–43, 48, **59**, 76
   AAQ-14 target 27, 42, 43, 44, 48, 60, 76
McDonnell Douglas (McAir) 26, 27
   E/A-18G Growler *see* Boeing
   F-4 Phantom II 30, 114
   F-4G "Wild Weasel" 33, 36, 70, 76
   F-15 Eagle 26, 64, 167, 168, 170, 177, 182, 185, 198
   F-15C 30, 36, 81, **101**
   F-15D 30
   F-15E Strike Eagle *see* Boeing F-15E Strike Eagle
   F/A-18 Hornet 36, 84, 104, 114–117, 119–123, 126–127, 129–131, 133, 137, 140–145, 147–148, 150–155, 157, 159, 167
      Advanced Tactical Airborne Reconnaissance System (ATARS) 117
      avionics 116–117
      Balkans operations 131, 137, 140–141, 144–145
      combat operations 131, 133, 137, 140–141, 144–145, 147–148, 153

      engines, General Electric F404-GE-400/F404-GE-402 116
      F/A-18D attack deltas 117
      Glass Hornet program 115–116
      Middle East operations 145, 147–148, 153
      nose wheel steering **123**
      Operation *Iraqi Freedom* 148, 153
      operators C/D 120–121
      operators E/F/G 126–127
      radar, APG-73 116
      Super Hornet – F/A-18E/F *see* Boeing F/A-18E/F Super Hornet
      variants 114–117, 119, 122–123, 127, 129–130
   F/A-18A 114, 119
      VFA-132 **115**
   F/A-18B 114
   F/A-18C 119, **133**, 137, 144, **145**, 153
      VFA-105 **123**
      VFA-106 **144**
      VFA-125 **159**
      VFA-195 **123**
      VMFA-106 **141**
      VX-23 **119**
   F/A-18C/D 114–117
      operators 120–121
   F/A-18D 117
      US Marine Corps **117**, **129**, 140–141, 144–145, 153
      VMFA-314 **117**
      VMFA-533 **129**
   F/A-18E/F Super Hornet *see* Boeing F/A-18E/F Super Hornet
   Hornet 2000 proposals 119
   SF/A-18C/D Hornet 116
McDonnell Douglas Helicopters AH-64 Apache 45
Middle East operations, F/A-18 145, 147–148, 153
*Midway*, USS (CV 41) 131
Mikoyan
   MiG-21 "Fishbed" 137
   MiG-23 "Flogger" 77
   MiG-25 "Foxbat" 107, 137
   MiG-29 "Fulcrum" 81, 194
Mil Mi-24 "Hind" 51–52
Milosevic, Slobodan 79, 144
Mission Planning Cells (MPCs) 99
Morrison, Capt Matt "Demon" 99
Mosely, Gen Michael "Buzz" 216
MPCs (Mission Planning Cells) 99

NASA 114
Nathman, Adm John "Black" **115**

NATO 52, 77, 79, 137, 140, 144
navigation pod, LANTIRN (low altitude navigation targeting infra-red for night) AAQ-13 27, 42–43, 48, **59**, 76
Nelson, Dave "Doc" **207**
Netherlands Air Force, Royal: No. 322 Sqn 81
*Nimitz*, USS (CVN 68) 121, 123, 127, **133**, 148, 155
North American F-100F Super Sabre 69
Northern Alliance 57, 59
Northrop YF-17 64, 114
Northrop Grumman 202 *see also* Grumman
　AAQ-28 Litening II Advanced Target Pod 42, 43–44, 71, 80, 108
　APG-77 AESA radar 82, 183, 186, 198–199
　EA-6B ICAP-III Prowler 129–130

O'Grady, Capt Scott 79
Oney, Capt Jerry "One-Y" 45–47
Operation
　*Allied Force* 52, **66**, 79, 81, 117, 137, 144, 194
　*Dead Eye South East* 140
　*Deliberate Force* 77, 79, 140, 141
　*Deny Flight* 52, 77, 137, 140–141
　*Desert Fox* 83–84, 145, 147–148
　*Desert Shield* 30–31, 33, 131
　*Desert Storm* 70, 75–77, 131, 133, 137, 150
　*Desert Storm* and F-15E Strike Eagle 36–37, 39, 45–48, **48**, 51–53
　　daylight strikes 45–47
　　first helicopter kill 51–51
　　losses 48, 51
　　mobile "scuds" 47–48
　　pivotal role in opening stages 52
　*Enduring Freedom* **15**, 53, **56**, 56–61, **61**, 83, **133**, **145**, 148, 150, 153
　　Combined Air Operations Center (CAOC) 56–57
　*Iraqi Freedom* 43, 44, 61, 67, 80, **123**, **129**, 142, 148, 150, 153, 154–155, 157, 159
　*Iraqi Freedom* and F-16 84–86, 94, 98–99, 101, 104–105, 107–108, 110–111
　　adaptable Weasels 101, 104–105
　　Block 40 and Block 30 exploits 105, 107
　　mission success 111
　　and RAM 01 86, 94
　*Noble Anvil* 79
　*Noble Eagle* 84, 163
　*Northern Watch* 52, 53, 76–77, 83
　*Provide Comfort* 52
　*Southern Watch* 52, 53, 76–77, 83, 86, 105, 107, 123, 150, 153
OPLAN 1003V 85, 86

Panavia Tornado GR.Mk 1: 36
Panavia Tornado GR.Mk 4: 98
Pave Tack, AVQ-26, target pod 26
Pentagon 64, 216
Piggott, 1st Lt Russ "Spicoli" 107
Pomeroy, Maj Steve 131, 133, 137
Pratt & Whitney engines
　F100 64
　F100-PW-220 29, 58, 65–66
　F100-PW-220E **85**
　F100-PW-229 30, 58, 70, 106
　F119 **173**
　F119-PW-100 198
　F135 208–209, 212
Predator UAV 59

Rambouillet peace accords 79
RAND Corporation 213
*Ranger*, USS (CV 61) 131
Raytheon APG-70 radar 26–27, 29, 42, 46, 220
Reconnaissance Pod, Shared (SHARP) 142–143
Reconnaissance System, Advanced Tactical Airborne (ATARS) 117, 145
Republic F-105G Thunderchief 69, 70
Riyadh, Saudi Arabia 31, 33
Roberson, Lt Col Anthony "Roby" 84
Rockwell B-1B 98, 99
*Ronald Reagan*, USS (CVN 76) 121, 155, 157
Royal Air Force 36, 98
Royal Navy 202
rules of engagement (ROE) 59–60, 86
Russia 216, 220

Sarajevo 140
Saudi Arabia 31
SCAR (strike coordination and reconnaissance) 142
Schaal, Capt Bill "Shadow" 45, 46, 47
SEAD (suppression of enemy air defenses) role 69, 98–99, 129, 131, 133, 137, 141, 152
September 11, 2001 terrorist attacks **20**, **39**, 153
　aftermath operations 53
Serbia 81, 140, 141, 144
Sherer, Capt Gene "Owner" 80–81, 98–99, 105
Shower, Lt Col Mike "Dozer" 184–185, 194, 198
Siberski, Maj Joe "Ramsty" 44
Simmons, Capt Tony "Jaws" 108
"Slokes" (F-15E pilot) 60
Sniper ER target pod 80
Sniper XR, AAQ-33, target pod **15**, 42, 44, 71, **111**
"Snitch" (F-15E WSO) 60
"Snort" (F-16CG pilot) 107

# Index

Soko G-2 Galeb  77
Spanish air force, 12/14 Ala  140
Sparrow, Lt Col William "Swapper"  108, 110–111
"Spear" (F-15E pilot)  56, 57, 59, 60, 61
Spear, Lt Eric "Papa"  98, 99
special forces, COBRA 25/25T  108, 110
special forces, "TF20"  108
Speicher, Lt Cdr Scott  137
Srebrenica  140
strike coordination and reconnaissance (SCAR)  142
Sukhoi PAK-FA  216
Sukhoi Su-30 "Advanced Flanker"  213, 220
Swiss Air Force  116

Tactical Air Control (Party) (TAC(P))  101, 104
Taliban  39, 53, 56, 57, 58–59, 60, **145**, 148, 157, 159, 216
target pods
    AVQ-26 Pave Tack  26
    LANTIRN (low altitude navigation targeting infra-red for night) AAQ-14  27, 42, 43, 44, 48, 60, 76
    Northrop Grumman AAQ-28 Litening II Advanced  42, 43–44, 71, 80, 108
    Sniper ER  80
    Sniper XR, AAQ-33  **15**, 42, 44, 71, **111**
*Theodore Roosevelt*, USS (CVN 71)  140, 144, 148, 159
Tomlinson, Graham "GT"  202–204, 205, 207–209, **209**, 212
TST (time-sensitive tasking) targets  56–57, 60
Tupolev Tu-95MS "Bear-H"  168
Turner, Capt Brad "Fletch"  99

Udbina raid (1994)  140
Ulmer, Capt Scott  104
UN Security Council resolutions  83
    Resolution 781  77
United Airlines Flight 93:  **20**
United States Air Force (USAF)
    Aerospace Expeditionary Forces (AEF)  53
    Air Combat Command (ACC)  32, 33, 64, 67
    Air Education and Training Command  67
    Air Expeditionary Group (AEG), 332nd  53
    Air Expeditionary Group, 363rd  84
    Air Force Materiel Command (AFMC)  32, 33, 67
    Common Configuration Implementation Program (CCIP)  71
    F-15E operators  32–33
    "Global Strike Task Force" (GSTF)  170
    Manned Destructive Suppression Program (MDSP)  80
    Pacific Air Forces (PACAF)  67, 168
    squadrons
        4th FS, 388th FW  84

4th TFS  64
7th FS, 49th FW  171
8th FS, 49th FW  171
14th FS, 35th FW  84
14th EFS "Samurais"  98
17th WS, 57th Wing  33
18th AGRS (Aggressor Squadron)  **64**
19th AGRS  **94**
19th FS, 3rd Wing  168, 170
19th FS, 15th Wing  171
22nd EFS  98
22nd FS "Stingers," 52nd FW  **65**, **69**, 81, 85
23rd EFS  98
23rd FS "Fighting Hawks," 52nd FW  **69**, 77, 81, 85
27th FS, 1st FW  163, 165, **168**, 171, **177**
27th TFS  30
40th FTS (Flight Test Squadron), 46th FTW  **20**, 33, **83**, **85**
43rd FS, 325th FW  **167**, 171
64th AGRS, 57th FW  **108**
77th FS "Gamblers," 20th FW  84, 86, 94, 98, 99, 104–105
79th FS, 20th FW  67
85th TES (Test and Evaluation Squadron), 53rd Wing  33
90th FS "Dicemen," 3rd Wing  165, 167–168, 170, 171, **173**, 173, 177, 180–181
94th FS, 1st FW  171, **173**
333rd FS "Lancers," 4th FW  32, 33, **47**
334th TFS/FS "Eagles," 4th TFW  30, 32, 33
335th TFS/FS "Chiefs," 4th TFW  30, **31**, 33, **39**, 56, 61
336th TFS/FS "Rocketeers," 4th TFW  30–31, 33, **59**, 61
336th TFS/FS "Rocketeers," 4th TFW: CHEVY flight  36–37
389th FS, 366th FW  33, 53
390th FS, 366th Wing  99
391st FS "Bold Tigers," 366th FW  33, **39**, 53, 56, 57–58, 60, 61
391st FS, 366th FW: CROCKETT 51/52 flight  60–61
393rd FS, 48th FW  81
411th FTS  171
412th FTS, 412th  171
415th FTS, 412th TW  33
419th FTS, 412th TW  33
422nd TES "Green Bats," 53rd Wing  33, 44, **101**, **163**, 163, 165, 167, 171, 184, **191**
428th FS, 366th FW  33
433rd Weapons Squadron, 57th Wing  171
492nd FS, 48th FW  **15**, **33**, 33, **52**
494th FS, 48th FW  **33**, 33
510th FS "Buzzards," 31st FW  **15**, 77, 79, 81, **98**

524th EFS  105, 107
524th FS "Hounds," 27th FW  84
525th FS "Bulldogs," 3rd Wing  **162**, 165, 168, 170, 171, 173, **187**
555th FS, 31st FW  77, 79, 81
Tactical Air Command  26, 30, 64
Tactical Air Control Center (TACC) (Operation *Desert Shield*)  31, 33, 47
"Thunderbirds" Air Demonstration Squadron  **108**
wings
   1st FW  165, **168**, 171
   1st TFW  30
   3rd Wing, Pacific Air Forces  168, 171, 173, 185
   4th FW  30, **47**
   4th TFW  30
   4th TFW  30–31, 48
   4th TFW (P), DODGE flight  36
   4th TFW (P), T-BIRD flight  48
   8th FW  67
   20th FW  67, 83, 84
   27th FW  84
   31st AEW  81
   31st FW  67, 77, 79, 81, **98**, **101**
   33rd TFW  30
   35th FW  67, 84
   46th FTW  67, **83**
   48th FW  33, 81
   49th FW  171
   51st FW  67
   52nd FW  **66**, 67, **69**, **75**, 81, 85
   52nd Wing  101
   53rd FW  67
   53rd Wing  33
   56th FW  67
   57th FW  67, **108**
   325th FW  **167**
   354th FW  67
   366th AEW  53, 61
   366th FW  33
   366th Wing  **29**, 99
   379th AEW  33, 85
   388th FW  67, 83, 84
   388th TFW  64
   405th TFW/FW  30, 33
   410th AEW  84
   412th Test Wing  33, 67
   455th AEW  33
   4404th (Provisional) Wing  83
United States Air Force Reserve Command
   Fighter Group (FG), 477th  168
   squadrons
      301st FS, 44th FG  171
      302nd FS, 477th FG  171
      307th FS, 414th FG  32, 33
      457th FS, 301st FW  84
      466th FS, 419th FW  84
   wings
      301st FW  67, 84
      419th FW  67, 84
      482nd FW  67
United States Air Forces Europe (USAFE)  32, 33, 67, **69**
United States Air National Guard  67
   Alabama  107–108, 110–111 *see also* US Air National Guard: 187th FW
   squadrons
      120th FS, 140th FW  84
      121st FS, 113th FW (Washington)  84
      149th FS, 192nd FW  171
      157th FS, 169th FW  85
      190th FS, 187th FW  84
      199th FS, 154th Wing  171
   wings
      113th FW  67
      114th FW  67
      115th FW  67
      122nd FW  67
      132nd FW  67
      138th FW  67
      140th FW (Colorado)  67, 84
      144th FW  67
      150th FW  67
      158th FW  67
      162nd FW  67
      168th Air Refueling Wing (Alaska)  **168**
      169th FW (South Carolina)  67, 85, 101
      174th FW  67
      177th FW  67
      178th FW  67
      180th FW  67
      187th FW (Alabama)  67, **75**, **79**, 84
United States Army  57
United States Marine Corps  114, 117, 131
   and F-35B  202, 205
   and F/A-18D  140–141, 144–145, 153
   MAG-11  121
   MAG-12  121
   MAG-31  121
   Marine All Weather Fighter Attack Squadrons (VMFA(AW)s)  120
      VMFA(AW)-121 "Green Knights"  117, 121
      VMFA(AW)-224 "Bengals"  121
      VMFA(AW)-225 "Vikings"  121

VMFA(AW)-242 "Bats" 121
VMFA(AW)-533 "Hawks" 121, 140
Marine Fighter Attack Squadrons (VMFAs) 117, 120
  VMFA-115 "Silver Eagles" 121
  VMFA-122 "Crusaders" 121
  VMFA-224 140
  VMFA-232 "Red Devils" 121, **133**
  VMFA-251 "Thunderbolts" 121, 140
  VMFA-312 "Checkerboards" 121, 140
  VMFA-314 "Black Knights" **117**, 131
  VMFA-323 "Death Rattlers" 121
  VMFA-332 144–145
  VMFA-333 131, 133, 137
  VMFA-533 **129**, 144–145
Marine Fighter Attack Training Squadron VMFAT-101 "Sharpshooters" 120, 121
MAW-1/MAW-2/MAW-3 121
United States Marine Corps Reserve
  MAW-4 121
  VMFA-112 "Cowboys" 121
  VMFA-134 "Smokes" 121
  VMFA-142 "Flying Gaters" 121
  VMFA-321 "Hell's Angels" 121
United States Naval Reserve Force
  VFA-204 "River Rattlers" 121
  VFC-12 "Fighting Omars" 121
United States Navy 36, 114
  Carrier Air Wings (CVWs) 120, 126
    CVW-1 121
    CVW-2 121
    CVW-3 121, 147, 159
    CVW-5 121, 126
    CVW-7 121
    CVW-8 121, 159
    CVW-9 120, 121, 157
    CVW-11 121, 147, 155
    CVW-14 121, 123, 153, 154
    CVW-17 147–148
  and F-35C 202, 205
  F/A-18C/D units 120–121
  Fifth Fleet 148
  Naval Strike and Air Warfare Center 121, 127
  Operation *Desert Storm* kills 137
  Sixth Fleet 144
  Strike Fighter Squadrons (VFAs) 120, 126
    VFA-2 "Bounty Hunters" 127
    VFA-11 "Red Rippers" 127, **155**, 159
    VFA-14 "Top Hatters" 123, 127, 154–155
    VFA-15 "Valions" 121, 131, 140, 148
    VFA-22 "Fighting Redcocks" 127
    VFA-25 "Fist of the Fleet" 121, 148
    VFA-27 "Royal Maces" 126, 127, 148
    VFA-31 "Felix/Tomcatters" 127, 159
    VFA-32 "Swordsmen" 127
    VFA-34 "Blue Blasters" 121, 147–148
    VFA-37 "Ragin' Bulls" 121, 147
    VFA-41 "Black Aces" 123, 127, 154, 155
    VFA-81 "Sunliners" 127, 131, 147–148
    VFA-82 131, 140, 148
    VFA-83 "Rampagers" 121, 131, 147–148
    VFA-86 "Sidewinders" 121, 131, 140, 148
    VFA-87 "Golden Warriors" 121, 131, 140
    VFA-94 "Mighty Shrikes" 121, 148
    VFA-97 "Warhawks" 121, 148
    VFA-102 "Diamondbacks" 126, 127
    VFA-103 "Jolly Rogers" 127, 157
    VFA-105 "Gunslingers" **123**, 127
    VFA-106 "Gladiators" 120, 121, 126, 127, **141**, **144**
    VFA-113 "Stingers" 120, 121, 148
    VFA-115 "Eagles" 120, 121, 122–123, 127, 153, 154, 155, 157
    VFA-122 "Flying Eagles" 122, 127, **159**
    VFA-125 "Rough Raiders" 120, 121, **159**
    VFA-131 "Wildcats" 121
    VFA-132 "Privateers" **115**
    VFA-136 "Knighthawks" 127
    VFA-137 "Kestrels" 127, 148
    VFA-143 "Pukin' Dogs" 127, 157
    VFA-146 "Blue Diamonds" 120, 121
    VFA-147 "Argonauts" 120, 121, 127
    VFA-151 "Vigilantes" 121, 131, 148
    VFA-154 "Black Knights" 127, 155, 157
    VFA-192 "Golden Dragons" 120, 121, 131, 148
    VFA-195 "Dambusters" 120, 121, **123**, 131, 148
    VFA-211 "Fighting Checkmates" **21**, **114**, 127, **141**, 157, **159**
    VFA-213 "Black Lions" 127
  Test Wing, Atlantic 121
  VAQ-132 "Scorpions" 130
  VX-9 (Air TES Nine) "Vampires" 121, 122, 127, **147**
  VX-23 "Salty Dogs" **119**, 127
  VX-31 "Dust Devils" 127, **151**
  Weapons Test Wing, Pacific 121
United States Special Forces (SF) 51, 52, 58

Venice **101**
Vietnam War (1954–75) 69–70
Virginia Beach **159**
Vogel, Lt Col James 165, 167
Voigt, Chf MSgt 105
Vought A-7 Corsair II 36, 114

Walters, Capt 105
warfare, irregular 216, 220
weapons
    ATFLIR (Advanced Targeting Forward-Looking Infra-Red) **119**, 130, 143
    bombs *see also* weapons, JDAM
        BDU-33 training **27**
        BLU-118/B thermobaric 56
        EGBU-15 (Enhanced Guided Bomb Unit) 2,000lb 56, 58
        GBU-10 laser-guided (LGB) 2,000lb 51, 58, 60, 107
        GBU-10C laser-guided **59**
        GBU-12 Paveway II laser-guided 500lb **26**, **48**, 57, 58, 59, 60, 107, 108, **123**, **133**, 140, 141, 148, 150, 153, 155, 157
        GBU-16 laser-guided 1,000lb 141
        GBU-24 laser-guided 56, 57, 58, 60, 107
        GBU-28 5,000lb "Bunker Buster" **37**, 56, 57, 58, 86, 107
        GBU-38 small diameter (SDB) 250lb 157, 162
        GBU-38 SDB practice **199**
        GBU-39 SBD 500lb 162, 183–184, 198, 199, **220**
        laser-guided (LGBs) 26
        Mk 82 500lb low drag general purpose (LDGP) 31, 36, 37, 57, 58, 108
        Mk 84 2,000lb LDGP 31, 58, 76
    cannon
        GAU-22/A 25mm 205, **207**, 209
        M61A1 Vulcan 20mm **29**, 58, 59, 104, 107, 150
        M61A2 Vulcan 20mm 150, 182, 198
    cluster bombs/munitions 57–58, 107
        CBU-87 58, 76
        CBU-103 WCMD 71, 105
        Mk 20 Rockeye 31, 36
        Wind Corrected Munitions Dispensers (WCMDs) 71, 101, 104, 105, 107
    F-15E 58
    F-16C Block 50: 107
    F-22A 183–184, 198
    F-35 205, **207**, 209
    F/A-18E/F 150–152
    JDAM (Joint Direct Attack Munition) 101, 104, 107, 155, 162
        GBU-31 2,000lb 58, 71, 105, 107, 108, 148, 153, 205
        GBU-32 1,000lb 148, 153, **183**, 198, 205
        GBU-32 practice **199**
        GBU-38 500lb **15**, **26**, 58, 107, 111, **133**, 148
        GPS-guided 150
        Laser **20**
    MANPADS (man-portable air defense systems) 53, 57, 104
    of mass destruction (WMD) 83
    missiles

AGM-65 Maverick 58, 76, 105, 107, 150, 151, 152, 153, 155
AGM-65E **129**
AGM-84 Harpoon anti-ship 150, 151
AGM-84E Stand-Off Land Attack (SLAM) 127, 140, 150, 151
AGM-84H/K SLAM-Expanded Response (SLAM-ER) 150, 151–152, 153
AGM-84L Block II/III Harpoon 151
AGM-88 HARM (High-speed Anti-Radiation) 66, 71, 75, 81, 94, 98, 105, 107, 129–130, 131, 140, **145**, 145, 147, 150, 151, 152
AGM-88 HARM practice **69**, **75**
AGM-88C 150
AGM-130 56, 58
AGM-154 Joint Stand-Off (JSOW) **123**, 130, 150, 153
AIM-7 Sparrow 58, 127, 140, 150
AIM-7F 31
AIM-9 Sidewinder 31, 58, 75, 77, **117**, 127, 137, 140, 150, 198
AIM-9M 36, 107, **123**, 182
AIM-9M training **75**
AIM-9X 107, **133**, 209, **220**
AIM-120 advanced medium-range air-to-air (AMRAAM) 42, 58, 65, 66, **69**, 77, 81, 107, 117, 127, 130, 140, 150, 182, 198
AIM-120 training **75**
AIM-120C 205, 209
AIM-132 advanced short-range air-to-air (ASRAAM) 209
Iraqi "Scud" 33, 36, 45–46, 76
Iraqi "Scud" mobile 47–48
JASSM (Joint Air-to-Surface Stand-off) 209
MBDA Meteor air-to-air 209
SA-7 shoulder-mounted 57
Storm Shadow cruise 209
Tomahawk Land Attack (TLAM) 94
Westinghouse AN/APG-66 radar 64
Wild Weasel role development 69–71
Wright, Orville and Wilbur **31**

Yugoslavia, Federal Republic of 79
Yugoslavia, former, F/A-18 operations 131, 137, 140–141, 144–145